Explore the World

NELLES

KU-524-735

CROATIA

ADRIATIC COAST

Authors:
Alexander Sabo, Darja Peitz-Hlebec

*An Up-to-date travel guide with 143 color photos
and 18 maps*

**Second Revised Edition
1999**

Dear Reader: Being up-to-date is the main goal of the Nelles series. Our correspondents help keep us abreast of the latest developments in the travel scene, while our cartographers see to it that maps are also kept completely current. However, as the travel world is constantly changing, we cannot guarantee that all the information contained in our books is always valid. Should you come across a discrepancy, please contact us at: Nelles Verlag, Schleissheimer Str. 371 b, 80935 Munich, Germany, tel. (089) 3571940, fax. (089) 35719430, e-mail: Nelles.Verlag@t-online.de

Note: Distances and measurements, including temperatures, used in this guide are metric. For conversion information, please see the *Guidelines* section of this book.

LEGEND

★★ ★★	Main Attraction *(on map)* *(in text)*	Vabriga **Basilika**	Places Highlighted in Yellow Appear in Text	National Border
★ ★	Worth Seeing *(on map)* *(in text*	✈	Airport	Expressway
❽	Orientation Number in Text and on Map	♣	Nature Reserve	Principal Highway
		Obzova (568)	Mountain (altitude in meters)	Main Road
▨	Public or Significant Building	\ 13 /	Distance in Kilometers	Provincial Road
■	Hotel	❸❸❸ ❸❸ ❸	Luxury Hotel Category Moderate Hotel Category Budget Hotel Category *(for price information see "Accomodation" in Guidelines section)*	Secondary Road
▨	Shopping Center			Pedestrian Zone
▨ O	Market			E 94 70 Route Number
✝	Church			Railway
				Car Ferry

CROATIA – ADRIATIC COAST
© Nelles Verlag GmbH, 80935 Munich
 All rights reserved

Second Revised Edition 1999
ISBN 3-88618-121-9
Printed in Slovenia

Publisher:	Günter Nelles	**Translation:**	Judit Szász, Chase Stewart,
Managing Editor:	Berthold Schwarz		Marton Radkai
Project Editor:	Alexander Sabo	**Cartography:**	Nelles Verlag GmbH
English Edition		**Color Separation:**	Priegnitz, Munich
Editor:	Chase Stewart	**Printed by:**	Gorenjski Tisk

TABLE OF CONTENTS

TABLE OF CONTENTS

TRAVEL INFORMATION

SLOVENIA

CROATIA

LIST OF MAPS

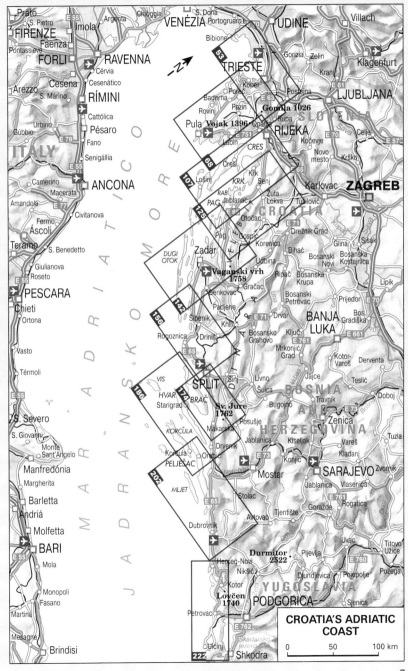

CROATIA'S ADRIATIC COAST

0   50   100 km

HISTORY AND CULTURE

ISTRIA

These days, Istria is one of the most popular destinations for international tourism on the Adriatic. As early as prehistoric times numerous peoples mixed and mingled on this peninsula, giving rise to vivacious cultural exchanges. Yet in spite of these multifarious ethnic influences, one in particular did manage to leave its special stamp on Istria: the urban civilization of Venice, which ruled this territory for over 500 years.

Prehistory and Antiquity

The Istrian peninsula is one of Europe's oldest areas of settlement. Finds made in the cave of Šandalja in southern Istria show conclusively that prehistoric humans lived here as early as 800,000 years ago in the Paleolithic Era. Later, in the Neolithic Era – between 6000 and 2000 B.C. – the main thrusts of Neolithic culture spread from the Near East to the southeastern part of Europe. A few traces of Neolithic culture have also been found in Istria; painted pottery, stone vessels and tools.

The Indo-Germanic tribe of the Histri-Illyrians (whence the name of the peninsula) migrated to central Europe in the late Bronze Age. The Histri were hunters and fishers and were also acquainted with agriculture and animal husbandry.

Nature offered especially advantageous preconditions for these pursuits: the fertile valleys of the Mirna, Dragonja and Raša rivers were ideal for cultivating

Preceding pages: Architecture on the Dalmatian coast was influenced by Venice (here the town of Trogir); a mosaic of Byzantine splendor in the Euphrasius Basilica of Poreč. Left: The "Valun Panel" in Cres.

fields; the forests were good hunting grounds; the clearings were good for livestock. Easily accessible but protected bays provided for fishing and shipping, and for busy trade with the Dalmations, Greeks and Etruscans.

The many isolated hillocks and mountaintops in the heartlands of the peninsula proved to be excellent, easily defendable locations to found walled-in villages. The special way in which the Illyrians built their settlements is known as the *Gradina Culture*. Sanctified districts and rulers' houses were built on the summit of a hill or a mountain, and the peoples' houses were constructed like a ring around the central rulers' residences. The entire area was defended by a massive wall rather like a fortress.

This settlement pattern has marked the urban build-up of many towns to this day. The wily Romans quickly recognized the strategic advantages of the Illyrian towns, and only applied the traditional Roman system, with its right-angled street grid, to new constructions.

The Illyrians also evolved a very advanced tribal culture with a social hierarchy and labor leadership. The social structure of that era is graphically illustrated on such items as *situlae*: vessels of bronze in the shape of a bucket, often decorated with typical vignettes from the day-to-day life of the Histri.

The drawings on the situla from Vače (Slovenia) suggest a patriarchal system. It shows a woman, possibly a priestess, offering a sacrifice to a male person; a nobleman or a god. The Histri introduced the art of metalworking to the peninsula in the second millennium B.C., and made wide use of it in a great variety of manners.

The situlae also reveal Illyrian skill at crafting metal. Similar objects were also found in Italy (Bologna and Este), which raises the issue of whether the Illyrians actually developed their handicraft skills themselves, or whether they adopted

them from another culture. It is also possible, as a number of historians believe, that Etruscan craftsmen at some time moved to Illyria to work.

Thanks to their advanced civilization, the Illyrians were soon able to subjugate the entire western section of the Balkan peninsula. They even managed to establish a toe hold on Italian soil – in Apulia, to be precise. Trade between their settlements developed more and more, and soon the local trade in wares no longer covered the demand. Contact was sought with other Mediterranean and continental peoples.

Economic ties were expanded internationally, especially with the Hellenistic world, but also well to the northeast: products from the Baltic made their way to the Mediterranean over the famous Amber Road, one of the oldest of the great trade routes, which crossed Europe

Above: The Illyrians had extensive know-how when it came to metal working (bronze belt covering from the 5th century).

from the Baltic Sea over the Carpathians and the Alps, through Istria and Cres, all the way to Corfu and Hellas (Greece). Amber was highly valued, not only for jewelry and as a currency, but also for its alleged magical powers.

The ancient Greek chroniclers made mention of Istria and the Kvarner region as early as the 6th century B.C. *Gnatya* ware, a kind of pottery excavated north of the Alps and in Greece, and Greek coins and sculptures found in Istria bear witness to the far-flung trade contacts entertained during antiquity.

Istria under Roman Rule

The arrival of the Romans brought about major changes. After conquering the Appenine peninsula, they set their sights on the Adriatic area. Their excuse was an alleged "call for help" by the Greek communities of central Dalmatia. By the 3rd century B.C., the Romans had succeeded in terminating piracy by the Illyrian tribe of the Delmata, and soon

had placed further areas along the Adriatic coast under their control. The process evolved as follows: After building the fortified town of Aquileia on the Gulf of Trieste in 181 B.C. to stem the barbarian tides, the Romans pressed on into the rest of Istria. Thanks to their better military organization, they ultimately broke the resistance of the Histri. Under the command of their chief, Epulon, the latter retreated to the heavily fortified town of Nesactium on the southern tip of the peninsula. But even this last bastion fell after a long siege, and all of Istria became Roman.

The new occupants then started systematically installing an efficient transportation network connecting all of their bases in the region. They built fortified military towns over the former Histri settlements, of which Pola (Pula) and Parentium (Poreč) were considered the most important. The two towns developed into major administrative centers and, owing to their protected maritime locations, important trade centers as well.

Under the Roman yoke, the Illyrians lost their land to Roman veterans and large landholders, and were turned into serfs or sold into slavery. Numerous rebellions failed to expel the Romans, but after the last great troubles, in 121 B.C., Istria was declared a colony, a status that at least improved the situation of the native inhabitants. When Augustus became emperor (27 B.C.-A.D. 14), all Istrians were granted civil rights, and the cities were declared *municipia* and incorporated into the Roman province of Histria.

Thanks to its geographical location at the northern tip of the Adriatic basin, its geopolitical situation and good connections to Italy, the city of Aquileia rapidly grew into one of the most important commercial intersections of all significant land roads and waterways in the Roman Empire.

The *Via Postumia* began in Aquileia and led to Emona (Ljubljana) and Pannonia. Another Roman road led through Tergeste (Trieste) to Tarsatica (Rijeka); other roads then went on to

Siscia (Sisak), and along the coast to the province of Dalmatia.

The *Via Flavia* began in Tergeste and ran along the Istrian coast. It gave rise to flourishing trade, especially with Italy. The great harbors of Pola and Parentium were transshipping points for olives, oil, wine and other products of the Istrian land to Gaul, Rhaetia (Switzerland) and Pannonia (Hungary). Archeologists have found amphoras with Istrian marks of origin in Rome. Significant examples of Roman architecture are also extant on Istrian territory, especially in the area around Pula, like the amphitheater, the Temple of Augustus, or the royal Villa Rustica on the Brijuni Islands.

By the 2nd century A.D., the Roman tradition was so deeply entrenched on this side of the Adriatic that even a couple of emperors of Illyrian origin were al-

Above: The Temple of Augustus in Pula, a testimonial of Roman architectural design. Right: Emperor Justinian (6th-century mosaic from Ravenna).

lowed to rule over the empire. Toward the end of the 3rd century, a man from Salona, the capital of Rome's Illyrian province of Dalmatia, even climbed onto the Roman throne, namely Diocletian. It was thanks to his efforts that construction of the palace of Split was undertaken, and for a short while Illyria was considered the real hub of the empire (see also history of Dalmatia, beginning on page 25). The sheer size of the empire and the numerous parts where wars were being waged led Diocletian to introduce the tetrarchic system at the end of the 3rd century. It called for dividing power between two *Augusti* (High Emperors) and two *Caesares* (Low Emperors), who ruled the eastern and western halves of the empire for a certain period.

When the Edict of Tolerance was promulgated in Milan in A.D. 313, guaranteeing religious freedom throughout the empire, the first Christian diocese appeared in Poreč, Pula, Novigrad and Koper. The bishoprics replaced the old municipia, taking over their former political, social and economic functions. Oratories were transformed into early Christian basilicas, giving rise to great masterworks of architecture over the centuries, such as the cathedral of Pula and the Euphrasius Basilica in Poreč.

In A.D. 395, the sons of Theodosius divided the Roman Empire into an Eastern Roman Empire and a Western Roman Empire. This step went well beyond the technical administrative division that had taken place under Diocletian a century earlier. Istria remained in the Western Empire, whose imperial seat was fixed in Ravenna.

Istria and the Great Migrations

A great migration at the end of the 4th century A.D. altered structures throughout Europe. The Visigoths, led by Alaric, marched through Istrian territory to Italy in 399. The Huns, under Attila, followed

in 452, coming from the Pannonian Plain. On their way to Rome they destroyed the wonderful city of Aquileia and caused economic havoc with the inland regions of the peninsula. Only the larger coastal towns were spared.

In 476, the Germanic military commander Odoacer took power in Italy after deposing the last emperor, Romulus Augustus. Eastern Rome – that is, Byzantium – took action to prevent his expanding into the eastern Adriatic. It sent the Ostrogoths under Theodoric (also known as Dietrich of Bern) to Italy. Odoacer's fate was sealed after he lost the decisive battle on the Italian-Slovenian border river of Soča to the north of Tergeste (Trieste). Soon after, the Ostrogoths established their rule over Italy and hence Istria.

The empire of the Goths fell apart right after the death of Theoderic. Byzantium under Emperor Justinian seized the opportunity to expand its territory westwards, with the ultimate aim of placing the entire Mediterranean region under its domination. In 555, Istria and Dalmatia became Byzantine. The Eastern Empire also founded the Exarchate of Ravenna as an administrative center and rebuilt Aquileia. This heralded a new cultural Golden Age in Istria lasting only a short while, but leaving traces that can still be seen today. The Euphrasius Basilica of Poreč, with its rich mosaic decoration, clearly shows its family ties to the mosaics found in Ravenna; it is quite possible that some of the same stone-setters were at work here.

Before Greco-Byzantine culture could totally replace Roman culture in Istria, another migration of peoples moved into the region. Around A.D. 500, large federations of Slavs crossed Pannonia from their homelands in the eastern Carpathians, along the Dnjestr and Danube, and settled the region between the Sava and the Drava. From there, groups of them consisting mainly of Croats continued on to the Adriatic coast, Istria and Dalmatia. From 600 onward, they settled the hinterlands of the coastal strip.

A correspondance between the Vatican and the Exarchate of Ravenna and the bishopric of Salona (Split) mention significant migrations in 599, 600, 602 and 611. Since the interior of the peninsula had by and large been destroyed by the migrations, and Byzantium had not yet completed setting up its administration, the Slavic tribes were able to settle large areas without being troubled by local resistance.

The Slav tribal structure did not consider related members of the tribe as part of the family. The tribal chief (*domaćin*, literally, "the head of the house") created a tribe (*bratstvo*) or a village community out of several individual families. Larger comunities (*župa*) were led by a prince (*župan*). A fortified city stood at the center of a župa, usually in a well-protected town (*grad*). Because of the way they had actually taken the land in widely dis-

Above: The Euphrasius Basilica in Poreč, a grand legacy of ancient Byzantine culture in Istria.

persed regions, many village communities were cut off from other Slavic tribes. A profoundly-rooted sense of particularism arose from this situation, and only seldom did several župas unite under one ruler (*knez*). The Slavs were also unable to spread into the tightly organized and well-defended Romanized coastal cities. These cities, in turn, were compelled to unite their forces in order not to be defeated in the short or long term by the superior number and strength of the Slav tribes. Byzantium, distant as it was, could neither stop the land-taking of the Slavs nor turn back the clock.

The Early Middle Ages: Lombards and Franks

When the Germanic Lombards invaded Istria in the 8th century, there was no single force strong enough to resist them. Even though they never ruled the entire peninsula, their occupation of the coastal towns made them the powers to be reckoned with. The Lombards estab-

History and Culture

lished a bishopric in Novigrad and turned it into their most important city. Istria continued being Lombard, even after the expansionism of the Lombards had driven them onward to northern Italy via Cividale in Friuli to Pavia south of Milan.

The Pope's request from Charlemagne to help defend against Lombard incursions on Roman territory resulted in a transition of power on Italian soil. The Franks seized the opportunity to swallow up the Lombard dominions, including Istria in 788, which had nominally been Byzantine up until that point. But the Church also took advantage of the situation to consolidate and extend its possessions. Contacts were still being maintained with Byzantium, and thus the Adriatic coast soon returned to the Byzantine fold. The Patriarchs found this to be a fine state of affairs, since the emperor was far away and the Franks were not yet strong enough to threaten the autonomy of the bishoprics. Churches underwent massive extension work, such as the Euphrasius Basilica in Poreč. New churches were also built, with impressive ornamental reliefs, elaborate capitals and wonderful mosaics.

In order to make sure they could hold on to the land they had fought so hard to aquire, the Franks unified the areas with a dominant southern Slav population under a powerful central government and recruited the services of some of the princes as margraves. Duke John, who received the new territories as a fief from the Frankish crown, introduced the feudal system to Istria. The legal norms by and large surviving from Roman antiquity in the cities were also adapted conveniently to the new power structures; in other words, the considerable autonomy of the coastal towns was curtailed. Older laws were only kept on the books inasmuch as they did not interfere with the excecution of power by the new rulers.

The economic and political goals of the powers that be were essentially focused on a single basic factor: the weakness of the cities, since they could expect no support whatsoever from those quarters. Newly-introduced taxes and other contributions, such as the church tithe and trade tariffs, punished above all the cities and the bishoprics. The duke additionally settled the fallow lands around the cities with Slavs.

The establishment of the feudal system led to the economic decline of the cities, since hitherto trade had run on the good old Roman tradition of hard currency. The exchange of commodities took place far more flexibly. The feudal system, on the other hand, was based on the backward principle of bartering. Rent, for example, was paid to the feudal lords in the form of work, or by delivering a percentage of the harvest.

Whatever money was in circulation ended up rapidly in the coffers of the princes or the Church. The Slavs were not nearly as critical of this system as the people living in the coastal cities, who had operated under a completely different system for centuries.

What also served to weaken the coastal towns was the build-up of larger communities in the country's interior, where the Slavs soon became a serious power factor. Illyrian settlements, such as Buzet, were greatly enlarged. Urban structures were positioned on hills and mountains: concentric ring roads and streets enclosed by walls spread out from a central marketplace like waves. This system is still found in many interior Istrian towns to this very day.

The Middle Ages and Modern History

The influence of the Croats, who poured in from Dalmatia heading north, grew so during the period leading up to the 11th century that a section of eastern Istria and the Kvarner region became part of the Croat kingdom. When the wars of succession raging throughout the Holy

Roman Empire came to an end, things in Istria settled down as well.

The struggle over the investiture in 1074 only affected Istria inasmuch as the Pope had promised the peninsula to the patriarch of Aquileia. This led to arguments over authority between religious and secular power. When the latter decided to transfer Istria to Louis IV of Bavaria in the 13th century, the patriarch protested. Bavaria was a powerful land which surrounded Aquileia, a fact that did not go down well with the church. Istria was then divided into two parts: the mountainous region, mostly covering the northeast, was granted to the Counts of Devina; the plains went to the Counts of Görz. Aquileia kept the coast.

As the power claims and attacks of Aquileia – and later Venice – grew bolder, the two noble dynasties placed

Above: The Slavs adopted the Illyrian way of settling the hilltops and surrounding their communities with a wall (Završje). Right: A Lion of St. Mark (Novigrad).

themselves in the hands of the Habsburgs, who promised to guarantee the protection of their territories.

In the 13th century, the empire, which was now ruled by the Staufen dynasty, entered its next crisis. Istria suffered a string of power struggles between the Counts of Devina and the Counts of Görz, as well as between Venice and Aquileia. Finally, in 1420, the maritime republic of Venice succeeded in annexing the coastal strip so coveted for its rich towns and salterns, and some of the more important inland cities, such as Motovun and Buje. Treaties of inheritance ultimately stripped the counts of the rest of the peninsula, which thereafter stayed under Habsburg rule until 1797.

The period during which the Lion of St. Mark ruled the region represented a cultural and economic Golden Age for Istria. Thanks to social and political transparency and generally peaceful times, trade flourished. This situation could have led to great cultural undertakings, but the Turkish wars and frequent plagues hin-

dered the easy spreading of the Renaissance – and later of the Baroque – movement throughout Istria.

Austria and Venice were deeply involved in battling the Ottoman Empire during the 16th century. The Uskoks, after being chased out of their native Klis (near Split) by the Turks, settled near Senj. From there they threatened the waters all around the Kvarner Gulf, and even conquered Rovinj in 1597.

With the help of the Austrians, these fearsome pirates succeeded in chasing the Venetians out of Istria in the Uskok War (1615-1617). But Venice had luck on its side: the Uskoks lost their Austrian protection and their central seat of power, so the coast once again fell to the maritime republic.

Nothing changed, thereafter, until the year 1797. Napoleon was the instrument of the turmoil. The Treaty of Campo Formio required Austria to surrender Belgium to the French in exchange for Venice, along with the entire peninsula, including Dalmatia.

After the defeat of the Austrians at the battle of Austerlitz (1805), these territories were once again turned over to the French, who now controlled all the former seaports of the enemy. The political upheavals also put an end to the feudal system. Nevertheless, freedom for all was seldom the result, as the feudal tradition was far too deeply anchored in the wealthier coastal communities.

On the other hand, the nationalist parties of the Croats, Slovenes and Dalmatians (and the Serbs) considered the principle of equality embedded in the ideals of the French Revolution as offering an opportunity to achieve at least some degree of economic independence as a way toward eventual political self-determination. Istria and Dalmatia were united with the eastern Tyrol, western Carinthia and Slovenia in the province of Illyria. The last scene remained to be written, however: after Napoleon's fall, the Congress of Vienna, held from 1814 to 1815, decided that it should go to Austria again.

A look at architectural history makes clear that new cultural influences only spread into Istria until the 15th century; after 1420, it was Venice that left the most noticeable mark, especially with its very particular interpretation of the Gothic. Urban loggias appeared all over the place (many of which are still being used as covered markets to this day), the most beautiful of which are in Koper and Pula. The Venetian-Gothic city palaces of the wealthy merchants demonstrate the increased activity and significance of trade. The campaniles erected during the Romanesque age were redone in Gothic style under Venice. The interiors of churches, too, were revamped and given new brilliance.

A school of painting with its own rustic style culled from various foreign influences evolved in the 15th century. Some impressive examples of this style are to be found in Hrastovlje (east of Koper) and Beram (near Pazin). The masters Ivan and Vincent from Kastav (Rijeka) worked there. Their treatment of the Dance Macabre motif proves that Istria had its own independent ideas of art.

The Renaissance had as little resonance in Istria as in Venice. The only place we find a representative square with a church, curia and city loggia as a typical urban composition from the Renaissance is the ensemble in Svetvinčenat, which was built in the 16th century.

The same applies to the Baroque age, which arrived in Istria around 1700, i.e., quite late. Neither money nor space were really available for the opulent decorative forms and ornamental techniques of the Baroque. In most cities, the older patrician houses were simply given a new Baroque exterior wrapping, the city hall of Rovinj being a perfect example of this disguising.

Right: The Italian poet Gabriele D'Annunzio storms Rijeka (Fiume) in 1919 to annex it for Italy, against the wishes of his government.

Glagolithic Script

Although Istria belonged entirely to the Roman sphere during the first half of the second millennium, and the Church acted as a cultural ambassador through its orders, it was the Slavs, particularly the Croats, who sought their own individual language and writing. The Glagolitic script thought to have been invented by the apostles Cyril and Method in the 9th century was the first Slavic script ever. The Croats later squared out his originally rounded letters.

Interestingly enough, Glagolithic writing, whose ancient form consisted of 38 letters, resembled no other European or Asian writing. It corresponded perfectly to the vocal system and served additionally as a numeric script. This brilliant creation by Byzantium's two missionaries appeared suspiciously like the work of the devil to the Roman Church, and even quite dangerous, since the Benedictine, Franciscan and Dominican friars sent by Rome could not offer the Croats anything similar. So Rome decided to prohibit and persecute Glagolitic writing without further ado. Many churches and village parishes possess Glagolitic inscriptions that prove, however, how long this writing was actually in use despite the opposition. Furthermore, it took a long time for Latin writing to finally establish its predominance in Istria.

The bulk of medieval Croat literature was printed in Glagolitic script. The most important printers were not in Istria by accident: the art of printing had established itself a lot quicker here than in southern Dalmatia. But even well prior to the invention of the printing press, there were numerous scriptoria that produced wonderfully illustrated codices, whether in Beram, Roč, Hum or Draguč.

Philosophy, too, had its share of proponents. Herman Dalmatin, born in the 12th century, was one of the first local thinkers. He focused his attention on Arabic

History and Culture

sources. In the 14th century, the *pope* (priest) Mikula from Gologica wrote the first set of laws derived from the Slavs' common law. But since the Croats had neither power nor a state system that could keep Venice, Austria or Hungary at bay in the long term, it was merely a matter of time before they lost their cultural independence. Certainly there were customs and traditions which influenced later folk art, but the great, visible cultural creations in Istria all go back to foreign rule.

Istria from the Nineteenth Century to the Present

German and Italian became the official languages when Istria fell to the Habsburgs in 1814. Using them was obligatory. During the 100 years of the Imperial and Royal Monarchy, the Slavs had to struggle for cultural survival. It was above all the population out in the country that succeeded in preventing its own language, Chakavian, from dying

out. The priests also played an important role in the preservation of the old traditions. In the mid-19th century, Bishop Ljudevit Gaj founded the Movement of National Rebirth, which was supported by the small class of Croat intellectuals.

The Habsburg laws on language also gave way to widespread illiteracy among the Slavs, as no school taught their language. Lacking proper training meant that the Slavs had no access to the lucrative jobs opening up in the industry built up by Austria. Croats and Slovenes were only allowed to perform manual work, which was poorly paid. But before the nationalist movement could achieve anything, World War One broke out, and all plans to build up a national community suddenly fell through.

The collapse of the Austro-Hungarian Empire gave the still young Italian nation the possibility of raising claims on the Istrian peninsula. A violent struggle arose around the important port cities of Trieste, Pula – Austria's number one naval base before the war – and Rijeka.

Austria still needed them badly as access ports to the sea, and losing them meant an end to all dreams of being a great power again. Gabriele d' Annunzio's famous putsch in 1919, which brought Fiume (Rijeka) into the Italian fold, prevented Austria once and for all from establishing a toe hold on the coast.

Under the protective shield of Italy, Fascism also spread into Istria. It was accompanied by further repressive measures against the Slav population. It was the armed resistance of all anti-Fascist forces of Istria that led to the liberation of the peninsula during World War Two. It was declared a free territory in Pazin in 1943. When Yugoslavia was re-established in 1945, Istria south of the Mirna was assigned to the constituent state of Croatia, and therefore became part of the Socialist Federal Republic of Yugoslavia under the leadership of Tito's Communist Party.

Above: Tourism has become one of the most important industries in Istria.

The harbors played a more significant role than ever after World War Two, when heavy industry was moved here. In the mid-1950s, a new and lucrative financial buttress was discovered: tourism. The centers of tourism along the coast, which remain important to this day, were either built up or extended back then.

In spite of Croatia's independence gained in 1991, the fate of the peninsula rests squarely on the future of political stability in the Balkans. Tourism, which is now the greatest source of currency and jobs, is very sensitive. Concern about the outbreak of armed conflict – as happened in 1994 when fighting broke out in Krajina, some 250 kilometers away – has kept tourists away.

But by August 1996, the hotels and camping sites of Istria and around the Kvarner Gulf were booked to the hilt once again. Countless new, private establishments, bars and pensions are bringing fresh wind into the world of tourism dominated hitherto by the old and somewhat creaky state-run businesses.

DALMATIA

Today's Dalmatia consists of the deeply cragged Adriatic Coast from Pag Island to the Bay of Kotor, the groups of islands lying offshore, and the western edge of the Dinaric Alps just beyond the coastal strip. This mountain range reaches an average altitude of 1,500 meters, a width of up to 300 kilometers in the south, and is neatly parceled up by valleys that run lengthwise.

The generally karstic landscape in the country's Dalmatian region and the Alps' strong declivity toward the Adriatic always made effective access to the hinterlands from the coastal roads difficult. This explains why the coast has retained its Western-oriented Roman culture, whereas the Slavic hinterlands were dominated first by Byzantium and later by the Turks. In terms of culture, the coast is less influenced by the Slavic Balkans; its close relationship to Italy is evidenced by cities such as Zadar, Šibenik, Trogir, Split, Korčula and Dubrovnik.

The karstic Dinaric mountains offer only poor conditions for agriculture. It is no wonder, then, that it was always thinly settled. Only a few larger towns in the hinterlands were able to make a name for themselves, like Knin, Mostar and Cetinje. But they, too, were dependent on trade with the coastal cities. During periods of conflict between the coast and the hinterlands these towns were particularly affected. The infertile soil was not enough to guarantee self-sufficiency to the local population, and isolated deliveries were frequently snatched by marauding gangs of bandits who could easily hide out in the numerous ravines of the Balkans.

The people of the hinterlands, who suffered continuous famines and plunderings, directed their energies toward the inland regions. They hoped to find especially fertile land in the Pannonian basin to the north, or in the neighboring water-rich Morava-Vardar basin. Moreover, ethnically related tribes had already settled there. An exodus took place and the Dinaric Alps became increasingly depopulated. Not until the 20th century did modern agricultural methods and an improved infrastructure provide an incentive to resettle the region.

The contrast between the coast and the hinterlands used to be mentioned in terms of nature; nowadays, the contrast generally has to do with newly-kindled nationalism. The coast is, for the most part, in Croatian hands; only a small section in the south belongs to Montenegro (Yugoslavia). The large inland territory is in Bosnian hands. A simple glance at the map suffices to show how the region's long and turbulent history has shaped its present-day borders.

From the Illyrians to the Romans

Just as they did in Istria, Illyrian peoples migrated into the coastal area and the Balkans over to Lake Ohrid around 1200-800 B.C. Some of the tribes even went as far as southern Italy (the Japygians, for example, who pushed as far as Apulia). Along the northern Adriatic coast it was the Istrians and the Liburnians, and the Delmata in the south. The name Dalmatia is obviously derived from them.

As opposed to their relatives in the north, the Delmata did not have a common system of state. Instead, they often fought wars amongst themselves. The reason for this was no doubt the precarious situation of supplies. Fields provided only little, partly due to underdeveloped methods of agriculture, and partly due to the winds that blew along the coast; from the north the *bora* and from the south the *sirocco*. When the harvest failed, it was common to go foraging in a neighbor's fields.

In light of these frequent mutual attacks, it is hardly surprising then that no uniform Illyrian system of government

came about. An "Illyria," if you will, only arose in the Bay of Kotor. At least, that's what the Greeks reported before they themselves conveniently annexed the territory.

Just as they did in Istria, the Illyrian peoples also headed first for the inaccessible, protected areas in their wild mountains. From the 6th century B.C. onward, the Delmata and the Liburnians began settling the peninsulas and islands, and founded the first towns. This paved the way for flourishing trade later on. Like the Histri in Istria, the Delmata also knew how to manufacture bronze, a fact evidenced by numerous discoveries of tomb gifts (helmets and vessels).

It is very probable that knowledge and raw materials reached Dalmatia through trade (with the Celts, perhaps) with the north over the Amber Road. The first

Above: Dionysus of Syracuse founded Greek colonies along the coast of Dalmatia (portrayed in a woodcutting from the 19th century). Right: Illyrian bronze sculpture, 3rd century B.C.

Greek merchants started making their appearance in the 5th century B.C. They were on the lookout for new commercial markets and commodities. While they brought fresh life to trade in the Adriatic region, they also invited piracy along the coast.

Not satisfied with trade alone, the Greeks also founded colonies. The most important of these was Vis, which goes back to Dionysus of Syracuse (4th century B.C.). The first toe holds on the islands followed foundations on the mainland, like Trogir, Aspalathos (Split), and Epidauros (Cavtat).

Many new settlements remained dependent on their "mother towns." These were in some cases large Greek islands such as Crete and Rhodes, and cities such as Athens, Epidauros (in Turkey) and Sparta, or in other cases colonies which had grown considerably and become independent in the course of time, like Syracuse on Sicily.

Dependency had its own benefits, however, namely protection from the attacks of Illyrian pirates, who had excellent hiding places in the islands and coves of the coastal strip. But the Greeks were unable to rid the Adriatic of piracy entirely, and trade remained a risky business. In the northern Adriatic, for example, the Greeks took a long time to penetrate as far as the Kvarner islands.

One thing is certain: the Illyrians adapted many elements of Hellenistic culture, for instance, in the areas of law, religion and technical innovation. Furthermore, they founded city-states on Greek patterns, and dominions that grew to become honest to goodness competition to the Greek colonies.

Ultimately, the expansion of Illyrian power led to armed struggle for supremacy along the coast. After 200 years of cohabitation, the Illyrians had sucked up so much of the superior culture of the Greeks that they could count on a major victory over their teachers. Since the Greek colonists were by and large on their own in the 3rd century B.C., because the mother cities had enough problems of their own to deal with, they called on the Romans for help.

Dalmatia under the Romans

Rome, which was just beginning its ascendency to becoming a world power, had a great deal of interest in controling the Adriatic Sea. And so it took this opportunity to ally itself with the otherwise Rome-shy Greeks and conquer the Illyrian cities, while at the same time wiping out the plague of piracy.

Rome's increased military commitment soon gave it supremacy over the entire Adriatic coast and its offshore islands. The final subjugation of the Illyrians only took place in 33 B.C., however, although most of Dalmatia had already been conquered by 168 B.C. To establish peace, however, took no less than six wars against the Illyrians.

For Dalmatia, Roman rule meant a Golden Age that was never to repeat itself. The Romans took over all Greek settlements and built them up to *municipia* administered by military officials. Towns in good strategic locations were fortified, and their urban development was extended according to Roman ideas of city architecture.

Besides creating a streamlined administration for their new territories, the Romans also went through great efforts to set up a functioning infrastructure. Their basis for this was the network of roads they had used to militarily annex the region from their original bases in Istria, and which allowed them to advance into the interior and southwards over Salona, the capital of the Illyrian province in central Dalmatia.

The denser network of roads not only enhanced troop mobility, but also allowed for quicker communications and better trade. The *Pax Romana*, the Roman legal system, and the introduction of Roman weights and measures – valid

throughout the empire – encouraged economic development in Dalmatia.

Romanization also meant that the local population was given Roman civil rights. Each person was thereby freed from the duty of paying tribute and had the opportunity to climb to the highest position in the ranks of military or government service. The most illustrious example of a Roman career is probably that of the emperor Diocletian, who was an Illyrian born in Salona.

The 3rd century A.D. was a veritable test of survival for the Roman Empire. Rebellions broke out in almost every far-flung territory, as the vassals serving as governors or advanced to kings hoped to achieve independence from the capital. The military once more gained importance: only its victories could keep the empire from falling apart. The soldiers

Above: Emperor Diocletian, Dalmatia's most famous Roman. Right: The ancient forum in Zadar has some decorative remains of Roman houses.

therefore only accepted emperors chosen from their own ranks. There were often several soldier emperors ruling at the same time. Their life expectancy, however, was usually extremely limited. Gaius Aurelius Valerius Diocletianus was one exception to the rule. He was proclaimed emperor on November 17, 284, by the guard in Nicomedia (Izmir), and immediately disposed of his predecessor and opponent Carinus. After Diocletian secured the recognition of the entire empire, he worked on shoring up its borders and undertook measures toward inner stability (among them the most severe persecution of the Christians).

Diocletian's most spectacular act, probably, was the naming of a co-emperor in 285. For the sake of administration, the empire was divided into two halves, each ruled by one emperor. In 293, Diocletian introduced the tetrarchal system. It was, up to that point, the capping of the most sweeping reform of the empire. Every emperor was given a deputy, and the period of reign was limited to 20 years. And just as he had promulgated, Diocletian abdicated in A.D. 305 in favor of his deputy.

In 308, Diocletian, who still had a great deal of influence, was offered the imperial rank again, but he declined. When he died, the tetrarchic system went with him. The emperors that succeeded him thought along dynastic lines; they preferred having their own sons in power rather than already-tested governors. Dalmatia's Golden Age also ended with the death of Diocletian. The former center of power, Spalato (Split), no longer had any importance, and no emperor ever again resided in Diocletian's splendid palace there.

In 324, Constantin emerged victorious from the power struggles that erupted after the passing of Diocletian. He proclaimed himself sole master, or *Totius Orbis Imperator*. When Byzantium was raised to the rank of imperial capital and named Constantinople, Dalmatia lost its

central position in the formerly huge Roman Empire and slipped to its edge.

The Edict of Tolerance proclaimed in Milan in 313 and the Council of Nice (325) allowed Christians to practice their faith and rebuild their churches as they pleased. That is how Christianity ultimately spread throughout Dalmatia, mainly in the cities on the coast. Roman culture traduced from the past now continued to evolve under the aegis of the Christians.

The Great Migrations

In 395, after the death of Emperor Theodosius, his two sons divided up the Roman Empire into an Eastern and Western Empire. Dalmatia at first fell to the Western Empire. Like Istria, the province of Dalmatia was also visited by the wandering peoples of the Great Migrations. The marauding Goths, a veritable plague upon the land, were nevertheless unable to capture the well-fortified cities left behind by the Romans.

Eastern Rome (Byzantium) succeeded in forging a temporary alliance with the Visigoths and Ostrogoths active on its borders and in the Dalmatian hinterlands, and thus in pacifying the region for a while.

The Visigoths, however, under the leadership of Alaric, failed to uphold their side of the alliance, started pushing southward, and tried to conquer Constantinople. The Byzantine troops did manage to beat Alaric back, however. The Visigoths then moved north again, headed into the Italian peninsula, and, in 410, invaded Rome.

Dalmatia became a province of the Eastern Roman Empire in the middle of the 5th century. The coast, with its cities still more or less intact and rich, was separated from the hinterlands, which were promised to the Ostrogoths if they agreed to settle down and found their own state. In return, they were asked to recognize the rule of Byzantium. As proof of their loyalty, and as a pledge to keep them in check, the tribal leaders were required to

send their children to Byzantium for their education.

Among these charges was Theodoric, who, after receiving the title of *Magister Militum*, or military master, was ordered by the eastern emperor Zenon to free Ravenna and Rome from the Germanic king Odoacer. He therefore moved to Italy – not without ulterior motives it appears – to fulfill his duty.

In 489, Theodoric annihilated Odoacer's troops, and in 493, the year of Odoacer's death, he added Italy to the Ostrogoth territories, declaring himself king at the same time. This was all sanctioned by Byzantium, which also expected that Theodoric, for his part, would continue recognizing the emperor and the supremacy of Eastern Rome. But after the death of Theodoric, Byzantium fought hard to retake Dalmatia, and the empire of the Goths soon fell apart.

Above: Theodoric (Dietrich von Bern), king of the Ostrogoths, depicted on a wood engraving from the 19th century.

After the restoration of the Roman Empire under Justinian, free maritime trade once again brought prosperity to the coast, but peace was short-lived.

Early Middle Ages

In 527, when Justinian acceded to the throne, the first Slavic tribes reached the Byzantine Empire in the wake of the Huns. These wild hordes at first raided the northern border for booty without showing any particular signs of wanting to settle. The Byzantine army built a number of fortified spots along the affected border, but these did not prevent further assaults. Almost every year some part of the Balkans was plagued by Slav incursions. In 574, they reached Thrace, in 547 and 548, they crossed the karst, invaded Dalmatia, and got as far as Durazzo (Albania). By the year 559, they stood at the gates of Thessalonica and Constantinople.

The Slav tribes only started settling down in the areas devastated by their own incursions when the Avars, the next human wave of migrators, reached the shores of the Danube and gave them a push.

Their taking of the land, however, was without any planning or internal coordination whatsoever. Every valley and every mountain range was turned into a *slavinie* that was jealously guarded against its neighbors. The individual tribes still stood under the influence of the Avars, who intended to pursue their goal of conquering Constantinople with the help of the Slavs.

In 626, the city was besieged by an alliance of Avars, Slavs and Bulgars. These "Barbarians," however, suffered a stunning defeat that broke the power of the Avars and also gave the Slavs something to think about. Incidentally, the Akathistos hymn, which is still sung to this day in the Orthodox Church to honor the victorious Mother of God, was written back then.

At about the same time, tribes of western Slavs came under the influence of the Franks, who also proved to be of assistance in shaking off the Avar yoke. But the Franks had their own set of ulterior motives and attempted to extend their borders as far as possible in order to gain access to the Adriatic.

When the Byzantine king Heraklios entered into negotiations with Dagobert, the king of the Franks, the Slavs' political position became obvious, namely, right between the Frankish and the Byzantine empires; that is to say, between West and East.

In the course of the 7th century, the Slavs gradually spread across the entire Balkan region, all the way to the Peloponese in Greece. The Byzantine Empire was powerless in the face of this expansion, as it had two other fronts to deal with at the same time: on the one hand the rise of Islam, and on the other hand, iconoclasm, which arose at the beginning of the 8th century.

Catholic or Orthodox?
The Schism of the Churches

Toward the end of the 7th century, the Croats penetrated the region bordered by the Sutla, Mura, Danube and Drina rivers, without initially making contact with the coastal towns. The latter were formally under Byzantine rule.

Contrary to the Istrian peninsula, the coastal strip of Dalmatia was not settled by Croats until the 8th century, because it was well protected by the Dinaric Alps. Since the settlement area of the Croats bordered on the kingdom of the Franks, Frankish influence was inevitable. Around 800, Charlemagne sent missionaries to Christianize the northern and central Adriatic area. The Museum of Croatian Archeological Monuments in Split has a baptismal font from around the year 800, inscribed with the name of the first Croatian prince, Višeslav. Around 860, the famous apostles of the Slavs, Cyril and Method, reached Dalmatia and Istria on their way to the Moravian Slavs. They brought with them the religious writing developed solely for the Slavic sounds, the Glagolithic alphabet, which formed the basis of all other Slavic scripts.

Where had the two missionaries learned Slavic? They were most certainly Greeks, and probably from Thessalonica, but it is thought that they had learned the language from Slav settlers in their homeland. Since the Gospel and the most important liturgical elements had already been translated into this script and hence into Slavic, Constantinople had a great advantage over Rome, which was also trying to win over the Croats for the Christian community.

The conflict between Rome and the Byzantine Church over religious leadership reached a climax in 847, when Pope John VIII prohibited the use of Slavic in the liturgy. With the assistance of the Franks, on whom the Croats were de-

pendent, the Vatican was able to firmly establish the Roman Catholic Church in Istria and Dalmatia. The Glagolithic alphabet did survive in some isolated regions, but the Roman liturgy was adopted everywhere.

Even when an independent Croat state was created at the end of the 9th century – which is a very significant event for the national consciousness of Croats even today – after heavy fighting against the Franks, Bulgars and Magyars, the Croat prince Branimir was granted papal recognition not least for his loyalty to the Catholic cause.

The Schism also led to an ethnic and linguistic split among southern Slavs. The Croats and Slovenes stuck to Roman Catholicism, with its Latin alphabet and occidental culture, while the Serbs and Bulgars adopted the Orthodox faith, the Cyrillic alphabet and Byzantine culture. Later political events served to widen these fundamental cultural differences even more.

Religious Architecture of the Early Middle Ages

In Dalmatia, the early Middle Ages were marked by significant pre-Romanesque church architecture, evidenced to this day by the Donat Church in Zadar and the Church of the Holy Cross in Nin, for example. These architectural monuments from the Carolingian era are by the same token the oldest ones surviving in Dalmatia, since nothing was left over from the Byzantine era. The churches are remarkable for their variety of ground plans: cloverleaf, Greek cross, rotunda and basilica were well known and widespread in Dalmatia.

Ancient Croatian draughtsmen also introduced their own ideas to the diversity of form. The Church of the Holy Cross in Nin is an excellent example: it is not only

Above: Cyril and Method, the "Slav apostles," (wood engraving, 1863). Right: The Church of the Holy Cross in Nin, an example of traditional Croatian architecture, 9th century.

a house of God, but also a clock and a calendar at the same time.

In addition to architecture, sculpture also developed at this time in Dalmatia. It reached its climax in the 12th century. There is no evidence of the development of a school of painting, however. While Roman culture continued to dominate the cities, in rural areas, where the Croats formed the majority of the population, Slavic culture took over quite firmly in Dalmatia.

Dalmatia from the High Middle Ages to the Renaissance

By the beginning of the 10th century, in spite of very violent incursions by the Magyars, the Croats had succeeded in consolidating their rule. Under Tomislav (910-928), a Croatian kingdom came into being in 925 which stretched from the eastern coast of Istria, over the Kvarner coast, to the (formerly Byzantine) *Thema Dalmatia* coastal strip. Northern Dalmatia, with the Bishopric of Nin headed by the Glagolithic Bishop Grgur, was regarded as the cradle of the this Old Croatian state.

In the years 926 and 928, a church synod was held in Split, during the course of which the Roman clergy was finally able to establish its supremacy over the members of the Croatian Church, which used Glagolithic as its own script. Besides building up a powerful military and an effective navy, Croatia's first king also attempted to lessen the divide created by the synod between the Romans on the coast and the Slavs inland.

The death of Tomislav signaled the end of the good times. Croatia was immediately shaken by dynastic struggles, and incursions by the Magyars and Venetians. The Serenissima, as Venice was known, had already cast a covetous eye on Dalmatia quite early in the game, because it was considered the key to the entire Adriatic. The famous Doge of Venice, Pietro Orseolo, ordered a campaign against the coast in the year 1000. By Ascension Day, his army had conquered the entire country; but in the long term, Venice could not maintain its hold.

Naval supremacy in the Gulf, as the Venetians called the Adriatic, was now solely in the hands of the Serenissima. Since Venice did not wish to prejudice its top-priority trade relations with Byzantium, which had granted it tariff-free status within the capital in 992, it gave itself the more modest title of "Protector of the Dalmatian-Byzantine Coast." This was nominal, at any rate, since Venice knew perfectly well that Byzantium could never recapture Dalmatia through military power without risking the weakening of its eastern border against the powerful force of Islam, and hence precipitating its own downfall. Announcing the protectorate was, therefore, nothing more than a diplomatic move.

When the Magyars annexed Croatia's possessions along the Adriatic, the Venetians sensed they were in the presence of quite a powerful opponent (they tried to mix into the Magyars' dynastic troubles following the death of their first king, St. Stephen, in 1038). Zadar placed itself under the protection of the Hungarian crown and turned against Venice. The town acted this way a total of seven times during its history, a prime example of its cantankerous spirit. The Doges retaliated with great brutality; even the local nobility, suspected of carrying the burden of responsibility, was deported en masse.

In the 11th century, the Croatian king Krešimir founded the port city of Šibenik to compensate for the loss of Zadar and to maintain Croatia's interests in the Adriatic. But the pressure from neighboring Hungary and Venice was too great, and Krešimir's successors on the Croatian throne were unable to keep the young state from collapsing. Even an alliance forged by King Zvonimir (1075-89) with the Normans under Robert Guiscard

Right: Lion of St. Mark– detail from a painting by Vittore Carpaccio, c. 1500.

against Byzantium and Venice failed to salvage the kingdom.

The last Croatian monarch, Petar Svačić, died in 1097 at the battle of Mount Petrova against the Magyars. After lengthy negotiations that aimed at guaranteeing Croatia's independence, in 1102, the Croatian nobility agreed to a dual monarchy with the Hungarians under King Kálmán. The treaty foresaw a Croatian viceroy (*ban*), whose function was to be that of representative of the king, and gave the Croats their own army, their own currency and their own tax system. The Hungarians, however, did not keep up their end of the agreement. They considered Croatia a province to be milked as much as possible, especially since the opening of oriental trade promised hefty profits for the cities along the coast.

The influence of the Hungarian crown on Dalmatia dwindled toward the end of the 12th century. In 1202, Venice invaded Zadar with the help of the knights of the Fourth Crusade. The entire coast was now in Venetian hands, while the pillaging raids of the crusaders considerably improved the travel budget for the crossing to the Holy Land. That, however, was only the start. In 1204, the crusaders and the Venetian army conquered Constantinople, overthrew the Byzantine Empire, and founded the Latin Empire, which survived until 1261.

As for Dalmatia and the Adriatic, even though it was under the rule of Venice starting in the 13th century, the Hungarians repeatedly raised claims to it. Dynastic conflicts and financial probems in the Hungarian royal house forced King Ladislaus of Anjou-Durazzo to relinquish all claims on Dalmatia to Venice for the sum of 100,000 ducats.

At this point, Venice set up a new colonial administration in all its territories. All important posts, be that of rector or of bishop, were filled by Venetian noblemen, and their job was to insure that

PAX VAN
TIBI GELI
MAR STA
CE /E MEVS

all new directives and laws were being obeyed to the letter. New taxes and tariffs were raised on trade and business, most of which flowed back to government coffers in Venice.

Quite understandably, these reforms gave rise to resistance, but Dalmatia was considered of such significant strategic importance to the new power brokers that the province was given its own *provveditore generale*, a special military authority to head the administration. The *provveditore* had his headquarters in Zadar. New buildings, governmental palaces, loggias and offices were built in the important towns, as well as piers and workshops. Unprotected cities were given new fortifications and well-armed garrisons. For Venice, the *Schiavoni*, or Slavs, soon became loyal subjects, and the regiments with Slav soldiers earned a reputation for being particularly effective in the struggle against the Turks, who were already moving up through the Balkans and sailing into the Mediterranean sea to challenge Venice.

Art and Culture in the Middle Ages and Renaissance

In spite of all the wars and the changes at the top, it was precisely during the Middle Ages and the early Renaissance that art and culture reached its climax in Dalmatia. The orientation toward Italy and the acculturation of the Croatian-Slavic and Latin peoples played a major role in the development of art and culture. The cultural barrier between the coast and the inland regions disappeared after a while. By not differentiating between the Latin and the Croatian-Dalmatian peoples, Venice supported this development – albeit while guided by economic interests.

The profitable Adriatic and oriental trade created an economic boom that the fine arts were able to profit from. Local ateliers opened in the cities to satisfy the demand on the part of the stratum of wealthy merchants and religious orders. Everywhere opulent palaces, indeed entire streets, were being built anew, and

churches and monasteries were being richly decorated, giving sculptors, painters and goldsmiths a great deal of employment.

Architecture, too, experienced a Golden Age in the 12th and 13th centuries. Outstanding examples of the Romanesque style are the cathedral of Trogir and the sculptures framing its portal, and the campanile in Rab. Dalmatia's Gothic masterpieces from the 14th and 15th centuries include the Franciscan and Dominican monasteries in Ragusa (Dubrovnik), as well as the Rector's Palace there, the cathedral of Zadar and, in particular, the cathedral of Šibenik.

The special influence of Venetian Gothic can be seen mainly in the carefully designed windows and house entrances of the secular buildings in the larger towns.

Above: One of the Romanesque masterpieces in Dalmatia – the Chrysogonus Church in Zadar. Right: A painting by a famous emigrant from Koper, Vittore Carpaccio (15th century).

At the beginning of the 15th century, both the economy and artistic growth stagnated. For lack of commissions at home, many Schiavoni moved to Italy during the Renaissance, where they continued to practice their well-known skills. Sculptors such as Ivan Dubrovnić, alias Giovanni Dalmata, and Franjo Vranjanin, better known as Francesco Laurana, could easily compete with the best in the field in Italy. There were famous painters, too, among the emigrés, notably Vittore Carpaccio. He was responsible for decorating the Oratorium San Giorgio degli Schiavoni in Venice.

Conversely, many Italian artists – not only from Venice – made their way to Dalmatia. Nikola Fiorentinac, who completed construction on the cathedral of Šibenik, is on that eminent roster.

Nevertheless, the cultural drain caused by the large-scale emigration of Dalmatian artists and craftsmen could not be stopped. In plain terms, the initiative to preserve Dalmatia from total cultural dependence on Venice and Italy was lacking, even if the Dalmatian people were permitted to maintain their Slavic identity in their customs.

Dalmatia Becomes a Venetian Province

After Venice acquired Dalmatia legitimately in 1409, the great maritime republic was constantly occupied by skirmishes right up until the 18th century. From the north, the Habsburgs were using every means to get a window on the Adriatic. The Ottoman Empire, coming from the south, the east and from the sea, was trying to gain more and more territory (and booty). In addition, local rebellions were frequent; but by and large, most of Dalmatia was peaceful, and many Schiavoni served the Lion of St. Mark as elite soldiers. The Schiavoni regiments consisted of Morlaks (Slavs from northern Dalmatia), the Bocchesi from Cattaro

(Kotor), Narentans (from central Dalmatia) and Christian Albanians.

The famous Giacomo Casanova, who observed the Schiavoni soldiers in the citadel where he was held prisoner for a while, described them as a horde of wild men who chewed garlic cloves all day as if they were candy.

They were indeed simple, loyal men who did battle with the French in Verona in 1797, and would have defended Venice from Napoleon's troops had their commander not prevented them from doing so. Venice was ultimately taken by Napoleon's troops without a single shot being fired.

Since Venice had been concentrating most of its attention on the military situation in Dalmatia, it had neglected public administration of the province to a certain extent. The governors (*rettori*, or rectors), mostly drawn from the lower, impoverished gentry of Venice, considered their job as a welcome opportunity to amass fame and considerable fortune as well. The people of Dalmatia were not safe from iniquitous acts by the rettori and the local privileged class.

It was no small wonder, then, that emigration increased, creating a significant social and economic drain. Even some Slavs, who had just fled from the Turks, preferred to return to the Ottoman yoke, which seemed no worse by comparison. Corruption, prejudice, pettifogging and neglection of duties seriously undermined public order, the economy and culture.

Normally, Venice should have sent inspectors (*sindici inquisitori*) to its provinces on a regular basis in order to keep a sharp eye on the doings of its local representatives. But the lower gentry, feeling its sinecures were being threatened, delayed the dispatching of the inspectors for nigh 130 years.

Thus, Dalmatia did not play an active or profitable role in the Venetian books during the last centuries of the city's supremacy. Venice had not cared as much for its agriculture as it had done for its other Levantine possessions. Cultivating the meager soil just seemed too hard an undertaking. Often the financial wherewithal was lacking, as it tended to go rather to the military for the expansion of citadels and the buttressing of fortified walls. The importance of these defensive measures, however, is perhaps best illustrated by Šibenik (Sebenico): the Turks besieged the Croatian city seven times in all. The area controlled by the sultan often began just beyond the first ridge, which thereby formed not only a political border, but a religious and cultural one as well.

The Turks conquered Serbia in 1459, the kingdom of Bosnia (which had lasted not even a hundred years) in 1463, parts of Croatia in 1493, and Zeta (Montenegro) in 1499. They then turned their attention to Venice's Dalmatian possessions. The 16th century started out as their best, so to speak: in 1537 they took the Croatian fortress of Klis, just eight kilometers from Split, and held on to it until 1648; and after defeating the Hungarians at Mohács in 1526, they set up shop in Budapest in 1541, and remained a threat to Vienna until 1683.

During the 16th century, pillage and arson became part of everyday life. Since all attempts at retaking the town failed, Split and its hinterlands fell into a kind of catatonic state. Even the great naval victory against the Turks at Lepanto only brought temporary relief in the long war against the sultans.

During the 16th century, the Uskoks living in Senj began threatening the Kvarner Gulf, with the help of the House of Habsburg, no less, which was bent on clipping Venice's wings. The Uskoks were a major force along the border to the Ottoman Empire, which nevertheless left them enough room for their own undertakings.

Right: Diplomacy and massive fortifications protected Ragusa (Dubrovnik) from Venetian incursions.

For Venice, Ragusa (Dubrovnik) was also a tough competitor in southern Dalmatia. Its high walls could not easily be climbed by soldiers, and the town also hammered out its independence thanks to some very cunning diplomatic moves. Ragusa's perseverance was a lot more painful for Venice than for the Turkish beys and pashas, who were quite open to financial gifts, since it could take the city neither militarily nor through bribery.

Venice's economic decline began when trade in the Mediterranean lost its importance thanks to the discovery of the New World and of new shipping routes to Asia. Venice only survived thanks to its mainland possessions and colonies. But the growing budget deficit started eroding those possessions. Even parts of Dalmatia had to be surrendered: the coastal strip at the foot of the Velebit range went to Austria-Hungary, and the mouth of the Neretva and the hinterlands of Split were given to the Ottoman Empire.

Cultural Developments during Venetian Rule

The numerous wars of this epoch were a major hindrance to Dalmatia's cultural development. Arts and letters only flourished as long as the aristocracy and the Church provided commissions. While literature still flowed from the pens of writers like Petar Hektorovič, Ivan Gundulič and Marko Marulič in the 16th century, and theater scored impressive marks with the works of Marin Držič, other artistic genres stagnated. Dalmatia increasingly sank into a deep provincial state.

The cities remained behind their defensive walls during the Middle Ages. Only a few palaces, churches and monasteries were adapted to the architectural style of the time. Often a Renaissance or Baroque façade – or sometimes simply a new portal – was added onto the massive town houses in order to go along with contem-

porary trends. The overall appearance of the city, however, was hardly altered; hence, to the modern observer, every Dalmatian old town still seems medieval.

Dubrovnik has a special status in this context. It experienced peaceful times very propitious for cultural life. Writers, philosophers, arists, scientists and architects all joined to create the special character that earned Dubrovnik the nickname "the Athens of the Balkans." For many travelers, Dubrovnik is the second pearl of the Adriatic after Venice.

CROATIA IN THE NINETEENTH AND TWENTIETH CENTURIES

Venice finally met its demise at the hands of Napoleon in 1797. He handed its Dalmatian territories to Austria, but then, in 1805, gave them back to Italy. In 1809, he founded the Illyrian Province, which consisted of Istria, Dalmatia, Kvarner and the Bay of Kotor. Thereafter, nothing really changed for the population of that strip of land and its islands until Dalmatia

was handed back for the next 100 years to Austria at the Congress of Vienna in 1815. The request by Croatian representatives to unite the coastal strip and interior regions (the narrow corridor designated a "military border against the Ottoman Empire," which runs between the present-day border of Slovenia and Bosnia-Herzigovina and Pannonian Slavonia) under a Croatian *ban* (governor) was not granted by the Viennese court.

In the new Europe, as it was recreated by the Congress of Vienna, Austria, with its newly-won east Adriatic coast and the developed free ports of Triest and Rijeka, rapidly developed in the 19th century into an important world naval power. Beginning in the mid-19th century, Pula was developed into the Austrian Empire's central military harbor. The harbor installations in the most important coastal and island towns were modernized, and shipyards were constructed for the servicing of the Austrian navy. In addition to new industrial complexes, residential areas soon sprung up, into which workers and

soldiers from the hinterlands and other parts of the empire soon moved.

Roads were built connecting the coastal towns with Budapest and Vienna, and later with Bosnia. With the expansion of railway lines and shipping routes of the Austrian Triestener Lloyd and the Croatian-Hungarian Steamship Company, predecessor of the Jadrolinija Shipping Company, Austro-Hungarian tourism firmly established itself on the Croatian coast. Civil servants were sent into the country, especially into the mostly Italian-speaking coastal cities, and schools and other educational establishments were constructed. Croatians received their first secondary schools, and they founded their own reading and cultural organizations.

In the face of the economic upswing enjoyed under their Austro-Hungarian

Oben: Dalmatia was given to Austria at the famous Congress of Vienna in 1815 (wood engraving). Right: Tito (Josip Broz), Yugoslavia's post-WWII leader (about 1960).

rulers, and as a consequence of the empire's political goal of Italianizing the coastal regions and of Germanizing and Magyarizing the hinterlands of the monarchy, the resistance of the majority Slavic population was awakened. A national movement was called to life which reached deep into the formerly Ottoman Balkan regions and encompassed not only Croatia and Dalmatia, but Serbia as well.

The concept of a common "State of Southern Slavs" – Yugoslavia – was at first merely a dream of Slav intellectuals. The Croat Ljudevit Gaj, the founder of Croatian National Rebirth (1830), also known as the "Illyrian Movement," worked on a standardization of the Croatian and Serbian written languages. In 1842, *Matica hrvatska*, an institution for the promotion of Croatian culture and science, was founded. At the same time, Zagreb developed into the cultural and political center of Croatia.

At the national assembly in Zagreb in 1848, *Ban* Josip Jelačić adopted the first

Croatian political program, in which, among other things, the constitutional independence of Croatia from Hungary – after a 700-year-long union – and the unification of all Old Croatian districts, from the Drau and the Danube all the way to the Adriatic, was demanded. The following year, Croatia became an independent kingdom.

Serious conflicts broke out between the pro-Hungarian and the pan-Slavic parties. In 1867, Rijeka and the Croatian coastal lands (the eastern coast of Kvarner) were reunited with Hungary; Istria and Dalmatia, on the other hand, came directly under the control of Austria.

In 1878, Montenegro succeeded in achieving independence. Its national boundaries were internationally recognized at the Congress of Berlin that same year. In 1881, a narrow land corridor in the Kvarner hinterlands, the military border, came under the direct control of Croatia. Bosnia and Herzigovina, once components of the Old Croatian state, whose borders with Croatia were established by the Treaty of Pozarevac in 1718 between the Ottoman Empire and Venice, was now, against the wishes of the Croatians, under the direct control of the monarchy.

Emperor Franz Josef I may have still been a popular holiday guest in the empire's spa town of Abbazia (Opatija), but general dissatisfaction with the monarchy, its politics and its administration was on the rise. The Resolution of Rijeka of 1905 called for an immediate break from the House of Habsburg and the formation of a state of southern Slavs. The Croatian-Serbian coalition formed at the time played an important role in Croatian politics until well into the 1980s.

After the end of the first Balkan war against the crumbling Ottoman Empire in 1913, the Kingdom of Serbia grew into a formidable Balkan power. With the assassination in Sarajevo of Archduke Franz Ferdinand, the successor to the

Austro-Hungarian throne, in 1914, the first sad chapter of 20th-century history began on the western edge of the Balkans: World War One. The archduke's assassin was a man named Gavrilo Princip, a member of the secret Serbian organization "Black Hand."

Austria was one of the losers in the war, and, as a result of the Croatian-Serbian coalition, the Kingom of Serbs, Croats and Slovenes (the so-called SHS State) was declared in 1918; later called the Kingdom of Yugoslavia, to which the Croatian coastal lands with the island of Krk, Dalmatia, Montenegro and most of the Dalmatian islands also belonged. The Italian nationalists were pacified with Triest and all of Istria, Rijeka and Zadar, as well as a few islands, during the interwar years.

The Kingdom of Yugoslavia was strictly centrally governed from the court in Belgrade. From the very beginning the country showed signs of instability and division through numerous inner conflicts, bloody demonstrations and politi-

cal murders and intrigue. This was a dark period for the Croatians (national and cultural identity had been denied, against all expectations, and national symbols were prohibited), in which tense relations between the Serbs and Serbia developed which remain to the present day. In 1929, Ante Pavelić founded the illegal Croatian *Ustasha*, which, together with Macedonian nationalists, assassinated King Alexander I of the Serbian Dynasty in Marseille in 1934.

The mismanaged and ruined Old Yugoslavia immediately capitulated during the Second World War upon the first attack by Nazi Germany in 1941. A barbaric civil war took place in the part of the country where Croats, Serbs and Muslims lived, between the "Independent State of Croatia" (which, with the excep-

Above: Rijeka was one of the industrial hubs of the Yugoslav republic. Right: Although the Adriatic coast of Istria and the Kvarner region were not theaters of war, local tourism experienced a serious crisis from 1991 to 1995.

tion of outer Istria, Backa and the Bay of Kotor, encompassed all enthically Croatian regions), with the Italian Fascists and the Nazi collaborator Pavelić on one side, and Old Yugoslavian officers, Chetniks (Serb nationalist guerrillas) and partisans on the other. Fifty years later, in 1991, an equally gruesome war began.

After Tito's successful partisan war, which many like-minded Croatians took part in, the Yugoslav multi-ethnic state was reborn in 1945 as the Socialist Federal Republic of Yugoslavia (SFRJ). Istria and Dalmatia were joined to Croatia; Montenergo became an autonomous republic. Tito's international successes as a statesman, which included the 1961 establishment of the League of Non-Aligned Nations and the idea of workers' self-administration, held the six culturally very different autonomous republics together until his death in 1980.

But, shortly after his death, the clamor for Croatian national independence suppressed hitherto bubbled up to the surface again.

By the time this independence was realized in 1991, the Croatian coast had already become one of Europe's most popular tourist spots. Germans, Austrians and Italians, above all, had become regular visitors to the beautiful coast and the offshore islands, which boasted modern hotels and vacation centers, as well as a good tourism infrastructure.

Croatia: Rise of a New State

Tito's death in 1980 evoked mourning throughout Yugoslavia. In socialist Yugoslavia, Tito was regarded as the embodiment of the quintessential freedom fighter. He provided the country with a symbol of identity and of integration. Today, especially in Istria, a few streets and squares pay homage to the former leader, and the Brijuni Islands have been declared a monument to Tito.

Josip Broz, known as Marshall Tito, became Yugoslavia's most important personality after World War Two, and one of the Cold War's most mercurial and brilliant figures. He was born on May 25, 1892, in the little village of Kumrovec to the north of Zagreb. His mother was a Slovene, his father a Croat. As an Austrian soldier, he took part in the Russian Revolution of 1917.

By 1927, he had advanced to the position of secretary general of the metalworkers union in Zagreb, but his political activities landed him a six-year prison sentence. In 1937, he became the secretary general of the outlawed Communist Party of Yugoslavia. During World War Two, he initiated and organized the partisan movement. Josip Broz was also the only commander-in-chief to actually fight, and was wounded at the front. Hitler put a price on the head of this much hunted but never captured fighter.

The international decisions made by this popular president, such as distancing himself from Stalin's policies in 1948, and his succesful economic and educational policies, became much more important than the settlement between the opposing warring factions – the Croatian

43

ian, was given a three-year sentence in 1981 and was banned from public speaking for five years because he denounced discrimination against the Croats in the official history books. The official number of victims of the fascist Ustasha regime during the war was much too high, he claimed, but the socialist government proclaimed them loudly for its own propagandistic purposes. Nevertheless, he was, and still is, accused of wanting to downplay the terror spread by the Ustasha regime.

In the 1980s, after Tito's death, everything seemed ready for the splitting of the Yugoslav state. Disapproval of the constant changing of the head of the State Presidium and economic scandal set the stage for the division of the country. The two highly industrialized states of Slovenia and Croatia were particularly disgruntled at being the golden goose for the development of the southern regions, such as Kosovo and Macedonia, and supplying the national economy with their hard-earned currency without having equivalent political representation in the committees.

nationalists and the partisans – in the period following the Second World War. There were always Croats who dreamed of national self-determination, but even after the fall of the proponent of "Yugoslav Patriotism," vice-president Aleksander Ranković, in 1966, the situation, according to Croatian patriots, hardly changed at all for "Croatians on Croatian soil."

In 1971, Marshal Tito had the "Croatian Spring" – an anti-Yugoslav independence movement – put down, and forced the pro-Croatian members of the Croatian Communist Party (KPH) to step down. A number of political dissidents, Croatian intellectuals, writers and scientists were charged with illegal activities against the state, and were persecuted and punished.

Today's president, Franjo Tudjman, a former general of the partisans and once upon a time a renowned military histor-

In 1989, Croatia introduced the multi-party system. The first democratic elections in 1990 were won by Tudjman's Croatian Democratic Union (HDZ) party. Shortly thereafter, an autonomous Serb republic was declared in Krajina, a predominantly Serb region in the Dalmatian hinterlands, because of their "denationalization in their own land."

After referendums in 1991, Slovenia and Croatia declared themselves independent states. After a ten-day war in June 1991, Slovenia managed to find a "common language" with Belgrade. The attempt of European Union negotiators, who met with representatives of the republic on July 8 on the island of Brijuni in an attempt to maintain the status quo in Yugoslavia, were fruitless; Slovenia and Croatia were internationally acknowledged in 1992.

Above: War damage is being repaired. Right: U.N. soldiers keeping an eye on Dubrovnik.

While political issues were being hotly debated, the Serb-oriented Yugoslav army, which saw itself as the savior of the state, was waiting in the stands and demanding a free hand in solving the problem. The State Presidium declared an ultimatum for the recanting of independence. The war of territorial claims on the western edge of the Balkans escalated; first between Serbs and Croats in open battles in Krajina and around Vukovar, and then, from 1992, also in battles between Serbs, Croats and Bosnien Muslims in Bosnia and Herzigovina. Thousands were killed and hundreds of thousands were forced to flee or were driven out on all sides. This was the terrible toll of the 1991-1995 war.

Istria and Kvarner, the western portion of Croatia, were not drawn into the war, but because of it they suffered from the disappearance of tourism. The Dalmatian coastal towns once crowded with vacationers, Zadar, Šibenik and Dubrovnik, were under constant grenade attack by the Yugoslav military.

In the summer of 1995, the Croatian army managed to win back large portions of Serb-occupied territories in Croatia, including the Krajina region, which made up a third of the Croatian state.

The Dayton Peace Accords, signed by Croats, Serbs and Bosnians in November 1995, and the U.N. SFOR troops stationed in the region, nowadays guarantee peace in Bosnia and Herzigovina.

Tourism in Istria and Kvarner had completely recovered by 1996; hotels and campgrounds were once again fully booked during the peak season. Dalmatia, too, and UNESCO World Cultural Heritage Sites, such as Dubrovnik and the Plitvice Lakes, are visited more and more. Many hotels in the more important resort towns have been privatized and modernized. The Croatian sea is today considered the cleanest in the world.

Maintaining the thousand-year-old cultural treasures of the region and protecting its ecology are today the main priorities of the forward-looking Croatian tourism industry.

SLOVENIA:
COAST AND KARST

KOPER
HRASTOVLJE
ŠKOCJAN
LIPICA
POSTOJNSKA JAMA
SLOVENIAN RIVIERA

Slovenia

*KOPER

Koper, ❶ a town of 25,000 inhabitants, has a beautiful old Venetian quarter, while at the same time it is the only modern commercial port in Slovenia. This fact makes it an important local entrepot for trade and industry.

Historically, the fate of Koper was mostly determined by outsiders. Three millennia ago, an Illyrian tribe named the Histri lived in the region, but it was the Greeks who founded the first official settlement on a small offshore island. This is mentioned under the name of Aegida and is generally considered the predecessor of today's Koper.

Some time during the 2nd century B.C., Istria was incorporated into the Roman Empire, and Aegida was overshadowed by its mightier neighbor Tergeste (Trieste). During Byzantine rule, Slavs arrived in the hinterlands of the settlement, then called Justinianopolis. Bit by bit, they drove off the Roman population, but were themselves ultimately conquered by the Franks, who gave the place

Preceding pages: The year's most beautiful days! On the beach of Baška on the island of Krk. Postojnska Jama, Europe's largest stalagtite cave. Left: Slovenia's pride and joy – Lippizaner horses.

the name *Caput Istriae* (Istria's Head). To this day the Italians still call it *Capodistria*.

For a long time the Franko-Germanic influence dominated, and in the wars against Venice for supremacy in the Adriatic, Koper always sided with the German Empire. It was rewarded for this in the 11th century by Konrad II with the right to self-government. But in the 13th century, Koper fell to Venice and quickly grew into an important emporium dealing in cereals and salt. The latter came primarily from the nearby salt mines of Sečovlje (Portorož). A great rivalry developed with Trieste, which was under Habsburg rule until World War One, but Koper grew strong and rich during this struggle. The most important buildings of the town were erected between the 15th and 17th centuries.

Trieste attained the status of a free port in 1719, and this meant the beginning of the end for Koper. Neither the Habsburgs, who reigned over the region between 1797 and 1918, nor Italy, which took the place of the Austrian monarchy as a protective power in 1922, could free Koper from the shadow of Trieste. One accomplishment of these years occurred in 1825, when the town was connected to the mainland by a causeway. In 1945, Yugoslav troops liberated Koper and

Trieste. The Western Allies did not recognize Yugoslavia's claim to this stretch of the coast, but Marshall Tito was not prepared to make any territorial concessions. Yugoslavia and Italy did not sign a peace treaty until 1947. Trieste was declared a free territory administered by the Allies. The Yugoslavs got Koper.

The frontier that came into being as a consequence of this partition was recognized as an offical border between Yugoslavia and Italy in 1954 in the Italian-Yugoslav treaty that was signed in London. Since March 8, 1991, Koper has been a part of the independent state of Slovenia.

**Koper's Old Town

A tour is best started at the **Brolo** (Brolo Square), the center of the old town with its most important sights: Koper's landmark is the ***Katedrala Sveti Naz-***

Above: Koper – a Venetian old town and a modern commercial harbor.

arij, with its remarkable Venetian-style bell tower. It dates from the 13th century, but was rebuilt several times in various styles. This is well illustrated in its façade; the lower part is late Gothic, but the upper part is in Renaissance style. A particularly precious item in this three-naved cathedral is the marvelous Gothic sarcophagus of the patron saint of the town, St. Nazarius (14th century), surrounded by a Baroque wrought-iron grille. This saint, who according to legend made Koper into a bishopric, is also remembered by a Gothic relief in the apse. Two of the paintings in the church come from the brush of Vittore Carpaccio, one of them is the *Madonna on the Throne*.

East of the cathedral is the oldest building on the square, the **Fontik**. It was built in 1392 as a granary. The structure, deeply indebted to Venetian Gothic, was rebuilt in the 16th century. The façade is decorated by the coats of arms of several *podestas* (mayors). A little further east, you come across the **Frančiškanski**

Slovenia

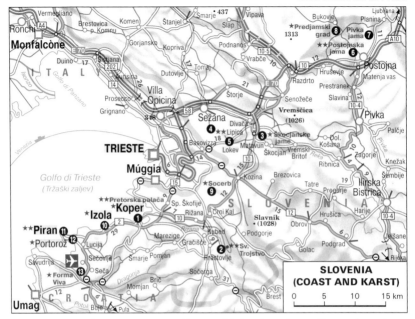

SLOVENIA
(COAST AND KARST)

0   5   10   15 km

samostan (Franciscan monastery) with a beautiful cloister.

If you follow Cankarajeva ulica to the east and turn onto Bazoviška Burlinova, you will come upon the small **Church of Sveta Ana**, which contains several precious paintings. The main altar painting, *Saints and Angels*, was done by Benedetto Carpaccio, a relative, perhaps even a son, of the famous Vittore Carpaccio (1455-1526). It is said of Vittore Carpaccio that he was born in Koper and was of Slav origin (in Slovenian Krpač; *krpa* means "scarf"). His place of birth is in the harbor right next to the oldest tavern of the town, immortalized in numerous paintings ever since it opened in the year 1619. On the other hand, it is known that Benedetto Carpaccio actually lived in Koper between 1538 and 1545.

On Tito Square in front of the cathedral is a remarkable *loggia in Venetian Gothic style. It was built in 1462 and currently houses a café. The other side of the square is flanked by the old **Pretorska palača** (praetorial palace). It has a splen-

did façade and actually consists of two separate buildings which were connected back in the late 15th century. The building on the left originally housed the offices of the port administrator and of the praetor; the one on the right held the local council.

If you walk down Kidrieva ulica towards the harbor (westwards), you will soon see on your left the **Palazzo Belgramoni-Tacco**. Built in the 16th century, today it houses the **Municipal Museum**. This museum contains a collection illustrating the history of Koper and Istria from Illyrian times to the era of settlement by the Slavs. Frescos, pottery, weapons, wrought iron objects and documents are exhibited.

Shortly before reaching the harbor, you will come upon the so-called **Justinian Column**, built in 1571 in memory of the famous sea battle of Lepanto. Venice sent a considerable number of boats to this battle, where, under the leadership of Don Juan de Austria, a son of Charles V, the West inflicted a major defeat upon the

Ottoman Empire. This battle not only secured Christian supremacy in the Mediterranean, but it also ridded the trade
routes of the plague of Ottoman pirates,
albeit only temporarily.

The **Vojkovo nabrežje** leads from the
harbor southwards to the **Muda Gate**,
built in 1516, the only remaining gate of
the once proud twelve town gates. On
Županieva ulica, close to Prešernov trg,
you will find what is probably Koper's
most beautiful house; **Almarigogna Palace**, built in Venetian Gothic style, whose
walls are decorated with frescos dating
back to the Renaissance.

HRASTOVLJE

The Ljubljanska cesta leads out of
Koper. After a drive of about twelve kilometers, you will reach Rižana. Turn south
(in the direction of Sočerga/Buzet) and

*Above and right: The beautiful fortified church
of Hrastovlje, with its fresco depicting the
Dance Macabre.*

follow the little road forking towards the
southeast until you reach the village of
Hrastovlje ❷.

The most interesting sight in this tiny
village of 140 inhabitants is the pretty
fortified church from the 12th-13th centuries, which stands on a hill overlooking
the community. The building, originally
in Romanesque style, was fortified in the
16th century as a means of defense
against the Turks. The inhabitants of the
village were "defense peasants," so-
called in the service of the House of
Habsburg, which gave them free use of
land and demanded no taxes from them.
In exchange for this, the peasants had to
defend the area if trouble was afoot. Since
peasant dwellings at this time were built
from wood, it was logical to fit the only
stone building of the area for special defense tasks and to surround it with a wall.
The church could not withstand a major
army, but might hold off marauding
bands.

Despite being a fortified building, the
interior of the **Church of Sveti Trojstvo**

(Holy Trinity) exudes a solemn atmosphere. It is decorated from top to bottom with frescos showing biblical scenes and images of the medieval world. The most interesting fresco is on the south wall and shows a **Dance Macabre**. Its message: In the face of death all men are equal, whether pope, emperor or beggar; how true, considering the devastating epidemics of the Middle Ages.

In the barrel vaulting of the side aisles are several small scenes from peasant life, among them vine-harvesting. These frescos date from 1490 and were painted by Ivan of Kastav. He belonged to a circle of local artists, and his works can be seen in other places in Istria, including the parish church of Beram.

**ŠKOCJAN

Only 35 kilometers from Koper – heading in the direction of Ljubljana – are the **Škocjanske jame** ❸ (Caves of St. Kanzian, whose entrance is in the village of Matavun), declared by UNESCO to be a World Heritage Site. Featuring a disappearing river and spectacular stalactites and stalagmites, this world-famous cave system is a product of the karstic phenomenon of underground drainage, and has still never been fully explored.

Between May and September there are one-hour tours in various languages led by specialist guides. The Reka River has created a cave system here about 2.3 kilometers long. The river seeps away into hollows more than 300 meters deep in places before disappearing completely a few miles later on. It then flows 35 kilometers underground and reappears only shortly before flowing into the Adriatic as the Timavo near Duino, north of Trieste. The fact that it indeed is the same river was proved by pouring dye into the upper Reka.

Both the cave and the area around the source of the Timavo gave birth to myths in ancient Greece and Rome. The entrance to Hell in Dante's *Divine Comedy* is at the Škocjanske jame.

**LIPICA

At Divača a little road forks off southwest to the green oasis of **Lipica** ❹, the home of the famous white Lippizaner stallions. It is worth stopping on the way at the Kraljeve Mesnine in the karst village of **Lokev** ❺, where *pršut*, a fine air-cured ham made from the meat of young pigs, is produced – sliced wafer-thin, it is a true delicacy.

In 1580, the Austrian archduke Charles, son of Emperor Ferdinand, bought 300 hectares of land near Lipica from the Archbishop of Trieste. Charles wanted to establish a stud farm here, although conditions for keeping horses were less than desirable: the karst region offered little water, and the ground was steep and dangerous and totally unsuited for paddocks. So the Habsburgs, undaunted by such petty things as the natural topography, adjusted the landscape to

the needs of the horses: the ground was levelled with red earth from nearby areas, and forests were planted to protect the animals from the cold, harsh bora wind. Appropriate water cisterns were also built for the animals, and finally the task of horse-breeding could start. The new breed of so-called Lippizaner, the pride of the Spanish Riding School in Vienna, came from crossing the undemanding and resistant local horses with the considerably fierier Andalusian breeds descended from Arabs. When born, the Lippizaner are almost completely black. At around the age of eight, their coats turn white.

The idyllic quietness of Lipica was disturbed quite frequently throughout its history. The stud farm had to move several times during the Napoleonic Wars. After the First World War, the imperial stud farm was closed down altogether and the 300 horses dispersed all over Italy, Austria and Czechoslovakia. After the Second World War, Yugoslavia was at first unsure of whether to continue the tradition or not; for the Communist state, it would have meant perpetuating a Habsburg heritage, and an expensive one at that. It is said that Tito put in a strong word in favor of the stud farm. Today, there are guided tours and dressage shows. Nowadays, you can spend a riding holiday in the Hotel Klub, where you can also play golf on a nine-hole course or try your luck in the casino.

POSTOJNSKA JAMA (Adelsberg Grotto)

Shortly after Divača the expressway to Ljubljana (E 70) begins, on which Postojna (known as Adelsberg in German) can quickly be reached. The road to the **Postojnska jama** ❻ is well signposted. The entrance fee is pretty high, but it is well worth it. A miniature grotto railway takes visitors to the starting point of the tour and back to the entrance. The guided tour lasts two hours (it's given in

Above: A good place for sailboats and their crews – the yacht marina of Izola.

several languages) and passes the most interesting calcifications in the caverns: bizarre stalactites (those hanging down from the roof of the cave, for those who don't know the difference) and stalagmites (the ones growing up from the floor) in charming lighting.

In a special pool there are plenty of blind, pale-skinned grotto olm salamanders. If they were exposed too long to the artificial light, they would suffer a "sunburn," so they are periodically released back into their dark freedom. The caves have a constant temperature of 8° C. Visitors should dress accordingly and also have sensible shoes because of the dampness. Shoes can also be rented at the entrance.

The caves of Postojna have been known since the 13th century. Geologists have figured out that they were washed out of the soft chalk and limestone by the Pivka River and its tributaries millions of years ago. During the guided tour, visitors are shown only the eastern branch of the approximately 20-kilometer-long underground system. The galleries you will walk along were washed out by the river only a few thousand years ago. The 500-meter **Paradise Grotto** is especially impressive, with its limestone sinter "curtain" and the perfect specimens of "diamond" stalagmites. Next to the Škocjanske Caves, the Postojnska Cave numbers among the absolute highlights of Slovenia's and Croatia's karstic landscape.

Another grotto is open to visitors 3.5 kilometers further north: it is the **Pivka jama ➐** which is more precisely part of a gorge measuring 6.5 kilometers in length cut into the limestone socle, and through which the Pivka River rushes.

Another six kilometers to the northwest the robber-baron Erasmus Lueger had a castle built right into a grotto: ***Predjamski grad ➑** is by far one of the most original "robber's dens" of the Middle Ages.

Socerb

Before returning to Koper, you should allow yourself a little side trip to the ***cliff castle of Socerb ➒**. The ruins of the mighty old fortress dominate the top of a rock growing out of the karstic upland directly on the Italian border. The location allows a marvelous panoramic view over the whole Bay of Trieste. They say that on a clear day you can even see Venice. The view is confined, however, to those visiting the cafeteria and the restaurant. But as the restaurant has very good food, combining the two pleasures is a very plausible option.

The castle changed ownership several times between the bishops of Trieste and the local barons, who often sold it to each other. The place was given its name by the Christian martyr Socerbus (*Sanctus Servilus*), who is said to have lived in one of the many karst caves which are found in the area.

SLOVENIAN RIVIERA
*Izola

Like Koper, **Izola ➓** was originally an island connected to the mainland by a causeway (hence the name *Isola*, Italian for "island"). It used to be a fishing village, but has developed into a holiday resort. No industrial port disturbs vacationers in their swimming pursuits. Worth viewing are the **Basilika Sveti Mauro** and the **Town Hall**, both from the 16th century. Izola has a few luxurious urban palaces to show, among them the restored ***Besenghi Palace**, as well as a new **marina**. Taking a slow evening stroll along the old harbor, with its many cafés and seafood restaurants, is one of the great pleasures in the town.

The products of the region – especially the **wine** – are well known all over Istria. Half of all Slovenian wines come from the coastal region (*Primorska*) and the neighboring karst (*Kras*). Wine grapes

tion, it soon became a sailors' stronghold. The name Piran is said to come from the Greek word *pyros* (fire), because the peninsula once boasted a lighthouse, which lit fires in order to guide vessels along the coast.

Illyrians, Greeks and Romans settled on the island until the time of the great migrations, during which mainly Slovenes settled here. Sea trade flourished, but growing wealth soon drew Piran into conflict with ambitious Venice. Despite its protected position, the town was conquered by the Venetians. Its independence was over, but not its trade: fishing and the extraction of salt from sea water remained the pillars of the economy, though the locals also lived well off smuggling.

Piran is considered one of the shining pearls of the Slovenian Riviera. The general impression is extremely harmonious, whether it is the well-run restaurants, cafés and bars in the sleepy little streets, or the practically unlimited subjects for photographers. The car-free old town invites the visitor to stay for good.

The heart of Piran is without a doubt *Tartinjev trg (Tartini Square). The most famous son of the town, the violinist and composer Giuseppe Tartini, was born here in 1692, the child of a Slovene mother and Italian father. His opus encompasses symphonies, religious works, and numerous works for violin, including the famous *Devil's Trill* sonata. His great claim to fame, however, was in reforming violin playing. The square was given its name on the 200th anniversary of Tartini's birth.

*Palazzo Benečanka, a Venetian palace on Tartini Square, is the most important example of Venetian Gothic architecture on the eastern Adriatic coast. The red-plastered façade is made up of lancet windows with marble sculptures. A lion holds a scroll between its paws with the inscription *Lassa pur dir* (Let them talk) – the locals say this is the response of a

are mainly grown in the areas around Koper, Sežana and Vipava. The best-known red wines are Merlot, Cabernet, Refošk and Teran. A remarkable white wine is Malvazija.

Of all the coastal wines, the Cabernet is the best quality, though many wines carry the quality mark DOC (*Denominazione Origine Controlata*). Altogether about 400,000 hectoliters are produced on 11,000 hectares of land, while private wine-growers collaborate with the state cooperatives in order to deliver a very good product. *Terra rossa* (red earth containing iron) is the characteristic basis for the preferred wines of the coast; teran, merlot and refošk.

**Piran

On a narrow, rocky peninsula is the picturesque town of **Piran** ⓫ (population 5,000). Thanks to its advantageous posi-

Above: Fishermen in Izola. Right: Venetian Gothic – Palazzo Benečanka in Piran.

Slovenia

rich Venetian merchant to those who were eternally jealous of him.

The new **Town Hall**, built in 1878, is also on Tartini Square. At the entrance you will see a polygonal stone on which the official measurements which were valid at the time are inscribed. Near the Town Hall, looking in the direction of the cathedral, the Town Café lures potential patrons with cappuccino and cream cakes, as well as with live piano music in the evenings.

On the square you will also find the house where Tartini was born, with a commemorative room, and the **Pomorskij muzej** (Maritime Museum), directly on the fishing and yacht harbor, where not only objects about the seafaring tradition of the town are shown, but, in addition, documents on the salterns of nearby Sečovlje.

Piran is dominated by the Baroque ***Church of Sveti Jurij** (St. George), which stands on Cathedral Hill. The first cathedral was consecrated here way back in 1317. The free-standing campanile

was built in 1607 as a copy of the one in Venice. In 1637, work began on a Baroque cathedral, but it was never finished. Highly recommendable is the wonderful view from here over the sea, the town and Tartini Square, especially in the evening.

*Portorož

Portorož ⑫ is a modern holiday resort with an elegant Riviera atmosphere. A four-kilometer-long promenade connects it with Piran. The protected bay, which today hosts the most popular **yacht harbor** in Slovenia, and has an artificially-made sand beach, has been of greater significance throughout history than the settlement itself.

The town was first mentioned in the 12th century as "St. Lawrence," in connection with the Benedictine abbey of the same name. It was later given the name "St. Mary's Rosary," and also "Rose Harbor." It was not until the late 19th century that the name Portorož entered into general use.

In the year 1202, the Venetian Doge Dandolo was leading a war against Trieste and the Dalmatian towns when he needed shelter from a storm. He arrived with his boats in this bay. On this occasion he also visited Piran, where envoys from Trieste voluntarily handed over the town.

The Venetian navy often sailed into these very protected waters to make repairs to its boats or just to recuperate from storms and battles. A rather prominent figure came to call in 1522: Emperor Charles V stayed in the Benedictine abbey, where he signed a decree putting the whole area directly under his authority after the death of the Patriarch of Aquileia.

The **Palace Hotel** started functioning as a spa after a doctor from Piran, named Lugnana, found a way to cure rheumatic illnesses in 1879. He experimented in the nearby *****salterns** of Sečovlje and Lucija,

Above: Spending time in the sun can make you thirsty – a typical seaside café in Portorož.

where he discovered the healing effect of salt-mud baths. A sanitarium was founded, and the 600-year-old saltworks suddenly found a brand new function and significance.

The health business boomed here: by 1890 a joint-stock company had been founded to finance the construction of further hotels. Initially, only rich people could afford the treatment; and, of course, Portorož got a casino – today located in the Hotel Metropol and very popular with Italian tourists. The spa services offered today include mud baths, massage, acupuncture, etc., and the place remains popular during the winter months, too. Portorož overflows in summer with Slovene day-trippers, as well as bathers from neighboring countries who frequent one of the 19 modern hotels and countless pensions.

On the cape south of the Lucija yacht harbor, the **Forma Viva Sculpture Park** ⑬, showing works of local and international artists, is an interesting place to visit.

KOPER (066)

Triglav, Pristanška 3, tel. 23771, fax. 23598; **Žusterna**, Istrska 67, tel. 284385, fax. 284409.

Restaurant Skipper, with a seaside terrace and yacht harbor, and very good food. Numerous restaurants, snack bars, cafés and shops, all geared to the tourist trade, are located along the shore promenade (Obala).

HRASTOVLJE (066)

Visits to the **fortified church** can be made by asking at house No. 30, tel. 59309.

ŠKOCJAN (067)

Hotel Triglav, in Sežana, tel. 31361; **Motel Kozina**, tel. 82611.

Škocjan Grotto (Škocjanske jame), year-round; June to Sept up to seven tours a day (in foreign languages, too), entrance 1500 tolar. April-October 10 a.m. to 5 p.m., November-March 10 a.m. to 3 p.m.

LIPICA (067)

KTC Lipica, Sežana,Lipica 5, tel. 31580.

The **Hotel Maestoso** belongs to the stud farm, has 150 beds, and features an indoor pool and a sauna, tel. 31009; the adjacent **Klub Lipica** is noticeably cheaper.

POSTOJNA (067)

Hotel Jama, 270 beds, tel. 24168. **Hotel Kras**, Tržaška 1, tel. 24071.

CAMPING: **Autocamp Pivka Jama**, four kilometers from the Postojna Grotto.

Adelsberger Grotto (Postojna jama), June 1-Sept 30 up to eleven guided tours daily (from 9 a.m.); two to four a day in winter. Expensive, but worth the fee: adults 1600 tolar, children (6-14 years) 800 tolar, in the peak season.

Predjama Fortress (Predjamski grad), same peak season opening times as Postojna; up to six tours daily in winter, from 9 a.m. Adults 800 tolar, children (6-14) 400 tolar.

IZOLA (066)

Hotel Sirena, Morova 6a, tel. 66221; **Hotel Marina**, near the yacht harbor, tel. 65325; **Hotel Rivi-**

era, Prekomorskih Brigad 7, tel. 62921, from June to September only.

CAMPING: **Autocamp Jadranka**, at the edge of town, tel. 61202, partially shady, shop and restaurant, cement shore.

Restaurant Ribič, the name says it all (*ribič* means "fish") – here you will find plenty of fish specialties, Veliki Trg 3, near the harbor; **Gostilna Canova Verdi**, cozy, pleasant establishment, horse meat among other specialties, tel. 65216.

PIRAN (066)

Maona, Cankarjevo nabrežje 7, tel. 746228.

Hotel Tartini (currently the top hotel in town, thanks to a total renovation), Tartinijev trg 15, tel. 746221; **Hotel Piran**, Stjenkova 1, tel. 746110, comfortable hotel.

Fiesa, tel. 73473, renovated, about 20 rooms, on the rocky cliff west of the center.

Pension Korotan, Obala 11, tel. 73050, toward Portorož, after Bernerdin.

Located between **Piran** and **Portorož** is the large **Bernardin Hotel Complex**, with the **Emona** and **Bernadin** hotels, Obala 2, tel. 4755104, fax. 475491.

The **Verdi Restaurant** is known for its fish dishes and its somewhat high prices, located at Verdijeva 18, near Tartinijev trg, tel. 75194. Also at Tartinijev trg is the **Kavarna Tartini**, a café with a gallery. A known gathering place for locals is the **Bistro Pergola**. Located near the lighthouse, this is an inexpensive restaurant featuring fish specialties.

Marine Museum (Mornarice muzej), Cankarjevo nabrežje 3, open Tue-Sun 9 a.m.-noon, model ships and paintings.

PORTOROŽ (066)

Turistične informacije, Obala 16 (on the shore promenade), tel. 747015.

Grand Hotel Metropol (with casino), Obala 77, tel. 740950; **Grand Hotel Palace** (with spa facilities), Obala 45, tel. 746950, fax. 746893; **Hotel Slovenija**, tel. 747051, fax. 747239.

CAMPING: In **Lucija**, at the southern edge of the harbor promenade, young crowd, a lot going on. Slovenia, tel. 747051, fax. 747239.

Marina, at the yacht harbor, tel. 471317, standard of fare and prices set to clientele on the yachts; **Ribič**, Seča 143, tel. 70790, an inviting establishment near the saltworks, featuring both good Italian and Slovenian cuisine.

Slovenia

ISTRIA

THE WEST COAST:
FROM UMAG TO PULA
EXCURSIONS INLAND
THE EAST COAST:
FROM PULA TO OPATIJA

CROATIAN ISTRIA

The landscape that presented itself first in Slovenia – fertile valleys, rich Mediterranean scenery, and hills crowned by picturesque little villages – continues in Croatian Istria and is enriched by the many sights to be seen in its wonderful coastal towns.

The charming and quiet inland region offers a pleasant contrast to the hustle and bustle of the coast, especially during the peak season (from April to September). Sleepy medieval places such as Motovun, Grožnjan, Roč and Hum, among others, have been able to maintain their charm over the centuries.

The proximity of the peninsula to Austria, Italy and southern Germany – Munich, for example, is only eight hours by car from Poreč – resulted in the past in huge floods of visitors, especially in the summer. In 1990, the number of overnight stays was a very impressive 16.2 million. When the Yugoslav conflict started the following year with the breaking away of Croatia (*Hrvatska*) from the republic, this number suddenly shrank to a mere 3.8 million.

Preceding pages: Feeding the seagulls against the beautiful backdrop of Rovinj. Left: View of the atrium of the Euphrasius Basilika in Poreč.

The great potential of Istria as a tourist magnet was recognized early on. The Yugoslav state supported the development of the infrastructure there beginning in the 1960s. Today, the peninsula has the largest capacity for accommodations on the entire Adriatic coast. On the other hand, the local economy became heavily dependent on tourism (which can be quite fickle). Most jobs are related in some way to the industry. Even the processing of some local raw materials (mineral coal and quartz sand for Murano glass, for instance) cannot relieve the lopsided job situation of the 200,000 inhabitants of the peninsula.

Istria isn't one of those Mediterranean holiday resorts likely to attract visitors all year round. Despite its Mediterranean climate, the winter can be pretty depressing because of the constant rain. In inland areas and in the Učka Mountains, temperatures at times fall below freezing, though it can also be cold on the southern and western coasts. In spring, when temperatures reach 15° to 22° C, the peninsula is transformed into a colorful sea of flowers. The rich greens of the meadows and fields don't hint at the barren karstic soil beneath. Everything that the earth seems to give to people here has been painstakingly wrought from it by generations of farmers. As opposed to the Dal-

matian region in the south, summers in Istria are not very hot; with an average of 26° C and a fresh breeze, a stay on one of the pretty bays or on one of the islands is a very pleasant experience.

In autumn, it gradually becomes quieter and the region reverts again to the locals – an ideal time of year for those who would like to spend their holiday away from the masses. The sea is still pleasantly warm for swimming, and prices tend to start dropping.

It is advisable to visit in September and October at grape harvesting time; investigate one of the vineyards and try the powerful Teran or Merlot, together with the excellent Istrian ham (*pršut*) and fresh olives. But beware: the traffic police know what kind of effect the local wines can have, and they ruthlessly confiscate the driver's license of anyone driving over the legal limit.

Above: Keeping the atmosphere lively – an accordion player in Buje. Right: Umag – pirates ahoy!

THE WEST COAST

Buje

The winding road from Portorož to Pula meanders across mild hills with big vineyards and leads first to **Buje ❶**, a good starting point for the drive along the west coast. The historic town is situated 220 meters above sea level, and its tall church spire shows visitors the way.

This hilltop was already settled in prehistoric times. When the Romans came, they called the place *Bullea*. In the Middle Ages, Buje was part of the Margravate of Istria. Essentially, its medieval structure has survived to this very day: it has a central square where the church stands surrounded by a circle of buildings, and then comes the town wall and its towers. The predominant building style is Venetian, but a modest provincial variety of it. It can be seen in many of the historic buildings that stables and store rooms were on the ground floor back in the old days, with living quarters above.

On the main square there is a beautiful Gothic **palace** with frescos from the 15th century. The façade of the Baroque ★**Parish Church of Sveti Servul** is unfinished. The surprise in the interior is the original organ from 1791.

The **ethnographic collection** shows folk art from the region. The **bell tower** of **Sveta Marija** (St. Mary's Church) is decorated with the coats of arms of Venetian rectors and a Lion of Saint Mark. Before leaving the old town, it is worth stopping in for a coffee or a snack at the Pod Voltom Restaurant. The terrace has a surprisingly delightful view.

The colorful 140-meter-deep ★**Baredine Jama ❷** karst cavern, six kilometers south of Buje between Baredine and Nova Vas, was opened to the public just a few years ago.

Umag

Umag ❸ is the center of a 20-kilometer-long stretch of coastline that is especially devoted to tourism. To give you an idea, in Croatia it holds third rank for the number of overnight stays. In Roman times, the settlement of *Umacus* occupied this flat peninsula. Despite all the upheavals throughout its history, it never changed in one respect: it has always been the biggest port for the export of Istrian wine.

Umag has an attractive old town with narrow streets and houses from various epochs. The coast from Kap Savudrija to Dajla is full of pretty bays, and it was perhaps unavoidable that Umag would become a tourist haven with more than 50,000 inexpensive hotel beds. Holiday resorts and camping sites line the coast right up to Savudrija in the north.

At **Cape Savudrija ❹**, in 1117, the Venetians won an important naval victory against the fleet of Frederick Barbarossa and Pope Alexander III. But few sunbathers think of history as they lie near the shadows of the pine forests that run down to the coast in places, and where the spicy smell of resin mingles with that of *čevapčići* and other delica-

CROATIAN ISTRIA

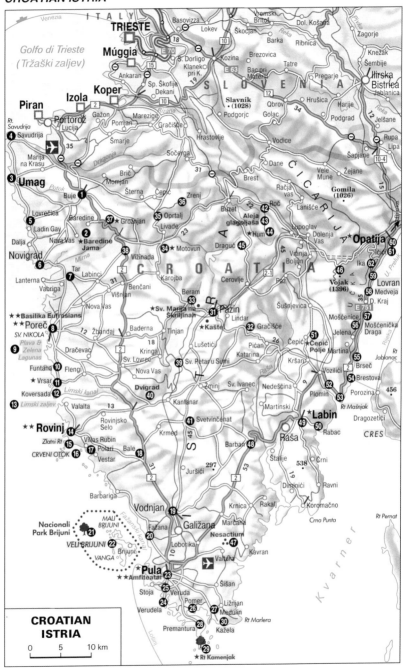

cies. Recreation is the name of the game in these parts.

The harbor bay north of Umag is home to the largest **marina** of the ACY, the Adriatic Yacht Club. Umag also has an international **tennis center** located in the resort village of **Stella Maris**. It offers a total of 18 courts plus a beautifully laid out center court. There are another 80 clay courts available in the area.

Every year in July/August, the **Croatian Open** tennis tournament is held here, where a number of top-notch players compete for the respectable prize money of US $400,000. One shouldn't forget, after all, that Goran Ivanisevič and Iva Majoli are Croatian. Maybe a few tennis lessons at one of the coaching centers here could bring positive results.

In front of the nearby Laguna Restaurant there is a real lagoon: a **sea-water-swimming pool** with a slanting pebble beach ideal for children.

In August, the Umag coast is no place for a quiet holiday; you have to like the turmoil. In the evenings, a miniature rubber-wheeled train collects holidaymakers from along the coast and delivers them to the **old town**.

In the seafood restaurants – mostly historic buildings along the waterfront – you should try the various recipes for perch or spaghetti *vongole* (with a light clam sauce), and then move to the *piazza*, near the Venetian campanile, for an after-dinner espresso.

Those who don't find Umag entertaining enough can make trips during the peak season to Venice, Trieste, Grado, Brijuni or Postojn. Tour operators even pick guests up at their hotels.

Novigrad

If you follow the coastal road to the south, you will pass **Lovrečica** ❺, a shallow bay good for swimming and the **Ladin Gaj** camping site, one of the many where nudism is allowed. Sixteen kilometers down the road you reach the picturesque and richly-endowed town of **Novigrad** ❻.

Novigrad is full of ice cream parlors, restaurants and cafés, which, together with the countless boutiques and souvenir shops located hereabouts, try hard to please the visitor. You shouldn't miss an opportunity to have a glass of the locally-produced *Malvazija* wine. The *old town is closed to cars in July and August. There are good places for swimming on the western and northern sides of the old town. Big hotels and holiday centers have been built here, too.

Novigrad was founded by the Romans and called *Aemona* by them. It was first referred to in written documents as *Neapolis* (New Town) in the 5th and 6th centuries. In the Middle Ages, the by then Slavic-named Novigrad was elevated to the rank of bishopric, a position which it retained until 1828. Novigrad was under Venetian rule from 1270 on. It was probably for this reason that it became the subject of a devastating Turkish attack in 1687. Until the 18th century, Novigrad was an island town separated from the mainland by a narrow tidal inlet.

Despite the damage done by the Turks, the town managed to retain a lot of its medieval character. Some parts of the fortifications are well preserved. The buildings inside the old town wall were gradually rebuilt in the Venetian Gothic style. In the **Palazzo Rigo** of the Urizio family there is a **lapidarium** with a collection of ancient tombstones from Novigrad and surroundings. The Byzantine and medieval fragments of guilloche ornaments, as well as fragments of stone church furniture and decorative sculpture, deserve special attention.

The Romanesque **Parish Church of Sveti Pelagij** (St. Pelagius), with its typical Venetian campanile, has a *late-Romanesque crypt below the presbytery. The vestry houses richly-decorated psalm books from the 15th century.

Istria

The road from Novigrad to Poreč runs past the big Maestral and Laguna hotels, as well as a camping site. A bit further on, the coast road crosses the Mirna River, which was navigated in earlier times using wooden rafts. From the old peasant village of **Tar ❼** there is a small road leading to the Bay of Tar (*Tarski zaljev*), where you will find camping and seafood restaurants.

Poreč

In the more than 2,000-year-old **Poreč ❽**, with its wealth of cultural monuments, beats the pulse of Istria's western coast and of its hinterland, called Poreština. About 22,000 people live in this region, but in the peak season Poreč and its surroundings are host to millions of tourists. The landscape of gently rolling hills with vineyards, olive groves and fertile fields, and little oak and pine woods here and there, constituted the basis of Poreč's earlier wealth.

Today, Poreč possesses by far the most developed tourist infrastructure in all of Croatia, where no fewer than 120,000 hotel and pension beds are available. In the bays south of the town, which are called "**lagoons**" ❾ by the locals – the "Blue" (**Plava**) and the "Green" (**Zelena**) – big holiday resorts were erected. They are rather more like small towns, with hotels, their own marina and shopping centers. Guests will find everything they need here for their vacationing. A great number of trips are offered, both by bus and boat.

Between July and September, the place is as busy as a bee hive. Many international festivals – including a pop music festival and a film festival – concerts of classical music in the basilica, a fishermen's festival, folkloric shows and sporting contests offer a broad range of amusements.

Right: Sunbathing on the rocky beach of Poreč.

To the south are many offshore islands. The landscape here, plus the extremely clean water and the advantages of the climate, make this part of the Riviera very popular. Some visitors might be intimidated by the masses, others, though, will enjoy the excitement.

About 800 B.C., Illyrian-Histri settled here and built a port. Finds of lower-Italian and Etruscan ceramics suggest it was a lively trade center in the 6th and 5th centuries B.C. In 177 B.C., Rome took the capital of the Illyrians, *Nesactium* (Pula) and subsequently conquered the whole peninsula. Following the building of roads in the new colony, the significance of *Parentium* (Poreč) increased. During the rule of Tiberius, Parentium was given the status of a colony – *Colonia Julia Parentium*.

Up until the 3rd century, Christianity found more and more followers here. In the 6th century, Slav tribes settled here together with Avars. With the decline of the Roman Empire, the Byzantine Empire gradually took over and developed Parentium into one of its most important strongholds. The wonderful Euphrasius Basilica, of which more is mentioned later, was built in this period.

In 1267, the Venetians took control over the town. Poreč was devastated several times in subsequent years by the Genovese, Turks and Uskoks. Plagues introduced by trade ships sailing from the Orient also savaged population numbers. In the 17th century, Poreč's inhabitants numbered only 100. Venice colonized the depopulated town with immigrants from Dalmatia, Bosnia, Montenegro and Albania.

After the fall of Venice (1797) into Napoleon's hands, the town came under Austrian rule. During the 19th century, the proportion of Italians increased rapidly, and after 1918, Poreč and the whole of Istria was given to Italy. During the Second World War, Allied bombing caused considerable destruction in Poreč;

75 percent of the buildings and numerous monuments were damaged. Immediately after 1945, rebuilding started according to old plans.

The Euphrasius Basilica

The most important monument here dates from Byzantine times and is unique to Croatia: it is the **Basilika Eufrasiana** ❶ (Euphrasius Basilica), with its gorgeous Byzantine mosaics. If you follow the main road, the Roman *Decumanus* leading into the town, you will find the basilica on Sveta Eleuteria, on the right-hand side.

This architectural complex has a special place in early Byzantine art. When Bishop Euphrasius commissioned the building in the 6th century, he employed craftsmen from Constantinople and Ravenna. They created a work of art consisting of an octagonal baptistry, a square atrium, a vestibule, a three-aisled basilica and a memorial chapel with a trifoliate outline. The present church stands on the foundations of several previous buildings; in the interior of the church the mosaic has been broken up in places to show parts of the foundations.

Unfortunately, the violent history of the region left its trace on a great part of the interior ornamentation. A lot of the work on the western façade in particular was lost. But above the portico between the round-arched windows there are still original mosaics to be seen depicting various saints.

Behind the three-arched vestibule, a modest door opens into the three-aisled **basilica**. The nave is separated from the aisles by two rows of marble pillars. The wide variety of Corinthian and Byzantine capitals is remarkable. The most impressive ***mosaics** are in the apse. The choir is divided from the nave by a railing of carved marble plates.

The altar is shielded by a ***ciborium** richly decorated with encrustations dating back to the 13th century. At the front you can see the **Annunciation** and, above the triumphal arch, Christ on the throne.

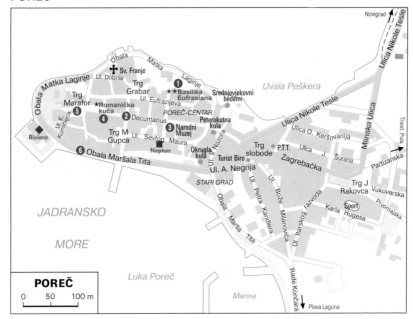

He is surrounded by the Twelve Apostles clad in long white robes. The round arches immediately underneath are decorated on each side by six medallions showing saints, in the middle the Lamb of God is accentuated.

The eye of every viewer is inevitably drawn to Mary on the throne on the domed ceiling of the apse. She is holding the Christ Child in her lap and is surrounded by saints and angels. From left to right they are: St. Maurus, patron saint of the town, Bishop Euphrasius, founder of the church, who can be recognized by the model of it, and Archdeacon Claudius, brother of Euphrasius, who is holding the Gospel.

Two angels are followed by three martyrs. In the middle of the apse some of the important scenes from the life of Mary can be seen: the Annunciation, for example, and the Visitation. In one very charming little detail in the Visitation, a

Right: The old town of Poreč is a great place to do a little shopping.

servant girl shyly pulls a curtain aside to observe the scene.

The lower part of the apse is decorated with geometric patterns made of marble. The mosaics in the apses of the Euphrasius Basilica excel in the variety of their colors and shades, and the detail of the presentation. In the soft light of a late afternoon the golden background shines in unearthly glory.

The **baptistery** dates back to the 5th century and to a previous building that once stood on the site of the basilica, but it was subject to enlargement and other changes in the 6th century. It is an octagonal building with the font in the center. The font has an octagonal bowl in which those baptized – until the early Middle Ages they were adults – were fully submerged. The octagonal form was chosen because of the symbolic meaning of the number eight: it stands for rebirth, a new beginning. Do not miss the climb up the ***bell tower** behind the baptistery: the view will be well worth the march up all those steps!

Next to the basilica stands the **Bishop's Palace**, which is accessed by going through an arcade. It dates originally from the 6th century, but was rebuilt several times and has a remarkable portal from 1464.

A Stroll through the Old Town of Poreč

Refreshments – and, as you will see, a little secular entertainment – are in order following a visit to the basilica. The ice-cream parlors along *Decumanus ❷, the main street in town, are famous, though not so much for the quality of their ice cream – which is in fact quite good – but, rather, for the antics of the barmen and waiters. Balls of ice cream come flying through the room and are caught in the mouth of a waiter, another waiter juggles with the cones, while huge bowls of ice cream are artfully decorated. If you order coffee, you need strong nerves. Grinning perfidiously, the waiter will bring the cup and suddenly stumble at the last minute, letting out a desperate cry as the cup sails towards the guest, followed by general uproar in the room. For a split second the guest will think his or her clothes are about to be ruined, not to speak of the thought of hot coffee on the skin; but it was all just a well practiced and choreographed trick – the cup was empty, and you are left with a rapidly-beating heart and a sheepish grin.

Directly opposite the street leading from Euphrasius to Decumanus is the former **Sinčič Palace**, dating from the 17th century. No nobles live there today: it houses instead the **Narodnij muzej** ❸ (National Museum) of the Porečtina region, with a lapidarium showing sculptures and capitals. The Hermes Monument, with its representation of grape and olive harvesting, the prehistoric and medieval collection, and a small art gallery are among the most recommendable items here.

Istria

A bit further down Decumanus, right before Marafor Square, is **Romanička kuča** (Romanesque patrician's house) ❹, with a wooden balcony and Gothic windows built some time later. Along the main axis of the old town are many buildings from the Romanesque period, mostly modernized with Gothic elements.

Decumanus ends at the main square of Poreč, **Trg Marafor** ❺ (Marafor Square). It was originally the Roman forum, measuring precisely 45 by 45 meters. This was the exact size of an *Insula* (island), which is what the Romans called their apartment houses. The Roman pavement has survived in several places here.

In the numerous alleyways around Trg Marafor, half-hidden restaurants specializing in fish and grilled meats have opened for business. The beach promenade, **Obala Maršala Tita** ❻, is also lined with restaurants.

Rakovča Square holds a colorful fruit and vegetable market every day. This is a good place to get a sense of the life of the town beyond the tourist scene.

From the old town harbor, shuttle boats take you in a few minutes to the island of **Sveti Nikola**, covered in pines and evergreen oaks.

Vrsar and the Lim Fjord

To continue visiting Croatian Istria, take the coastal road that runs from Poreč further southeast via the fishing village of **Funtana ⑩**, with its many restaurants, and ultimately arrives at the lively holiday resort of ★**Vrsar ⑪**.

This is a small picturesque town with a Romanesque church (St. Mary's) from the 12th century. Vrsar harbor is in a wide bay strewn with little green islands. In nearby **Koversada ⑫**, only the naked facts count: this is Croatia's biggest nudist colony, with hotels, bungalows and a camping site. Koversada is at the mouth

Above: Harvesting grapes for wine around Vrsar. Right: The Lim Fjord is home to an abundance of mussels, clams and fish – a prime destination for gourmets.

of the ★**Limski zaljev ⑬** (best translated as the Lim Fjord). The karst hills are overgrown with cypress and pine trees, and you can easily spot the fjord's lucrative mussel and oyster farms.

The further you advance up the fjord (on foot only), the higher the surrounding hills, until the walls of the canyon finally reach an impressive height of 100 meters. The cliffs here are covered in maquis; on the southern shore grow oak and ash; on the sun-bathed northern shore, evergreens.

The Lim Fjord is rich in fish. Because of the low salt content and the high concentration of oxygen in the water, the flora and fauna are highly developed. Many species of fish come here every year to spawn.

The road does not continue further from Koversada into the fjord. The only closer approach by car is on a road at the end of the fjord forking off westward from Highway 2 (Buje-Pula). This road ends at a motel with a restaurant, serving mussels and clams guaranteed to be fresh. Although the fjord looks like an inviting place for a swim, bathing is strictly forbidden.

★★Rovinj

Rovinj ⑭ is one of the finest jewels of the Istrian coast, not an easy boast by any means. The place was populated by Illyrian-Histri in antiquity, and was then conquered by the Romans in 129 B.C. They gave it the name *Ruginum*.

Rovinj was one of the first towns on the peninsula to recognize Venetian supremacy in the region. In spite of this, or indeed because of this, during its long history Rovinj was ravaged several times by the Genovese, pirates and epidemics. When more peaceful times finally arrived, the town spread onto the nearby hills of the mainland. In 1763, the narrow channel separating the island from the mainland was filled in.

Today, the town numbers more than 11,000 inhabitants. The silhouette of Rovinj as seen from the Adriatic is the hallmark of the whole Croatian coast: no townscape could be more harmonious. The narrow houses are clustered on the sides of an oval-shaped limestone rock, dominated by the Church of St. Euphemia and its campanile. Since the Middle Ages, the town center has been protected by a wall, three of the original seven gates of which survive. Picturesque alleys and the richly decorated portals of the palaces recall at every step the eventful past of the town.

A Stroll through the Old Town of Rovinj

The best place to begin a tour is undoubtedly on Trg Maršala Tita. **Bregovita ulica** begins here, a pretty street dating back to the 18th century. With its arcaded passageways and frescoed vaults, it is really the most picturesque street in the town. ***Ulica Grisia**, used by local artists as a center for galleries, also begins on Trg Maršala Tita and leads to the town's landmark, the campanile of the ***Church of Sveta Eufemia**.

On the highest point of the former island the inhabitants built a parish church in the 18th century, following the plans of a Venetian master builder, Giovanni Dozzi. They used the walls of a Romanesque predecessor. The campanile, very similar to the one in Venice, had already been standing for 70 years before the actual church was started. The campanile itself took 26 years to build, and when it was finished it was the highest in Istria, measuring 60 meters. It is decorated at the top by the figure of St. Euphemia, which was designed to serve as a weather vane as well, and shows the wind's direction from its dizzying height.

In the interior of the church you will find the valuable sarcophagus of the town's patroness saint, modeled on late-classical patterns from the 4th and 5th centuries.

According to legend, St. Euphemia is a martyr who, in the year 304 under the rule of Diocletian, was thrown to the lions in Chalcedon. The lions, however, had no appetite, so she was broken on the wheel. Her body was taken to Constantinople, but it disappeared during the chaos that followed the sacking of the city, and reappeared in a miraculous way on July 13, in the year 800, on the shore of Rovinj where it was swept up by the sea. A fresco close to the sarcophagus depicts the scene.

Since then, the church has been a place of pilgrimage for people from all over Istria. They come especially on the saint's day, September 16.

The church has a number of other treasures besides the sarcophagus, among them paintings by Giovanni Contarini, a pupil of the great Italian painter Titian. The sculptures come from the workshop

of another Italian master, Gerolamo Laureato.

The **Museum of Local History** is located on the harbor promenade. It hosts art exhibitions and stays open in the evenings during summer.

The oldest building in Rovinj is not in the historic old town, but is on the "mainland" close to the present-day bus station by Trg Oslobode (Liberation Square). It is a Romanesque heptagonal **baptistery** dating back to the 12th century. Why the builders deviated from the classical octagonal form will probably forever remain a mystery.

Rovinj is situated between two bays, on the north *Valdibora* and on the south *Katarina*. This gave rise to the two very different appearances of the town. The northern side seems massive and forbidding, with the houses forming an impenetrable high wall. The southern side, with the harbor and the pretty promenade, is really quite friendly. Cars are forbidden in the old town, so that long, meditative walks can be enjoyed undisturbed.

Above: Rovinj, a picturesque townscape exemplifying Venetian architecture. Right: Rovinjsko Selo is known for delicious ham.

If you would rather not visit one of the islands for a swim, you can find a nice place in the rocks beneath the shore promenade where the Hotel Rovinj stands. There are stairs leading down to the waterfront.

South of Rovinj, at *★Zlatni Rt* ⑮ (Punta Corrente), is a park dating back to 1860, with exotic plants and some very well laid-out walking paths. A regular shuttle boat connects the two offshore islands, **Sveta Katarina** and **★Crveni otok** ⑯. Crveni otok has a special climate and evergreen vegetation; the laurel and myrtle give off a sweet pungent smell that envelops everything. The island has traces from Roman times, and a monastery from the 6th to 7th centuries (with a restaurant and gallery).

In the 19th century, the entire island, including its buildings – which had become quite dilapidated over the years – was sold to Baron Ivan Georg Hütterrodt, who built a park and restored the monastery. The small chapel and the castle show paintings by Alexander Kirchner, who concentrated on depicting the development of the Austrian merchant marine and naval forces, and maritime travel from Rovinj. Before the naval harbor in Pula was established in the 1860s, Rovinj was the most important Austrian base on the Adriatic coast.

The coastal area around Rovinj is varied, with rich forests of evergreen oak and Aleppo pine. It is excellent countryside for long hikes, as there are almost no paved roads. There is a coastal road to **Villa Rubina** and to the nudist colony of **Polari** ⑰. **Camp Veštar** is a bit further south.

Between Rovinj and Pula

On the way to Pula you will drive through **Bale** ⑱, a little town on a karst plateau which has succeeded in maintaining its typical medieval look and feel. The **fortress**, which used to belong the the

Venetian families of the Soardos and Bembos, stands sentinel right at the entrance to the town. The center of Bale is dominated by a church, which simply seems to be too big for the place, and its spiky campanile.

The area around **Vodnjan** ⑲ is intensively cultivated. Grapes and olives are grown, as well as tobacco, and wine is made here, too. One of the most recommendable sights here is the Baroque **★Parish Church of Sveti Vlaho** (St. Blasius) in the old town center, which boasts a valuable stock of paintings, a collection of religious artworks of all kinds, and some enigmatic mummies. The town also has some beautiful examples of Gothic and Baroque architecture.

There is a road leading from Vodnjan to **Fažana** ⑳, from where the ferries to the Brijuni Islands depart.

The ★Brijuni Islands

The Brijuni Islands, better known by their Italian name *Brioni* (and which in

the time of Josip Tito were a closed area) are formed by two principal and eleven smaller islands and have, since 1983, constituted the **National Park of Brijuni** ㉑. They are all covered in typically rich Mediterranean vegetation.

With its 690 hectares, **Veli Brijun** ㉒ is the biggest island of the archipelago. Historians have shown that it was already populated in prehistoric times. There have been finds of stone and metal tools here. The islands came into Roman hands around 177 B.C., with several new settlements serving the Romans as summer resorts.

In 1893, the industrialist Paul Kuppelwieser, who came from Merano, bought the islands in order to build hotels and holiday resorts. He also built a race course, a casino, golf and tennis courts and a water pipeline from the mainland.

Above: A narrow lane in Bale, charming in the rays of the afternoon sun. Right: A school outing to the Byzantine castrum on the island of Veli Brijuni.

Kuppelwieser's vision was to turn the Brijuni Islands into a meeting place for the great industrialists of his day, an Adriatic Monte Carlo, though far more discreet. He created a luxurious tourist complex that attracted the upper crust of the time. After the First World War, Kuppelwieser's death and a few other unfortunate events (fires, Italian sanctions, etc.), Brijuni entered a period of major crisis. Second World War bombing destroyed much of what was was left.

Yugoslav premier Josip Broz Tito visited the islands for the first time in 1947, and quickly added up their resort value. The relics of cultural history and the mild climate, together with the restored luxurious tourist facilities, were tailor-made to help the president and his circle of friends, political cronies and guests relax. The islands provided the perfect background for important – and secret – conferences.

There are day tours to Veli Brijun from all tourist centers on this part of the Istrian coast, and there is a regular boat

from Fažana. The authorities aim to preserve the select atmosphere of the islands, so they are closed to cars. Luxury and middle-quality hotels offer restaurant dining, tennis courts and golf courses – even a conference center – creating the best conditions for a pleasant stay. Island hopping on local boats is a very popular activity here.

Veli Brijun has many interesting sights which can be easily reached on foot, by bicycle or with the local electric railway. The zoo and the safari park have deer, bison, zebras, lamas, giraffes and even a "holy" cow and a camel. Many of these animals arrived here as presents for Tito. The vegetation, which can be investigated closely thanks to numerous trails, yields Scots pine, eucalyptus, cedar, stone pine, cypress, and a thousand-year-old olive tree, plus a rich selection of Mediterranean flowers.

The parks are masterpieces of garden landscaping. It is said that there are more than 600 species of plants alone on the main island. There are about 200 species of birds, many coming here to spend the winter.

Near the bay of **Zaliv Verige** are the ruins of a ***Roman villa** from the 1st century A.D. The mooring place and the number of buildings arranged on terraces sloping down to the shore prompted the theory that it must have been the villa of an emperor. There is a religious area with three temples, priests' lodgings and a storehouse for votive offerings. The floors in the villa show remains of multicolored mosaics, and the walls have remnants of frescos.

In the bay opposite is a ***Byzantine castrum**, a structure unique to the whole Croatian coastline. Within is walls is a small town that was inhabited until the 16th century; this is why the foundations and other structures have been so well preserved.

In **Gospa Bay** stand the remains of an early Christian **basilica** with a three-aisled structure. Benedictine monks built an abbey near this church, which they abandoned after a plague in the 14th cen-

tury. The square fortified **watchtower**, a medieval construction dating to the 12th century, stands not far from the harbor in the midst of the little settlement of Brijuni. Next to it is a Venetian **fortress** from the 16th century, which was rebuilt in 1955 and now houses a **museum** and a little Gothic chapel. The museum contains materials relating to local archeology, as well as to natural history. There are also exhibits on the most recent period in the history of the islands, entitled "Tito on the Brijuni Islands." It notes the significance, for instance, of the year 1956, when the three independent leaders, Tito, Nasser and Nehru, signed the Declaration of Brioni, the founding document of the League of Nonaligned States.

All over the island are valuable sculptures created by contemporary Croatian artists. West of Veli Brijun is the island of **Vanga**, which was formerly Tito's summer residence.

Above: The Pula Opera Festival is held in the Roman amphitheater every summer.

*Pula

Pula 23 lies almost exactly at the southernmost point of the Istrian peninsula. It is a town of more than 60,000 inhabitants, making it the biggest community in Istria. It stretches along the southeastern shore of a five-kilometer-long and over two-kilometer-wide bay, whose very broad opening to the sea allows access for even the biggest ships.

The surrounding hills protect the port from stormy winds; the bora, for example, which can strike throughout the year. Its geographical situation proved ideal for the development of Pula into one of the most significant commercial, political and cultural centers in northwestern Croatia.

Pula is said to be the oldest town on the eastern Adriatic coast. It was first mentioned by the Greek historians Kallimachos and Lykophron in connection with the founding of a settlement by the Argonauts. According to Lykophron, the foundations for the "town of refugees" were laid by snakes, after Jason and Medea stole the Golden Fleece, fled over the Danube (*Hister*) and came to this spot. In their language, the name of the settlement was Pula.

So much for the legend. What is known is that the name Pula, meaning castle or spring, has its origins in pre-Roman times. Archeological finds prove a 3,000-year-long history of continuous occupation – something rare in Europe. Near the town fort, the remains of a cyclops wall were found; a wall built out of very big and irregular square-hewn stones. In the 1st century B.C., the town was fortified by the Histri. Their capital was the nearby Nesactium; Pula served only as a harbor. The significance of the town grew in the second half of the 1st century B.C., when the Romans finally managed to conquer the Histri and take over the entire peninsula.

About 40 B.C., Pula achieved the status of a colony. Under Emperor Augustus the damage suffered during the fighting was put right, and Pula obtained a new face. As an administrative center, the place attracted representative structures, such as triumphal arches, a theater, an arena, a forum and a temple.

Given that Pula was an important cultural and trade center on the route between Aquileia and Asia Minor, Christianity spread pretty early here – even though many of those first Christians actually ended up in the wrong section of the Roman arena. In A.D. 425, Pula became the seat of a bishopric. On the site of the present cathedral there was a single-naved church dating from the 4th century.

During the time of the great migrations, and following attacks by Goths, the fortifications were strengthened. The building materials used by the locals were the already hewn stone blocks from the Roman theater and arena. But all this activity was to no avail against the subsequent attack of the Ostrogoths. Pula's fortunes revived in the 6th century when it

came under the sphere of influence of Constantinople. It was mainly churches and monasteries that were built here now.

The influence of the Eastern Church upon the fate of the town was to survive until the 13th century. In 1331, Pula was forced to place itself under the protection of Venice, which prevailed over the Patriarchy of Aquileia. Their common hardship under Venetian rule brought the town's Slav and Roman populations closer together.

But Pula's development continued being hampered by wars and epidemics, so that by the 16th century the town had only 1,000 inhabitants. Since the ancient classical monumental architecture fulfilled no contemporary role and mattered little to the locals, it swiftly became dilapidated and fell into ruin. What did not collapse was taken to Venice, which decorated itself with marble pillars, sarcophagi, mosaics, fountain balustrades, tomb plates and sculptures.

Pula almost turned into a ghost town; in 1631 only 300 people lived there.

When the Congress of Vienna gave Istria to Austria, little changed immediately for Pula.

Only in 1848 did the town acquire a certain degree of strategic significance. Shortly afterwards, in 1853, Pula was made the most important port of the Habsburg Empire. The Austrians built a completely new town, but only to fulfill their requirements for a military base. It is no wonder that the amazing increase in the number of inhabitants (from 1,126 in 1842 to more than 40,000 by the end of the 19th century) was not accompanied by any significant enrichment of social or cultural life.

The lack of an autonomous urban culture proved especially negative for the Slav population. The official language was German, the language of the shipyards and businesses was Italian. The Austrian policy of Italianization did not allow Croatian to be taught in the schools. In 1904, James Joyce came to Pula, where he worked as an English teacher. In his letters, Joyce describes Pula rather unflatteringly as a "godforsaken nest," and a "Siberia on the sea."

During the two World Wars, Pula and its port suffered major damage. After 1947 and the incorporation of the town into Yugoslavia, rebuilding work was started. Pula flourished again as an industrial center; the region was opened up for tourism.

Discovering Pula on Foot

The most important sights go back to Roman times, with the **★★Amfiteatar ❶** (amphitheater) being the strongest magnet for visitors. The three-storied amphitheater, built under Augustus and enlarged under Vespasian, is the sixth in size among the Roman arenas to have

Right: Taking a break during a stroll through the town of Pula at Republic Square (Trg Republike), once the Roman forum.

survived. It once held 23,000 spectators who could follow events in the 133 by 105 meter oval. The outer wall, with two stories of arcades and a third story above with square windows, reaches to a height of 32.5 meters. The amphitheater's exterior ring is almost completely preserved. Two main and four secondary entrances in the towers funneled the crowds onto the double stairs leading to the terraces. Corridors from the basement, where rooms for the "technicians," the gladiators and the wild animals were located, ended in the arena.

Games were held here until the year 404, when gladiator fights were abolished. The arena served afterwards as a market place. The Venetians then used it as a stone quarry, which was one of the more common fates of Roman buildings all across Europe, but obviously not for too long. A plan to take down the amphitheater and rebuild it in Venice was even discussed for a while, but it was ultimately voted down by the Senate of Venice in 1583. Senator Gabriele Emo, who had a decisive influence on this decision, is honored by a memorial plaque on the northwest tower.

Today the arena is dedicated to more bloodless shows: in summer it hosts the **Pula Opera Festival**. One opera that has become a standard of the festival is Verdi's *Aida*. Spectators have the firm promise of glorious evenings like those enjoyed at the opera festival in the Verona arena. In the vaulted cellars there is an exhibition on the growing of vines and olives in Roman times.

Following the coastal road Riva winding around the old town, you will reach the **★cathedral ❷**. It was built in 1640 on the foundations of several earlier churches, the first dating from the 4th century. There are mosaics from the 5th and 6th centuries, as well as a Roman sarcophagus from the 3rd century. The campanile was built out of stone quarried from the amphitheater.

A walk along the shore will lead to *Trg Republike ❸ (Republic Square), which was the site of the old forum during Roman times. Near the **Gradska palača** (Town Hall), decorated with coats of arms and small sculptures dating back to the Renaissance, there is the well-preserved **Augustov hram** (Temple of Augustus). The harmonious building opens onto the square, its vestibule majestically supported by six pillars. The walls are built out of regularly-hewn limestone blocks. Above the Corinthian capitals is a decorated frieze with a dedicational inscription, originally done in bronze. Under Byzantine rule, the temple was transformed into a church.

Strolling another 200 meters down Flaciusova, you will soon see on your left the **Kapela Sveti Marije Formoze ❹**. This diminutive Byzantine chapel, dating back to the 6th century, was once a section of the St. Maria Formosa (del Canetto) Basilica that stood here, and was designed in similar fashion to the Euphrasiana in Poreč. The simple chapel, which has the floor plan of a Greek Cross, contains some modest remains of a mosaic and mural paintings.

The **Sergijevaca ❺** (pedestrian zone) begins on Trg Republike and cuts through the town center to the Sergius Arch. In the backyard of **house number 16** in the pedestrian zone, a large *mosaic from the 2nd century was uncovered in 1959. The central part of the mosaic's 40 sections is occupied by a mythological depiction of the "punishment of Dirke." The other sections are decorated with geometrical ornamental patterns, rosettes, dolphins and birds.

The *Slavoluk obitelji Sergi ❻ (Sergius Arch) was built between 29 and 27 B.C. in honor of Sergius Lepidus, Gaius Lucius Sergius and Gnaeus Sergius. All three held high miltary and civilian offices. The Sergius Arch is not, in fact, a triumphal arch (which was the sole prerogative of emperors), but rather an oversized memorial stone.

The arch is decorated only on the side showing towards the town. Slender pillars with Corinthian capitals form the frame for the arch's interior panels, with a little frieze above decorated with winged and wreathed Victorias, cherubs, a chariot and weaponry.

If you keep to the left of the Sergius Arch, which is also referred to as the *Porta Aurea*, you will bypass the **Herkulova vrata** ❼ (Hercules Gate, or in Latin *Porta Herculea*), whose origins go all the way back to the 1st century A.D. Nearby, very much in the spirit of all these ancient monuments, stands the ★**Arheološki muzej** ❽ (Archeology Museum), which guards countless archeological finds from the excavations of southern Istria.

Right next to the museum is the **Dvojna vrata** ❾ (Twin Gate, in Latin *Porta Gemina*), built during the 2nd century, and the remains of the medieval town wall.

Behind the museum, a road leads up to the **castle** ❿. Up here was the first Illyrian settlement, followed by a Roman capitol and a medieval fortress. The present building goes back to the Venetians and the 16th century. The hill where the castle of Pula stands offers a sublime view of the entire area. The monumental proportions of the amphitheater are best appreciated from here.

Swimming around Pula

At the clifflike Zlatne stijene around **Verudela** ㉔ are Pula's nearest swimming bays. Naturally, plenty of accommodations are on hand here for the flocks of visitors who come every summer like migratory birds. There are countless camping sites, private pensions and holiday apartments located hereabouts. The Hotel Histria is the only five-star hotel on the Istrian east coast. The well-equipped marinas of **Veruda** ㉕ and **Pomer** ㉖ in

Right: The long-awaited spring sun draws people out for coffee and fresh air.

protected bays offer sailors good points of departure for trips to the offshore islands, among them Cres.

On the two southern tips of Istria are the tourist centers of **Medulin** ㉗ and **Premantura** ㉘, featuring a variety of sports and recreational facities. There are several miles of beach with shallow stretches, popular above all with families with children. In July and August, many beaches near camping sites and hotels require an entrance fee, for example, at the ★**Rt Kamenjak** ㉙ nature park on Istria's spectacular southern tip. Near **Kažela** ㉚ is a big nudist colony with a beautiful sand beach.

EXCURSIONS INLAND

Pazin

Pazin ㉛ (32 kilometers east of Poreč) is the geographic and administrative center of Istria. The town was first mentioned in 983 in a document of Emperor Otto II, confirming Pazin to be the property of the Bishopric of Poreč.

The strategic significance of the place is best demonstrated by the castle, which dominates the junction of Istria's main inland roads. Pazin – *Mitterburg* in German, meaning "Central Fortress" – grew in the Middle Ages into a significant margravate, whose feudal lords tended to change with fair frequency. Most of the lords came from the German Empire and were loyal vassals to their kings, as the names of the burial slabs in the castle façade reveal: Eppenstein, Andechs, Wittelsbach, Görz. By the 16th century, no fewer than 25 settlements and adjacent lands had been subordinated to these lords. But the town declined thereafter, and today Pazin is a small industrial center containing the largest number of schools in the region.

The ★**castle** overlooking the 120-meter-deep Fojba Gorge goes back to the 9th century and is the oldest building in

Istria

Pazin. Its present form dates back to the 14th century. The four wings of the building are grouped around a large interior courtyard and a central water cistern, a necessary construction in case of siege. The entrance to the castle is secured by a drawbridge.

Today the castle houses the **Istarski etnografski muzej** (Istrian Ethnography Museum), documenting the development of agriculture and fishing. It also has a department showing a collection of jewels, furniture and peasant costumes.

At the southern fringes of the town is the **Parish Church of Sveti Nikola**, from the 13th century. The interior has wonderful frescos painted by a Tirolean artist who worked here in the 15th century, and numbering among the highlights of Istrian medieval art. The **bell tower** was added only in 1705.

Gračišće

It is worth stopping about eight kilometers east of Pazin in the romantic, half-ruined village of **Gračišće** ㉜. This place must have enjoyed better days in the Middle Ages, as evidenced by the huge **campanile**, a small loggia and the **Solomon Palace**. There is a beautiful view over the rolling countryside from the old cemetery behind the church, which stands at an altitude of 450 meters. Creature comforts are catered to by the traditional *Konoba Marino* near the town gate. In August, the day of the village's patron saint is celebrated with a traditional donkey race.

Beram

Only five kilometers west of Pazin on the road to Motovun you will reach **Beram** ㉝. This town is situated on a hill rising from a fertile valley, like nearly all settlements in this area. As a castle where the local population could find refuge in times of strife during the Middle Ages, Beram originally had a wall.

What is truly worth seeing, however, is about one kilometer east of town: the small ***Sveta Marija na Škriljinah**

(Church of St. Mary on the Stone Tablets). If you want to visit the church, you must ask for the key in the village (a gratuity is always appreciated). You will then be accompanied by a villager.

The interior of this Gothic building dating from the 15th century was once completley covered in frescos. In the course of several modifications, some of these frescos were destroyed, however. Despite this, the surviving cycle is considered the most complete in Istria.

The frescos were painted by the master Ivan of Kastav in the year 1474. In 46 pictures he depicts the lives of Mary and Jesus. In addition, on the west wall Adam and Eve are shown, plus a wheel of fortune, and a **Dance Macabre** very similar to the one in Hrastovlje. A remarkable feature on the north wall is the arrival of the Magi at the scene of the Nativity.

Above: Fresco in the Church of Saint Mary in Beram painted by master Ivan from Kastav in 1474. Right: Motovun was built to watch over fields and vineyards.

*Motovun

A beautiful stretch of road winding through fields and vineyards leads north to **Motovun** ❸❹. Shortly before reaching your destination, you will come across a charming view of this picturesque medieval fortified town sitting on a solitary hill 277 meters above sea level.

The Illyrians had settled here, and when the place came under Venetian rule in 1278, it was surrounded by a great **fortified wall**, which serves today as a walkway. You can enjoy rare views from here: it is said that on a clear day you can see as far as the Učka Mountains.

When the fortified hilltop became too overcrowded, the people started working on a suburb below the inner town on the southwestern side of the hill, and also a town gate with Romanesque and Gothic elements. The older and narrower inner gate, surmounted by an unmistakable Lion of Saint Mark, leads to the main square with the **Church of Sveti Stevan** (St. Stephen's). It was built according to plans by the famous Andrea Palladio. As with the entire town, time on the attached campanile seems to have stood still; at 1:24 p.m. to be precise. That's when you may be tempted to join the lunch guests of the **Hotel Kaštel** for dessert beneath the shade of the trees on the piazza. If you walk past the **Renaissance fountain** on the right, you will reach the walk along the town wall which has those beautiful views mentioned above.

On the other side of the Mirna Valley, the remains of **Motovun Forest** recall past industrial pursuits. It served in the past as a source of wood for Venice. The logs were bundled into rafts and floated down the Mirna to the coast. This forest was different from others in Istria, and in the karst region generally, for having a rich stand of oak (*Quercus robur*) normally only found at the foot of the Alps. This wood was ideal for the pilework of Venice and for shipbuilding.

Today, only ten square kilometers survive, 2.8 square kilometers of which are under special protection. The forests around Motovun are also known for their rare and valuable truffles (*Tuber magnatum*). The "truffle pigs" here are dogs, though.

Oprtalj

A little north of Motovun, spread over a nearby hillside, is **Oprtalj** ㉟, another jewel of a town. In the Middle Ages, this small community was the property of various feudal lords until 1209, when it was handed over to the Bishopric of Aquileia. Oprtalj did not come under Venetian rule until 1490.

The **town walls** have survived remarkably well here, too. At the entrance to the town, visitors are met by the **loggia**, dating from the 17th century. The labyrinth of alleyways, squares and vaulted passages concentrically arranged around the main square kindles a good feel for the atmosphere of the Middle Ages.

Oprtalj's central square is dominated by the **Church of Sveti Juraj** (St. George's), whose free-standing campanile overshadows the entire square. Inside, you can admire valuable altars and paintings from the 16th and 17th centuries – products of artisits from the school of Carpaccio.

There are four more little churches in the area exhibiting beautiful frescos. In 1471, in the **Brotherhood Church of Sveta Maria**, below Oprtalj, the master Clerigin of Koper painted scenes of Mary's life in Renaissance style on the round arch and on the south wall. In the **Church of Sveti Leonard** (St. Leonard's) is a *Pala* (alterpiece) by Žoržo Ventura from Zadar (17th century). In the **Church of Sveti Roč** (St. Roch's), Anthony of Padua, an Istrian master of the 16th century, painted numerous saints. Finally, in the single-naved Romanesque **Church of Sveta Helena** (Saint Helen's; located about one kilometer south of Oprtalj on the road back to Motovun), Clerigin of Koper was again active.

Only 4.5 kilometers away to the northwest is the village of **Zrenj** ㊱. The road leading there has little traffic and you might think of walking it. Some researchers think Zrenj is identical with the ancient town of *Stridon*; the birthplace of St. Jerome (Sophromius Eusebius Hieronymus, circa A.D. 347 to 420). He was the author of various religious writings and of the *Vulgata*, the first Latin translation of the Bible.

*Grožnjan

To the west of Oprtalj, perched on a hill about 288 meters high, is the settlement of **Grožnjan** ㊲. It was first mentioned in 1103 and, like Oprtalj, was for a long time in the hands of the Patriarch of Aquileia. During the centuries that Venice held sway here, the town became the administrative center of western Istria. Defensive walls and towers were renovated and enlarged; but only a **city gate** has survived from this effort. After walking through it, you will find on your left the **loggia**, with its upper story serving as a *fontik* (granary). In the center is the **Parish Church of Sveti Vid i Modesti** (St. Vitus and Modestus) from the 18th century. It has Renaissance-style choir furnishings clearly influenced by local folk art.

But it's not only the historical buildings that are the attraction of Grožnjan. It is more the special atmosphere of the place – young life within old stone: every summer the town hosts the *Jeunesse Musicale*, a school with courses for young musicians, concerts and lots of street music. Many artists have settled here, renovating decayed houses and building studios and galleries.

On days with a clear view, you can see to the east the Učka Mountains, to the north the Julian Alps and to the west the

Right: Vižnjan, an old village in the hills northeast of Poreč.

coast and its often wonderful sunsets. The Ladonja Restaurant is an excellent place to have a meal, and there is a market in town as well. You can take nice walks on farm tracks starting from Grožnjan. There are even a few marked routes (with red triangles). On the other side of the Mirna, atop a hill, is the typical Istrian village of **Vižinada** ㊳.

Between Pazin and Rovinj

Southwest of Pazin, after traveling about eleven kilometers towards Rovinj, you arrive at the **Sveti Petar u Šumi** ㊴ settlement. Benedictine monks built a monastery here in the 13th century, but abandoned it two centuries later. The complex was taken over by the Paulines (actually Minorites from the community of the Franciscans). The **samostan** (monastery) was enlarged throughout the 18th century, and the Church of Saint Peter and Saint Paul was decorated in highest-quality Rococo style.

From Kanafar it is worth making a detour to the ghost town of **Dvigrad** ㊵ (*Duecastelli* in Italian). The name reminds one of the fact that the place had two fortresses or, more specifically, that it consisted of two settlements. In 1631, the plague forced the locals to abandon the village and move elsewhere. Nobody ever returned, and Dvigrad decayed. In the picturesque complex you can see the remains of defensive walls and towers, and ruined houses.

A further side trip to be recommended is the one via Kanfanar to **Svetvinčenat** ㊶. Worth visiting there are the **Kaštel Grimani** and the frescos in the **Church of Sveti Vincent**.

Roč

Take the well-improved road along the Ćićarija Range, which reaches heights of up to 1,000 meters, and then turn off at the small, unexpectedly-appearing exit to

Roč ㊷. This town was first mentioned in a document of Henry IV who, in 1064, gave it to Margrave Odolricus. As Roč was strategically important, it was surrounded by a ring wall, as were all similar settlements in the area, irrespective of their size. Only the **city gate** has survived, however, with the guard's room on the upper floor.

The Parish Church of St. Bartholomew and the adjacent small **Church of Sveti Antun** (St. Anthony's) dominating the center testify to the former significance of Roč as an economic, cultural and religious site. The parish church is simple on the outside, but the interior is richly decorated in Baroque style. St. Anthony's Church is to the right of the main entrance and is often thought to be just a side aisle. On the right-hand wall is a Glagolithic alphabet from the 12th century carved into the votive cross. Roč was indeed a center of Glagolitic writing – the old Slavonic script used in the liturgy. Many codices, manuscripts and Gospels to be found today in Zagreb, Vienna and elsewhere,

came from here. The key to the church is kept with the priest's housekeeper in the building to the left of St. Bartholomew's. She also has the keys to the **Church of Sveti Roč** by the town gate, where you can see fragments of frescos from the 14th century and Glagolithic carvings.

From Roč to Hum:
The *Glagolithic Alley

As a means of recalling the close associations of the Roč region with the foundations of Croatian literature, the **Aleja glagoljaša ㊸** (Glagolithic Alley) was created along the route to Hum. Before setting off from Roč, it is advisable to have something to eat in the town's only restaurant; it is renowned for its cuisine, and many tourists on their way to Rijeka stop here for a memorable meal.

The monument section of the Alley stretches for seven kilomters; it was built in 1977 with the aim of fostering a sense of the literary-cultural tradition of the Croatian people. Eleven monuments on the route offer symbolic representations of important events or people associated with the Glagolithic writing so important to Croatian national sentiment.

In Roč, right at the turnoff to Hum, you can see the **Pillar of the Čakav Parliament** (*Čakavskog sabora*), a reference to Croatian autonomy and the Čakav dialect. The letter "S" is depicted in Glagolithic script. "S" stands for *slovo*, meaning intellect or reason.

The second monument shows the **Three-legged Table before Two Cypresses**. The trees are symbols of the missionaries to the Slavs, Cyril and Method. Monument three recalls the **Assembly of Kliment of Ohrid**. Kliment was a pupil of the two missionaries, and he founded the first Slav university near Lake Ohrid in Macedonia.

The fourth monument is the **Lapidarium** in front of the village church in Brnobiči: Glagolithic inscriptions from all regions of the former Yugoslavia were hewn into the stone wall here.

Monument five points to the **Gorge of Lucidar**: in the Middle Ages, a Croatian encyclopedia was written which regarded the Učka Range as the Croatian equivalent of Olympus. This fragment of wall depicts the peak of Mount Učka buried in the clouds.

Monument number six is the **Grgur Ninski Observation Point**: the block of stone with the Glagolithic, Latin and Cyrillic alphabets was erected in memory of the 10th-century bishop Grgur, who fought against Rome for a national church. Monument seven represents **Istarski razvod**, the document of the inspection of Istria's borders.

Monument eight is dedicated to Croatian Protestants and heretics. The **Resting Place of Žakan Juraj** is monument nine. A huge stone block here stands as the symbol of the first

Right: The old town of Labin. Statue of St. Francis from Labin's church.

Glagolithic missal dating from the year 1483. Monument ten is devoted to **resistance and freedom** over the centuries. Three stone blocks at the entrance to Hum represent the three historic periods of Antiquity, the Middle Ages and the Modern Age. Each block has inscriptions from the times it represents.

The eleventh monument is the **town gate** of Hum: the twelve medaillons on the gate represent the months of the year with typical activities of the season, be they in the fields or at home.

This strange memorial route ends in **★Hum ㊹**, probably one of the smallest towns in the world, with only a dozen intact houses. This fortified hilltop position was a border station between the Venetian and Habsburg territories. And, like Roč, it was a center of Glagolithic culture. The **Cemetery Chapel of Sveti Jeronim** (St. Jerome) has frescos from the 12th century worth seeing, and also one of the oldest Glagolithic inscriptions (from the late 12th century).

The interior of the big Parish Church of Sveti Jeronim (19th century) is also richly decorated, as in Roč. The reason why St. Jerome is so intensively worshipped here probably dates from the time of the persecution by Rome, when the Croats tried to save their writings by attributing them to the saint, who was a figure also recognized by the Western Church.

Few people live today in Hum, and those who do subsist mainly through agriculture. The cozy Humska Konoba Restaurant, with its hearty Istrian specialities, is popular among gourmets and is a good place to take a break. We recommend the *pršut* (ham) and the strong local wine. Every June a major celebration is held in the village for the mayoral elections.

Draguč

The picturesque village of **Draguč ㊺** is walking distance from Hum – only about four kilometers. If going by car,

though, you have to return to Roč and then continue via Buzet or the new highway via Cerovlje. The medieval town is situated on the side of a mountain, and the houses are crammed along its only street leading to the village church. The village's walls recall the time of the "defense peasants," the status given to locals retained by the emperor to fight off pillaging Turks and Uskoks.

At the entrance to the village is the **cemetery chapel**, with frescos from the 13th and 14th centuries. The votive **Church of Sveti Roč** (St. Roch's) is decorated by murals of the Istrian master Anthony of Padua (they recall the settlement of Kasčerg). He decorated the church almost entirely by combining Renaissance elements and folk art.

The Učka Range

On the way to Opatija, you will drive through Istria's biggest mountain range, the **Učka**, with the **Vojak** as its highest peak (1,396 meters). The mountain range

flattens out towards the south until it reaches sea level at Plomin. In the north, the Učka Massif is partly covered in thick forests and penetrates into the Ćićarija mountain range. In just about all of the holiday resorts between Opatija and Mošćenice, avid hikers will find marked paths leading away from the coast up into the massif.

In summer, the Vojak peak is the starting point for hang gliders. In winter, skiing is possible here. On a clear day, the view from the Vojak is spectacular, ranging from all the big islands in the Kvarner Gulf to the Julian Alps and the Slovenian Triglav Massif.

THE EAST COAST

The Pula region contains many remains from ancient times; even Odysseus is said by legend to have been here. To the north, via **Šišan** and **Valtura**, you will reach the ancient Illyrian settlement of **Nesactium**, the most important archeological site aside from Pula itself.

In one small area are finds from prehistoric and Roman times, as well as from the early Middle Ages. In pre-Roman days, the place was the political and religious center of the Istrian Illyrians. When the Slavs and Avars descended on Istria in the 7th century, they destroyed the town completely. But the remains of the thermal baths, a forum, the foundations of two Roman temples and the ruins of the Illyrian fortress are still quite easily discernable.

*Labin and Rabac

The road towards Opatija leads via Marana to the charming old village of **Barban ④⑧**, with its picturesque square with a loggia and clock tower. Every August since 1696 they have staged a jousting tournament on this square. The road to **Labin ④⑨** continues through lands

Above: Preparing for a sailing regatta in Lovran. Right: Spiny lobster is one of the great gastronomic delicacies of the coast of Istria.

which are under intensive agricultural development.

The pretty medieval town of Labin is on a hill 320 meters above sea level. The ground falls away steeply towards the sea along the course of the Rabac River. There was a settlement here in ancient times; the Illyrians built themselves a fortress and the Romans developed the place and called it *Albona*. Then came the Slavs. When Venice took over, the population started to split into two camps; the Romanic and Slavic-speaking groups. This corresponded pretty much to social rank; patricians and plebeians respectively.

The narrow streets of the picturesque **old town** invite you to take a leisurely stroll. Beautiful old palaces and the city gates offer marvelous backgrounds for photographers. The **Narodni muzej** (National Museum) housed inside the Baroque Palazzo Battiola-Lazzarini, shows archeological finds from Illyrian and Roman times, and also an exhibition on work in the coal mines. The Matthias

Flacius Illyricus collection in the birth-place of **Matija Vlačič**, the famous son of the town, is of special interest. Vlačič taught at many universities as professor of theology, and was an important collab-orator of Martin Luther. He founded the German Protestant movement of Flac-ianism, fighting ruthlessly against any concessions to Rome, the emperor or the German princes.

On the nearby coast is the one-time fishing village of **Rabac** ⑩, now a busy tourist center, with hotels and a big camp-ing site. The bay, with its much-visited pebble beach, is well protected from the feared bora wind, which occasionally sweeps in across the Kvarner Gulf. Tour-ists often use an old mule track to make the hour-long trip to medieval Labin.

The Coastal Road from Labin to Opatija

Driving north on the E 751 from Labin, you can make an interesting side trip near the village of Voziliči to the **Čepićko Polje** ㉛.

A *polje* is an oval depression in the karst; this particular one runs northwest-southeast along the line of the Dinaric ridges formed by the earth's tectonic movements. Fertile clay brought down by rivers helps to retain moisture above the barren karstic ground, and this has there-fore become a profitable base for agricul-ture in this otherwise barren region.

The view of the **Plominski zaljev** (Plomin Fjord) leaves mixed impres-sions: looking seawards, you take in an idyllic landscape, with the most promi-nent sight being the silhouette of medi-eval **Plomin** ㉜. Looking back, the eye meets the tall smokestacks of an ore re-fining plant – a powerful legacy of the former Socialist fetish for heavy industry – even if it meant sticking it in the most unlikely places.

At **Kap Mašnjak** ㉝ you will encoun-ter a first glimpse of the greenery of the

Kvarner island of Cres. Shortly after-wards, you will reach a steep road leading down to the little bay of **Brestova** ㉞, with a harbor from where the Jadrolinija ferries make the 30-minute crossing to the island (they operate all year round; in the peak season even at night).

On the winding coastal road towards Opatija there are a number of lovely views across the Kvarner Gulf, especially in **Brseč** ㉟. A narrow mountain road run-ning parallel to the main road but a bit higher up, along the eastern flank of the Učka Massif via Martina and Jelena, opens up new perspectives for bycyclists and motorcyclists.

The historic town of ***Mošćenice** ㊱, sitting at 173 meters above sea level – and thus well-protected against pirates in the old days – offers not only a beautiful pan-orama across the Kvarner Gulf, but also an **Etnografski muzej** (Ethnography Museum) exhibiting, among other things, an oil press several hundred years old.

Mošćenička Draga ㊲ is a picturesque fishing village that awaits its visitors with

an inviting pebble beach, a camping site, two hotels and the traditional seafood restaurant Benito.

It's worth stopping in **Medveja** ❺❽ for its beautiful pebble beaches flanked by shady pines. Parking problems, which begin here during the month of August, get increasingly worse as you approach Opatija.

Near Opatija, **Lovran** ❺❾ is the best-known tourist resort on the Istrian Riviera. Its name derives from the laurel tree (*laurus*). The two towns have now practically merged. They both share noble villas, rich green vegetation of cypresses, palm trees and flowering hedges, and gardens. These are especially charming in spring and summer, with their rich colors and scents. It is said that one of the first people to show his appreciation of Lovran was a Roman nobleman who built himself a villa here. In October, in the old

Above: The promenade – called Lungomare – in Opatija is a fine place to take a break for coffee and refreshments.

town, the two-week *Marunada* chestnut festival is celebrated.

★Opatija

Opatija ❻⓿ (population 13,000) is the epicenter of the more than 40-kilometer-long Riviera running along the Kvarner Gulf. Protected by the Učka Range, the whole Riviera has a very favorable climate: cool air streaming down from the mountains reduces the heat of summer and keeps away the cold Alpine air in winter.

In the 11th century, the Benedictine Abbey of Sveti Jakov was founded here, giving the place its name – *Abbazia* (monastery). The touristic development of Opatija began in 1844, when the ★**Villa Angiolina** (today the seat of the resort's administration) was built. The Italian Iginio Scarpa from Rijeka built it as a summer house and named it after his wife. Scarpa had a **park** built around his villa and sailors from all over the world brought him exotic plants to put there.

Ban Josip Jelačič, the governor of Croatia, was the first high-ranking visitor to be invited to the villa in 1850. A few years later, the former Austrian emperor Ferdinand and his wife Maria Anna spent the whole summer season in the Villa Angiolina. Nowadays, open-air concerts are regularly held in the villa's park in summer.

It didn't take very long for the Austrian aristocracy to start getting interested in this new spa town. They were followed by the usual entourage. Doctors attested that the air contained an unusually high concentration of aerosol and praised the therapeutic effects of the mild, humid climate. The small fishing village and its abbey soon became a popular winter retreat and spa resort. And so began Opatija's evolution into a health resort for the upper crust .

In 1873, the *Wiener Südbahn* (the Vienna Southern Railway Company) extended its Vienna-Trieste line by adding a connection from Pivka and Matulji to Rijeka, bringing more tourists to Opatija. A clever businessman from this company bought the seaside vineyards of a Croatian and, in 1883, built the first hotel here, the Quarnero (Kvarner). It was followed by other noble establishments: Crown Princess Stephanie (today the Imperial) and the Hotel Quississana (today the Opatija). Parks, promenades and beaches followed.

Almost all members of the Austrian imperial family visited Opatija – again and again. Europe's high aristocracy was at home here: Italy's King Umberto, the kings of Serbia, Montenegro and Greece, the Bulgarian czar, the Swedish-Norwegian king Oskar II and the German emperor Wilhelm II.

Not only the aristrocracy, but also artists, musicians and writers came, such as the Czech violonist Jan Kubelik, the Austrian composer Gustav Mahler, the Italian tenor Beniamino Gigli, the Hungarian operetta composer Franz Lehar, the French Lumière brothers, pioneers of film technology, and the father of psychoanalysyis, Sigmund Freud.

All these prominent visitors also spawned a luxurious lifestyle. In 1895, Opatija got electrical power, followed by water mains two years later. In 1898, a film was made here – only three years after the first moving pictures were shot in Paris.

Abbazia soon grew into the "Austrian Nice," until, in 1918, it came under Italian rule and was thus given an additional touch of *dolce vita*. The Yugoslav takeover in 1947 did nothing to damage the character of Opatija, in fact, the Socialist government was enthusiastic to develop its touristic potential very carefully and unintrusively. The new hotels were designed in the style of the existing buildings from the turn of the century.

Opatija today has more first class hotels than any other place on the Croatian coast. The tastefully-renovated villas and hotels of the *Belle Époque* – all in harmony with each other – reach all the way down to the seaside and truly make up the the charm of the place. Yachtsmen are also attracted here. The tourist program in the peak season meets all tastes: live music from pop to classical, trendy discos (*Palladium, Madonna*) and a casino in the Hotel Adriatic.

On the famous ***Lungomare**, the twelve-kilometer-long promenade, you can walk along the seafront – passing the marina of **Ičići** 🔟 and the pebble beach of **Ika** 🔢 – all the way to Lovran.

The only little disappointment, perhaps, is the fact that swimming is somewhat limited hereabouts. Nets placed in the water to divide up the beach areas also serve to prevent swimmers from floating too far out to sea. There have been incidents with sharks reported, which sometimes follow the ships heading for Rijeka. Surfers don't seem to mind this one bit; they are all perfectly at home in the bay of **Preluk**.

Istria

UMAG (052)

i **Turistička zajednica Umag**, tel. 741363, fax. 741649.

Hotel Kristal, tel. 700000, fax. 700199, elegant city hotel, large breakfast buffet; **Hotel Koralj**, tel. 741514, fax. 741076, beach, indoor and outdoor pool, fitness room, sauna, restaurant with vegetarian food, sports.

Hotel Aurora, tel. 741346, fax. 741289, five km outside of the city, private beach, no frills hotel; **Hotel Istra**, tel. 741589, fax. 741185, private beach, restaurant with vegetarian food, extensive sports activities; **Holiday Complex Stella Maris**, four km north of Umag, tel. 741051, fax. 741524, private beach, pool.

CAMPING: **Stella Maris**, tel. 741424; **Ladin Gaj**, before the town of Karigador, tel. 741128, comfortable establishment with nudism; **Finida**, six km before Novigrad, tel. 741684, fax. 741535, beautiful quiet establishment, private beach; **Kanegra**, Umag-Kanegra. tel. 741270, fax. 741282, nude sunbathing, sports; **Pineta**, Savudrija, tel. 759518, fax. 759526, sports.

Konoba Amfora, Riječka 45, reasonably priced restuarant with terrace; **Restaurant Stella Maris**, with **Coffee Bar Laguna**, on the main street of the Stella Maris complex, tel. 752145, large menu, fish specialties.

Umag is a competitive center for tennis. The modern tennis center offers courses with qualified teachers, tel. 741704, fax. 741513.

NOVIGRAD (052)

i Ulica Rotonda, tel./fax. 757075.

ccommodation

Rotonda della Rivarella, old town, tel. 757736, fax. 757468, pleasant, but expensive, indoor and outdoor pool, good fish restaurant. **Hotel Emonia**, tel. 757160, on the dock; **Hotel Maestral**, outside of the city, tel. 757557, fax. 757314, private beach, restaurant with vegetarian food, convention center, sports. *CAMPING:* **Camping Sirena**, near Hotel Laguna, tel. 757159. **Mareda**, tel. 757798, fax. 757988.

Bonanza, next to Aquarius discotheque, small and lively, terrace, delicious food. **Mandrač**, on the dock, terrace, fresh fish and very crowded.

MARINA: **Marina Novigrad**, Mandrač bb, tel. 757077, fax. 757314.

POREČ / VRSAR (052)

POREČ

i **Tourist Office**, Zagrebačka 9, tel. 451293, fax. 451665.

The Zelena Laguna is one of the biggest tourist areas, with plenty of hotels – various amenities allow guests to be independent from the city; **Hotel Parentium**, Zelena Laguna, tel. 451500, fax. 451536, this hotel features a private beach, restaurants and casino, sports, marina.

Hotel Neptun, central, tel. 451711; **Hotel Kristal**, Brulo, tel. 451277; **Hotel Diamant**, Brulo, tel. 451566.

CAMPING: **Zelena Laguna**, tel. 451696, fax. 451044; **Ulika Naturist**, a favorite spot for nudists, tel/fax. 436325, partly shady place with private beach, rental cars, launching slips for boats. **Bijela uvala**, Zelena Laguna, tel. 451278, fax. 451083.

Restaurant Istra, B. Milanoviča 30, tel. 434636, fish specialties; **Restaurant Spaghettoteca Barilla**, Eufrazijana 26, tel. 452742, 11 a.m.-1 a.m.; **Restaurant Jadran**, Obala M. Tita, Tel. 434743, fish specialties and grilled food.

MARINA: **Parentium**, Zelena Laguna, tel. 452210, fax. 452212, 200 berths in quiet bay, accommodation for ships up to 10 tons.

Along the coast and in the hills, for example, there are excursions to Motovun, Pazin and Grožnjan. Hunting is possible in the hinterland (by reservation only).

BOAT TRIPS: Excursions from Poreč and Rovinj are offered by hydrofoil to **Venice** and **Trieste**. Also day trips to **Pula** and the **Brijuni Islands**.

In July Poreč holds a big summer festival with lots of concerts featuring music of every sort, also theater and folklore.

VRSAR

Hotel Pineta, tel. 441131, private beach, extensive recreational activities. **Koversada**, tel. 441171, nudist hotel, bungalows, camping; **Funtana**, tel. 441511, beautiful location, sports.

CAMPING: **Porto Sole**, tel. 441198, fax. 441122, permanent winter camping spots, beach, tent rentals, marina, nice, partly shady place with sanitary facilities; **Turist**, tel. 441330. **Valkanela**, tel. 441515.

MARINA: 180 berths in the bay. Boat rental at the harbors and marinas of the city. Many hotels offer waterskiing and rent windsurfing boards.

LIMSKI FJORD

Restaurant Limfjord, Limski Kanal, tel. 448222, fish and seafood dishes.

ROVINJ / PULA (052)

BRIJUNI

Hotels Neptun and **Istra**, tel. 525807; **Hotel Karmen**, tel. 525400, the former convention center of the upper political circles now consists of three hotels, three restaurants, all amenities, also golf.

CRVENI OTOK

🛏️ 💲💲💲 **Sv. Andrea**, **Hotel Istra**, tel. 813055, fax. 813484, a picturesque location on the island.

FAŽANA

🛏️ CAMPING: **Pineta**, tel. 521088, fax. 521883, beautiful, shady, incredible beach, marina.

MEDULIN

ℹ️ Tel. 577145.
🛏️ 💲💲 **Hotel Naturist Kažela**, Medulin, tel. 576050.
❌ **Restaurant Sandra**, specialty: roast suckling pig; between Ližnjan and Medulin is **Ranch Libora**, a good restuarant with fresh fish, tel. 576 800.

PULA AND ENVIRONS

🚍 Matka Laginje 7, tel. 212987, fax. 211855.
🛏️ 💲💲💲 **Hotel Riviera**, next to the amphitheater, tel. 211166, fax. 211873; **Hotel Histria**, Punta Verudela, tel. 34777, fax. 214175, comfortable, directly on the sea, best hotel in the entire region, located on a peninsula, beach, pool, health center.
💲💲 **Apartments Punta Verudela**, fax. 22798, private beach, pool, sports; **Hotel Naturist Kažela**, Medulin, tel. 576050. CAMPING: **Puntižela**, tel. 517490, fax. 212926, shady place, recreational facilities, marina, car rentals.
❌ **Restaurant Adriatic**, at the yacht harbor, excellent fish dishes.
⛵ MARINA: **Marina ACY Pomer**, tel. 573162; **Marina Veruda**, tel. 33276.

ROVINJ

ℹ️ Obala Pina Budicina, tel. 811566, fax. 816007.
🛏️ 💲💲💲 **Eden**, tel. 811088, fax. 811349, beach and pool, restaurant serving vegetarian food, extensive sports opportunities, water sports, disco, casino.
💲💲 **Hotel Adriatic**, tel. 815088, fax. 813573, city hotel; **Hotel Montauro**, tel. 813088, fax. 813287, beach, indoor pool, fitness room, restaurant; **Hotel Rovinj**, center, tel. 811288, fax. 811257, beach.
CAMPING: **Veštar**, tel. 811431, fax. 811571, large, partly shady area with extensive sports. **Valalta**, tel. 811033, fax. 811463, large area just for nudists, private beach and marina, sports.
❌ **Konoba Cantinon**, Aldo Rismondo 18, tel. 816075, Istrian cuisine in historic vaulted cellar; **Istarska konoba Veli Jože**, Sv. Križa 8, tel. 816337, at the harbor, good drinks, traditional atmosphere.
⛵ MARINA: Tel. 813133.

STOJA

🛏️ CAMPING: **Stoja**, tel. 24144, fax. 212138, private beach and marina, extensive sports opportunities, permanent winter spots.

MOTOVUN (052)

🛏️ 💲💲 **Hotel Kaštel**, tel. 681735, restaurant (outdoor tables), in old town center; the view from here is fantastic.

RABAC (052)

🛏️ 💲💲 **Hotel Apollo**, at the harbor of Rabac, tel. 872222; **Hotel Fortuna**, tel. 87021, quiet, located on a hill over Rabac.
CAMPING: **Camp Oliva**, tel. 872258, no shade, beach, marina, open from May through Sept; **Camp Marina**, tel. 872301, fax. 872561, partly shady area located on a peninsula, dock and air tank refill station for divers, rocky beach.

OPATIJA / LOVRAN (051)

LOVRAN

🛏️ 💲💲💲 **Hotel Excelsior**, tel. 292 233, fax. 292989, comfortable rooms, beach, very good service, lots of sports activities.
❌ **Kvarner**, Maršala Tita 65, tel. 291118, fish restaurant with terrace located on the dock.

MOŠĆENIČKA DRAGA

❌ **Benito**, tel. 737502, traditional restaurant, fish.

OPATIJA

ℹ️ Tel. 271710, fax. 271699.
🛏️ 💲💲💲 **Hotel Ambasador**, tel. 271211, fax. 271772, beach, indoor swimming pool, restaurant with vegetarian food, a hotel with a lot of style; **Hotel Mozart**, tel. 271877, fax. 271739, small hotel with a lot of charm, near the beach; **Hotel Kvarner Amalia**, tel. 271233, fax. 271202, traditional hotel, located on the promenade near a park, private beach and indoor and outdoor pool, stylish dancing evenings in the café.
💲💲 **Hotel Belvedere**, tel. 271044, fax. 271484, beach, pool, sauna, tennis, beautiful classicistic building in the city center; **Hotel Jadran**, tel. 271700, fax. 271519, a lot of charm, on the main beach. **Hotel Bellevue**, tel. 271811, fax. 271964, pool, sauna, one of Opatija's best hotels.
❌ **Lovor**, Maršala Tita 160, tel. 271170, local food; **Maja**, Maršala Tita 158, pasta and pizza; **Zelengaj**, international cuisine, grilled food, fish.

RIJEKA AND THE KVARNER GULF

RIJEKA
KRK ISLAND
CRES AND LOŠINJ ISLANDS

The Kvarner Gulf

The Kvarner Gulf, which stretches from the Opatija Riviera and the Istrian coast down to Pag Island, covers a surface area of about 3,300 square kilometers. The main islands are Krk, Cres, Lošinj and Rab. The climate is generally pleasant, with warm summers and mild winters. The annual average temperature is 14° C.

The Kvarner Gulf is protected by the mountain ranges of the Učka and Velebit, which ensure enjoyably cool summer nights. The mistral wind brings a refreshing breeze in summer, but winter temperatures can drop quickly when the bora sweeps down from the hills. The bora brings cool air in summer, too, while the sirocco brings rain. The climate and its own special geographic disposition – the nearby Dinaric coastal mountains with their ski slopes on one side and the Adriatic on the other side – sometimes makes it possible between Christmas and Easter to actually ski in the mountains and swim in the sea on the same day.

The vegetation around the bay is abundant and green. In the undisturbed karst

Preceding pages: Valun – an idyllic fishing village on the island of Cres. Left: Façade of St. Mary's Cathedral in Osor (Cres).

landscape, laurels, palms and agave grow; many gardens grow exotic orange and lemon trees.

Despite lush springtime vegetation, there is a lack of fertile land for vegetables and moist meadows for cattle. The karstic terrain does not leave much room for profitable agriculture, either on the islands or on the mainland. But the Kvarner Gulf is rich in various species of fish, and the cuisine of the area specializes in seafood.

The name Kvarner, *Quarnero* in Italian, probably comes from the Latin *Mare Quaternatium*, meaning "sea of four parts." The Romans are thought to have been referring to the geographical position of the offshore islands: Krk, Rab and Pag run parallel to the Croatian coastline, while Cres and Lošinj shield the bay from the open sea.

The large number of sheltered bays actually made sea trade a risky enterprise in earlier days. In the Middle Ages, "Christian" seafaring meant that anybody could venture out and seize anybody else's vessel. Even the coastal settlements were not immune from piracy. It seemed that people were equal not only in the face of God, but also in the face of pirates. The Austrians made Kvarner an important strategic center during their attempts to expand their empire. The only fleet the

Habsburgs ever had cruised about in these waters; and this, too, is where the great imperial dreams of the Habsburgs sank.

Today, the islands, with the picturesque background of the Velebit Massif, are a paradise for sail and motor boats – but not pirates – and the only places where you might be relieved of your wealth are at the richly-stocked buffets of the hotels and restaurants.

RIJEKA

The capital of Kvarner, and the economic center of the whole region around the gulf down to the Zadar peninsula, is **Rijeka** ❶. The many names that Croatia's most important port has enjoyed reflect its eventful past: the town on the Rječina River has been known as *Tharsatica, Rika, St. Veit am Pflaun, Fluminus, Flumen, Fiume* and finally *Rijeka*.

At the estuary of the river, the Illyrians built a settlement which was destroyed by the Romans in the 2nd century B.C. Rome rebuilt the town, calling it *Tarsatica*. It was an important stop between Tergeste (Trieste) and Senj. Rome's frontier region, the Liburnian *Limes*, ran along here, and was meant to keep out the fractious Iapod and Delmata tribes.

In the early Middle Ages, Rijeka was part of the Kingdom of Croatia. Later, the town came under German influence and developed into an important free port. It was a thorn in the side of Venice, but the Serenissima never managed to permanently conquer Rijeka. The Turks were also a constant menace.

The Habsburg Empire made Rijeka the starting point of its so-called military border that stretched up to Hungary. In 1809,

Right: The Church of Sveti Vid (St. Vitus') in Rijeka, a 17th-century Baroque church built on an octagonal ground plan.

Napoleon annexed the town and added it to the Illyrian provinces that he had set up. Rijeka changed hands several times before returning once again to Austria. After the Turkish threat diminished and the military border lost its former significance, Austria decided to develop Trieste instead of Rijeka as a major port. The railway line from Vienna to Trieste bound it closer to the Habsburg power center than Rijeka.

Beginning in the middle of the 19th century, Rijeka enjoyed a period of economic growth: ship building, chemical industries, woodworking and machine building flourished. The coastal promenade, with all its monumental buildings and new districts, was built up during this opulent era.

During the First World War, Italy tried to enlarge its territory by taking Istria and Rijeka. Postwar treaties did give Italy a part of Croatia – but not Rijeka. So in December 1918, Italian troops entered the city to try and create a *fait accompli*. Unanticipated strong foreign pressure led the Italian government to contemplate withdrawal, but then Gabriele d'Annunzio, poet, writer and lieutenant colonel, seized a gunboat and "conquered" Rijeka with a small troop of 235 devoted soldiers and officers.

By this step, D'Annunzio hoped to force the Italian government to go through with its annexation of Rijeka. But Rome dissociated itself from the escapade of this peculiar egomaniac, who was on the lookout for publicity and was also one of the early supporters of Fascism à la Mussolini.

D'Annunzio didn't give up, however. He unilaterally declared Rijeka – now called Fiume – the free state of *Reggenza Italiana del Quarnero*. And he found a fair amount of support among the pro-Italian part of the population.

The free state existed for 16 months before the Italian government decided to end this unorthodox piece of nation-

building by sending a warship to Rijeka to shell D'Annunzio's headquarters. D'Annunzio had to flee and went into exile. When Mussolini, his ardent supporter, came to power in 1924, the poet was allowed back into Italy. And Rijeka was annexed by Italy that same year. After the Second World War, the town was incorporated into the Croatian Republic of Yugoslavia and grew into the biggest and most important port of the country. The conflicts of 1991 and Croatia's independence left Rijeka's status unchanged. Today, more than 200,000 people live and work in Rijeka.

A yearly media highlight attracting fans of motor racing is the Croatian International Motorcycle Grand Prix run, which takes place on Rijeka's popular Grobnik Circuit.

A Tour of Rijeka

The image of a busy industrial port does little to enthuse visitors to Rijeka at first sight. The façades of the – in part monumental – luxurious buildings and palaces from the turn of the century have been blackened by exhaust fumes, and their plaster is crumbling away from years of neglect.

For many tourists, Rijeka's position at the northernmost stop on the Adriatic coastal railway line and cruise ship docking point make it little more than a traffic crossing. But if one takes a closer look, Rijeka and its surroundings can offer much to the traveler.

When arriving from the west, from Opatija, follow the signs for the center (*Centar*) and you will pass the railway station at the end of Trg Žabica (Žabica Square). From here, the coastal road, the Riva, continues southeast. This is the center, and drivers are well advised to park their cars (preferably by the market to the right of the Riva by Riva Boduli).

The ***Tržnica ❶** (market), a roofed building consisting of several pavilions, was first opened in 1881. This construction of metal and glass was considered revolutionary at the time. There are a number of good, inexpenive restaurants and cafés to choose from around the market.

By the Mrtvi kanal (Dead Canal), the former estuary of the Rječina where small boats anchor today, stands the ***Ivan Zajc National Theater ❷**. The plans for the building were made by two famous Viennese architects, Fellner and Helmer, who specialized in building theaters all across Europe.

In 1885, the first electric light in the city was turned on in this theater. In 1981, the building was renovated to create an up-to-date space for the performance of today's plays, concerts and ballets. The Neo-Renaissance façade contains a group of figures by Augusto Benvenuti. It symbolizes drama and music.

The theater itself, with its three rows of boxes and a gallery, is faintly reminiscent of Baroque architecture. The ceiling is decorated with allegorical paintings by Franz Matsch and the brothers Gustav and Ernst Klimt. The first Croatian words heard from the stage were uttered in 1945. Shortly after that, Fiume changed its name back to Rijeka again, and in 1953, the theater was given its present name in honor of the "Croatian Verdi," Ivan Zajc.

Opposite the theater is the **Modelo Palace ❸**, also built by Fellner and Hellmer, and the former headquarters of the savings bank. Following Ivana Zajca ulica, you will ultimately reach the small Neo-Baroque **Church of Sveti Nikola ❹** (St. Nicholas'), built in 1790 by the Orthodox Serb merchants' colony of Rijeka. It has valuable icons inside originating from the Vojvodina region. North of the church is one of the town's special landmarks, the ***Gradski toranj ❺** (City Gate), dating from the 18th century. The old tower of the town wall was detroyed in 1750 by an earthquake.

In front of the city gate is the **Korzo ❻**, the pedestrian zone. Take the time to find a jeweler and ask for *Morčiči* or *Moretti*.

These amusing earrings with a Moor's head can be found only in Rijeka; the Moor has a turban of enamel and golden spots for eyes, mouth and ears.

Wearing this item of jewelry is a tradition for the women of the region. But why the head of a Moor? There's an ancient legend which explains that, in the 17th century, the Turks set up their camp on Grobnik Field above Rijeka and lay siege to the town. The famous Count Zrinski is said to have shot an arrow with deadly accuracy, hitting a Turkish Pasha in the temple. Having lost their leader, the Turks fled, but they were overcome when stones rained down upon them, completely covering them up and leaving only their turbans exposed.

Those who don't believe the legend and would rather stay closer to the facts, might recognize a close similarity between these earrings and the Venetian *mori*. During the Vienna world exhibition of 1873, the works of the goldsmiths of Rijeka came to be known and admired internationally, and many royal and aristocratic families ordered *Morčiči*.

Today, there is only a single goldsmith, **Antoni Gjon** at Užarka ulica No. 12, who makes these Moor's heads. In the History and Maritime Museum you can see copies and drawings of this piece of jewelry. If you follow the Korzo to **Trg Republike** (Republic Square) and then turn right, you will soon reach the former **Sveti Jeronim ❼** (St. Jerome's Church), the **Augustine Monastery** and the **Municipium**.

Construction of this church was commissioned by the counts of Duino in 1315, while work on the monastery began in 1408. The devastating earthquakes of 1750 and 1763 destroyed most of the complex. In the 18th century, it was rebuilt in Baroque style integrating surviving elements of the previous buildings. Especially worth seeing in the church is the **Chapel of the Immaculate Conception** for its Gothic vault and its frescos.

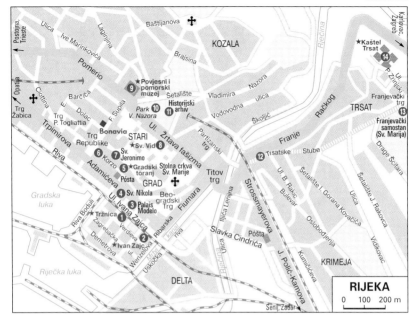

The monastery came to be the spiritual and cultural center of the town; the cartographer Ivan Klobučarič (1550-1605), worked here as a prior. The building ceased to be a monastery in 1786, and has served as Rijeka's City Hall ever since the 19th century.

Continuing in an easterly direction from the former monastery, you will come upon ★**Sveti Vid** ❽ (St. Vitus' Church), a 17th-century octagonal building in Baroque style. It stands in the vicinity of the Law Courts on Grivica Square. A church was first built here in the 9th century and was dedicated to Rijeka's patron saint. In 1627, the ruined building was granted to the Jesuits, who were just arriving. A rich Ursuline, Baroness Tannhausen, sponsored the building of the present church, which is modeled on Santa Maria della Salute in Venice. But in Rijeka's tumultuous subsequent history, building work remained unfinished.

On the marble altar stands a crucifix from the 13th century that is supposed to

have been the source of miracles at one time. Its story, and that of the stone next to it, runs as follows: When, in 1296, a man called Petar Lončaric rudely and loudly swore at the cross and threw a stone at it because he seemed to always be losing at cards, the ground suddenly opened and the sinner was swallowed up together with his playing cards. At the same time, the cross started to bleed. Since then, the crucifix has been regarded as miraculous.

Several hundred meters uphill, heading in a northwesterly direction, is the Neo-Renaissance building of the ★**Povjesni i pomorski muzej** ❾ (History and Maritime Museum), with exhibits of archeology, history, fishing and shipping.

In the adjacent **Vladimir Nazora Park** ❿ is the **Historijski arhiv** ⓫. The huge Neo-Baroque palace used to be Archduke Joseph of Austria's residence. The exotic plants in the park go back to his day.

Walking south (along the Žrtava fašizma) you will once again come across the Dead Canal and Titov trg (Tito

Square), and cross the Rječina. On the left are the **★Trsatske stube** ⑫, the steps leading to Trsat Castle. The Baroque entry hall (18th century) was built with the model of a triumphal arch in mind. A relief shows Mary and the Christ Child.

The building of the steps was started as early as 1531 by Petar Kruzič, a hero of the wars against the Turks. Labor continued on well into the 18th century. Eventually there were 561 steps for the pilgrims to climb. They lead up to Frankopanski trg, where the **Franjevački samostan** ⑬ (Franciscan monastery, 15th century) stands, along with its votive church, **Sveta Marija** (St. Mary's, 16th century), the pilgrims' destination.

The place is called by locals the "Croatian Nazareth," because the original house of Mary and Joseph is said to have stood here briefly. This allegedly happened in 1291, when crusaders returned

Above: Delivering mail in the more hilly districts of Rijeka is a job requiring good physical condition.

from the Holy Land with a little bit of sacred earth and stones from the house in Nazareth. They planned to rebuild the house in Loreto by Ancona, but somehow these materials ended up on the Trsat, where this "house" stood until December 10, when the stones were taken on to their final destination. The people grieved so much over the loss of their holy relics that, in 1367, Pope Urban V sent them as solace a **cedarwood icon** – allegedly painted by none other than St. Luke himself and possessing miraculous powers. The magical **triptych** with the picture of the Madonna and Child decorates the main altar of St. Mary's Church.

Petar Zrinjski Alley leads up to nearby **★Trsat Castle** ⑭. Here, 138 meters above sea level, the first fortress guarding the region was built in the 7th century. In subsequent centuries it was destroyed and rebuilt several times. The fortress and its pleasant café offer the best view over the city and the surrounding countryside. It is a charming spot for resting tired feet and quenching thirst after a difficult climb.

Kastav

Fifteen kilometers northwest of Rijeka, near Matulji, is the small town of **Kastav** ❷ – 378 meters above sea level. The town, which is still walled in as it was in the old days, has a loggia, narrow, winding lanes and a main square that all help to preserve its medieval character.

On the main square, called Lokvine, is an interesting cisterne with a stone tablet recalling the year 1666, when the locals pushed Captain Franco Morelli into the well because he levied excessive taxes and abused his powers. Whether that rebellious act spoiled the water remains an open question.

At any rate, the people of Kastav specialize in viticulture, and on the first Sunday in October they celebrate the *Bijela nedelja* **wine festival** which is known in the whole bay region, and

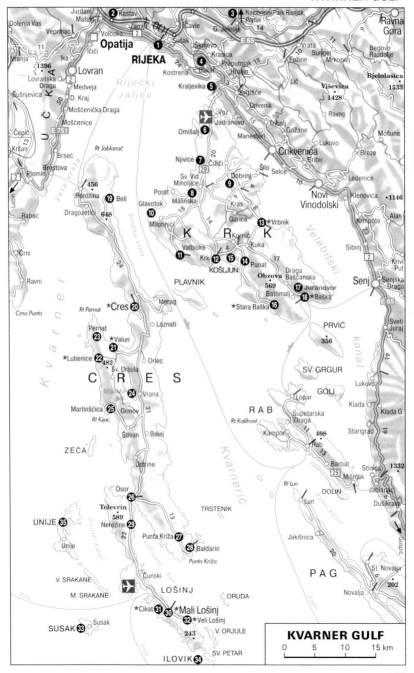

where people drink young local wine. In 1866, the first Croatian reading hall was founded in Kastav, where one of the most important Croatian poets, Vladimir Nazor, once taught. This was one way for the patriotic people of Kastav to make a statement against the Habsburg policy of Italianization. Another point for the traveler: Kastav offers excellent panoramic views of the surrounding area.

Risnjak National Park

Nature-lovers will find it worth making a side trip to inland regions, specifically to **Risnjak National Park ❸**, only 30 kilometers from Rijeka. The drive takes you through Gornje Jelenje in the direction of Lazac to Vilje.

A marked hiking trail begins there leading (in 90 minutes) to the peak of the **Veliki Risnjak** (1,525 meters). The karstic Risnjak is part of the Dinaric Mountains linking the Alps with the Balkans. It has rich flora, with fir and beech forests growing up until an altitude of 1,250 meters. The highest vegetation belt is made up of mountain pines.

There are many animal species, too; let us only mention the bird population and the chamois here. You are advised not to leave the marked trails. Wearing good hiking boots that support your ankles properly is recommended to avoid injuries that may occur by getting caught in one of the many fissures or crevices that mark the karstic floor of the mountain, if hiking off the trails.

Platak, standing at an altitude of 1,100 meters, is a recreational resort that nestles right at the edge of the national park, and which has skiing facilities and many trails leading into the mountains of the area. The climb to Risnjak from here takes about three hours.

Right: An entire fleet of ferries must be maintained to connect the islands of the Kvarner Gulf with the mainland.

Bakar

The main coastal road leading southeast, the Magistrala, can be very busy. **Bakar ❹** is accessible via a steep side road. The small harbor town has an idyllic location, but in 1972, during the communist era, its charm was somewhat compromised by the construction of a coal port and an ugly coking plant. Clearing-up work has started.

Kraljevica

On the way to Krk you will pass **Kraljevica ❺**, a small town with two castles. Its name, "King's Town" (*kralj* means "king"), goes back to the legend that states that the Hungarian King Bela IV sought refuge here in 1242 from a Tatar invasion. In the 17th century, the family of Count Zrinski built the first **Kaštel** at this strategically advantageous point. Today it forms the old castle with two interior courtyards and a chapel, and is situated in the middle of the town. A few decades later, the Zrinskis built a second set of fortifications on a peninsula in the direction of Bakar; Novigrad, "New Castle," which reminds one more of an Italian Renaissance palace.

The once luxurious imperial resort of Kraljevica lost much of its attraction in communist times due to the construction of an oil refinery opposite, but it is now being upgraded touristically.

KRK ISLAND

Since 1980, Krk Island has been reached over the 1309-meter Krčki most (Krk Bridge). Krk is the biggest island of the Yugoslav Adriatic, measuring 408 square kilometers; it is about 38 kilometers long and 20 kilometers at its widest point. Because of its closeness to the mainland, a certain amount of development was unavoidable. The contrast in the landscape between the eastern and

western parts of the island easily catches the eye: in the east the coast and the karstic hills lack good soil and vegetation because of the bora storms in winter. The western part, meanwhile, blooms in Mediterranean splendor; it is therefore no surprise that the most important settlements are on this side of the island.

Krk was the main feudal holding of the Croatian dynasty of princes of the Frankopans, which saw its best days in the 13th to 15th centuries. The coat of arms of the Frankopans – or Frangepans, as they were also called – points to the origin of the name: two lions are being tamed with a piece of bread (Latin: *frangere panem*).

Omišalj

The presence of the petrochemical industry on the island might irritate many visitors, but these plants are concentrated in the north. **Omišalj** ❻, the first place worth a detour, is situated like an Acropolis on an 82-meter hill and is one of the oldest towns on the island. The Romans called this place *Castrum Musculum* and had a small garrison here; in the Middle Ages, Omišalj was one of the four towns of the Frankopans. In the evening, you can see the lights of Rijeka, and the place has a beautiful atmosphere. Not far away are several small coves with rock and sand beaches. A coastal road leads to the yacht harbor. On the road south you can take a lunch-break in one of the restaurants of the modern **Njivice** ❼ resort situated on the oak-lined bay.

Malinska

In 1970, a big hotel complex called **Haludovo**, with a night club, a discotheque, parks and sports facilities, was opened here. It stretches north up **Malinska Bay** ❽ to the lighthouse, and was a luxurious place in its heyday. Today, more middle-of-the-road tourists promenade in the evening along the harborfront. You will get a better impression of the coast and its pretty bays if you

follow the *Rajski put* path. You can walk across to the village of Porat (three kilometers) and its Franciscan monastery.

Dobrinj

Heading east from Malinska, the road leads to **Dobrinj ❾**. It is the oldest place on Krk, and has been known by this name since the year 1100. Situated at 200 meters altitude in the middle of a forest of chestnuts and fig trees, it is surrounded by probably the most fertile land on the island.

The harbor of Šilo is not very far away, but people obviously felt more secure up on the hill. Instead of a town wall, it is the walls of the houses on the edge of the town themselves which provided protection. The panorama is fairly varied here, too, extending all the way to the Velebit Mountains. The prosperity of the place

Above: Beach life on the island of Krk. Right: St. Mary's Cathedral in the town of Krk, with its distinctive onion dome.

was based on salt from the salterns in the bay of **Soline**, where there is a sand beach today.

A road from Dobrinj, leading through vineyards to the northeast, takes you to **Šilo**, the erstwhile harbor where ferries departed for Crikvenica.

Glavotok

At the western tip of Krk is the small fishing village of **Glavotok ❿**. Those interested in Glagolithic writing should not miss the **Franjevački samostan** (Franciscan monastery).

In 1473, the Frankopans gave this spit of land to the tertiary Franciscans, who were Glagolithic. The church was built in the early 16th century, and was reconstructed several times after that. It houses numerous works by a number of Italian masters. The archive of the monastery is even more important, with its Glagolithic inscriptions. If after so much art and culture you want some leisure, you will find it on this corner of the island, with its cliffs and white beaches. Ten kilometers further south is **Valbiska** ⓫, with a ferry connection to Merag on Cres.

Krk Town

On the southern coast, protected from the storms of the bora coming down off the Velebit Mountains, is the harbor town of **Krk** ⓬. The Romans called it *Curicum* and gave it the status of a municipium. The strategic significance of the town also determined its fate in the following centuries. It was conquered, destroyed and rebuilt several times; it is not by chance that the defense walls count among the strongest on the Adriatic coast. Today, Krk is the administrative center of the island.

The *old town of Krk has been closed off to cars, and thus invites visitors to enjoy relaxing walks. The partly intact **town wall**, with its fortified tower and bastion, dates from the 12th century. In the same century, close to the harbor and not far from the mighty castle, the Romanesque cathedral was built. *Katedrala Sveta Marija (St. Mary's Cathedral), which was built on the ruins of a Roman bath, has a rather amusing and remarkable onion dome. In the 15th century, the Frankopans added a chapel with Gothic vaulting in the left aisle of the basilica.

The bishops of Krk are buried in the cathedral, in addition to several descendants of the Frankopans. The varied capitals of the pillars supporting the nave are quite interesting. Other valuable pieces of art that are worth having a look at are two reading desks dating from the Renaissance, a wooden pulpit and a silver *pala* (a decorated front altar panel), a gift of the Frankopans. The altar picture (a burial) is attributed to the most important painter of Friuli, Giovanni Antonio Pordenone.

The Romanesque **Church of Sveti Kirin** is right beside the cathedral. To-

Rijeka and the Kvarner Gulf

day, it has only two naves, the third having been lost when the street was laid. It was built in the 10th to 11th centuries, and has the oldest murals on the island. The main street leads from the two churches to the main square, surrounded by cafés, restaurants and souvenir shops.

*Vrbnik

The first section of the main road of the island, the Krk Magistrala, starts off in an easterly direction.

In Kuka there is a turnoff to the northeast to **Vrbnik** ⓭. This wonderful and picturesque town rises on the site of a prehistoric settlement on top of a steep cliff that sweeps sharply down to the sea. The narrow lanes that are a hallmark of the little town have survived so well that you almost get the feeling time has stood still for centuries here.

In the **Dinko Vitežič House**, some Glagolithic documents are kept. Vrbnik is the home of *Žlahtina* wine, a honey-colored heavy white wine.

Punat

The Magistrala leaving the town of Krk in an eastwardly direction leads along the inlet of Punat. On the right side of the road you will pass the small pre-Romanesque **Sveti Donat** (St. Donatus' Church), very similar to St. Donatus' in Zadar and the Holy Cross Church in Nin. It was built in the 9th century and is considered to be one of the most important monuments of the Croats. A bit further along on the right, a road forks south towards **Punat ⓮**.

In earlier centuries, the Punat inlet was counted among the most secure anchorages on the Adriatic, and therefore it is not surprising that even today it has a big **marina** with 800 mooring places. The former fishing village has turned to tourism and offers everything you need for a holiday.

Above and right: Baška, the center of summertime tourism on Krk, lies at the foot of typical karst mountains.

In the middle of the inlet is the idyllically-situated and perfectly photogenic island of **Košljun ⓯**, with an old Franciscan monastery, an abbey church full of art treasures, and neat, well-maintained gardens. If you are looking for peace and quiet, take a trip to the pebble bay of ***Stara Baška ⓰**, ten kilometers away.

*Baška

Beyond Punat, you will enter the foothills of Mount Obzova, at 569 meters the highest elevation on the island. Continuing on the Magistrala towards Baška to the south end of the island, you will be driving along a valley blessed with meadows, vineyards, olive groves and orchards, with oak and pine forests occasionally interspersed with some karstic land.

About one kilometer before Baška is **Jurandvor ⓱**, with the **Church of Sveta Lucia** from the 12th century. It used to house the famous Tablet of Baška (*Bašćanska ploča*), the oldest dated writing in

Croatian. The text mentions the Croatian King Zvonimir donating a piece of land to Abbot Držiha. It also relates how an abbot and nine monks built a church. The original tablet, which was discovered in 1851, was taken to Zagreb, where it is today. A replica was made for public display in the church.

At the foot of the barren, karstic hills, on a wide bay, lies **Baška ⓲**, a focus of tourism on Krk. The center of the town is marked by the parish church. On the square in front of it is the **Museum of Local History**. Narrow streets with colorful houses lead down to the quay. Along the harbor you will find a row of ice-cream parlors, cafés and restaurants, and you can dine while enjoying the view over the bay. The most beautiful beach on the island is on the ***Bay of Baška**; over a two kilometers of dreamlike beach covered in small, smooth pebbles, gently sloping off towards the sea and lined by green vegetation on its land side.

The four-kilometer-long *Lungomare* promenade leads along the sea. Hikers can enjoy 35 kilometers of well-marked trails in this area. You have the best view over the bay from a hill west of Jurandvor by Batomalj, with the Pilgrimage Church of Our Lady of the Mountain towering above. There is also a trail leading up there from Stara Baška on the west coast (circa two hours).

*CRES ISLAND

Cres is the second-largest island in the Kvarner Gulf after Krk. It has a surface area of some 404 square kilometers. Together with Unije, Susak, Ilovik and another 25 small islands, the double island chain of Cres/Lošinj measures about 513 square kilometers in all and constitutes the biggest group of islands in the Adriatic.

An 83-kilometer-long road runs north to south, with a swing bridge connecting the two main islands to allow masted vessels to sail between them. Along this road you can observe the change of vegetation as you drive south. In the north of Cres Island there are large forests of beech and various kinds of oak. Deciduous trees are predominant. The middle of the island consists of olive groves, vineyards and pastures. In the south there was originally little vegetation. Pine forests have been planted, but big areas of maquis (the dense scrub so typical of certain Mediterranean regions) remain.

The fauna of the double island is rich in small and winged game; in birds of prey and songbirds. You will even find white-headed goose vultures here – 60 pairs of them. These birds are monogamous for life. On Cres, the word for this animal is *orel*, and it gave the town of Orlec its name. Because of the scarcity of pasture, the locals' favorite domestic animal is the sheep. They are easily satisfied, and supply the meats and cheeses which count among the specialities of the islands. The underwater flora around Lošinj is known among divers as the most beautiful in the Adriatic.

In 1600 B.C., the Illyrian tribe of the Liburnians settled on the island and began building the 66 fortresses that can still be found spread around there. Many historians believe that the Liburnians dug the channel near Osor, splitting what had once been a single island into the two we see today.

The Greeks located one episode of the myth of the Argonauts here. After stealing the Golden Fleece, Jason and Medea are said to have fled to this region; but Absyrtos, Medea's brother, caught up with them. Cunning Medea managed to convince her brother to negotiate, but she was only waiting to kill him. Absyrtos's body was chopped up into pieces and thrown into the sea. This is said to be the origin of the many islands around Cres and Lošinj.

The Venetians ruled over the double island – apart from a brief Croatian inter-

Right: Dropping anchor together increases the enjoyment of a maritime holiday (Cres Island).

regnum – from 1000 to 1797. Already in those days, Osor and Cres were the most important harbors on the island, securing the prosperity of its people. The southern part of the island was very much neglected during these times, however, and the landscape ran to seed. This fact is graphically mirrored in the name Lošinj (*loš* means "bad").

But under Austro-Hungarian rule, it was actually Lošinj that flourished economically. In Mali Lošinj, six dockyards were built, making this the second most important military base of the imperial monarchy. The fleet of Lošinj is said to have numbered about 130 vessels. But after World War One, this navy and the empire it served were vanquished, along with Lošinj's economic base.

At the same time, the plant disease *phylloxera* swept through the region and destroyed all the grape vines, following which a big wave of emigration began. Things only started looking up again for the local population when tourism began to develop. Lošinj became a popular travel destination even earlier than Cres did.

The easiest way to reach the double island is by ferry from Brestova in Istria to Porozina on northern Cres. The only main road on the island begins at this spot and starts its southern journey winding around the island's peaks. Twelve kilometers after Porozina, a minor road doubles back to the picturesque northeastern settlement of **Beli** ⓳, once an ancient coastal fort.

The area was earlier called *Caput Insulae* (Head of the Island). A Roman bridge, restored in 1848, survives and leads across a twelve-meter-deep gorge to the town situated in splendid isolation on a cliff. The main square and the parish church occupy the highest point (130 meters). Below is a little bay where Roman galleys anchored 2,000 years ago.

★**Cres** ⓴ is also the name given to the capital of the island, and it is its most

attractive town. Cres town, which lies in a well-protected bay, has been an important harbor since ancient times. Remnants of the town wall and towers date from the Venetian era.

Life still hums in the old harbor; seafood restaurants and ice cream parlors beckon with their outdoor tables, and if you take an evening stroll along the waterfront and through the old town, you can soak in the medieval atmosphere. Romantic little alleyways lead from the water to the **Parish Church of Sveta Marija Snježna**. In the rectory are several paintings and a polyptych by Alviseo Vivarini. Not far from here is the main square, with the town hall and a **loggia**, under which market stalls offer fresh fruit.

In the nearby Arsan Palace is the **Gradski muzej** (Municipal Museum) of Cres, with a collection of antiquities and an ethnographic exhibition. Franjo Petrić was born in this palace in 1529. His family came from Bosnia, and it is no surprise therefore that Petrić became a de-

clared enemy of Venetian rule. He embraced Protestantism early on and had to leave the island.

His next stations were Labin, Ingolstadt, Venice and Padua, where he studied under Vlaći. He swiftly developed into an authority in the fields of Greek language, philosophy and literature. He wrote 13 books and translated numerous texts from Greek into Latin, among them the prophecies of Zarathustra. He died in 1597 in Rome and was buried in St. Onofrio's Church.

Another twelve kilometers away lies the small harbor of ★**Valun** ㉑. It is located on the edge of an inviting bay, with a clean, light pebble beach and clear turquois-colored water. In the middle of this picturesque fishing village is the church where the famous Tablet of Valun is kept. This is regarded as a very old testimony to Croatian letters. The inscriptions are in Glagolithic and Latin characters, but are unfortunately only partly legible. Scholars believe they list the names of the benefactors of the church. A copy

cient dry stone walls and fallow fields. A steep track leads from there to the sea. Hikers in especially good physical condition can walk along the cliffs back to Valun. There is no path running along the cliffs here.

South of Valun is **Vransko jezero** ㉔ (Vran Lake), the only lake worth mentioning on the islands in the Kvarner Gulf. It is 1.5 kilometers wide, five kilometers long and an average of 60 meters deep. Its surface lies 13 meters below sea level. Since 1953, both the town of Cres and Mali Lošinj have received their drinking water from these 220 million cubic meters of fresh water. It is therefore quite understandable that swimming here is not permitted. It was once believed that the water arrived through subterranean channels from the mainland, but in actual fact it is rainwater.

The bumpy track 300 meters above the lake to the west leading through deserted, karstic uplands via Sv. Ursula and Grmov to the south might seem inviting, but it is fit only for jeeps, cross-country motorcycles and mountain bikes.

South of the lake, a side road leads west from the main road and soon delivers you to the small fishing and holiday village of **Martinšćica** ㉕. This village lies on an lovely pebble bay, and there are other attractive rock beaches nearby around Cape Kijac. The coast from here all the way down to Osor offers numerous opportunities for swimming, but only the bays near Stivan, Belej and Ustrine can be reached by road.

of this tablet decorates the old oil mill that was converted into a cozy *konoba taverna*. On the pedestrian harbor promenade are three good fish restaurants, with a large selection of seafood.

*Lubenice ㉒, a medieval mountain village perched at an altitude of 380 meters, is a popular destination. The speciality of the village bar is the delicious air-cured *pršut* (ham) – especially tempting for swimmers or hikers who climb up from the bay far below (the bay can only be reached on foot or by boat). Today, only a few old people live in this 1,000-year-old settlement, and they earn a little extra income by selling lambskins to tourists.

In two hours you can walk on a shepherds' track from Lubenice to the old, partly-inhabited country village of **Pernat** ㉓. The hike will take you past an-

Thirty-four kilometers south of Cres and 24 kilometers north of Mali Lošinj is **Osor** ㉖, in the past one of the most important towns on the island. Today, it has fewer than 100 inhabitants. Osor has a long and eventful history closely linked to the 100-meter-long and eleven-meter-wide channel. The Greeks called the place *Apsoros*, meaning the oldest settlement on the island. It was also a trading point on the Amber Road.

Above: An evening in the mountain village of Lubenice can be a magical experience. Right: The pebble beach of Valun is a treasure trove for collectors of pretty stones.

In Byzantine times, Osor was a base for the fleet of Ravenna. In those days – in the year 530 to be exact – it also became a bishopric. In the 9th century, Saracens burned down the port and the town. Later, when shipbuilding technology allowed for larger vessels, the harbor proved to be too small and the waters here too shallow, and the place lost its importance as a port. The main attraction here is the 15th-century **Sveta Marija** (St. Mary's Cathedral). Its pretty Renaissance façade was renovated in 1969. In summer, the square surrounding the historic building plays host to concerts of classical music. You can also admire sculptures by the Croatian artists Meštrović and Krsinič on the square.

If you are on the lookout for some particularly nice beaches, then head for the south of Cres; walk eastward from the village of **Punta Križa** ㉗ for about 20 minutes until you reach an absolute dream of a bay. A popular place for recreational vehicles is the camping site on the bay of **Baldarin** ㉘.

LOSIJN ISLAND

After crossing the 2,000-year-old channel of Osor – if the bridge has been opened to let sail boats pass through, you may encounter a considerable traffic jam – you will be on **Lošinj Island**. Thanks to the mild climate, it has rich vegetation; the severe winter winds blowing across from the mainland have generally lost their strength by the time they reach this island. Four kilometers beyond the bridge is the resort town of **Nerezine** ㉙, with a yacht marina. You can also set off from here to Televrin; at 589 meters, the highest peak on Lošinj.

The tourist center and the biggest town on the island is ★**Mali Lošinj** ㉚ (population 7,000). In the 15th century, the Venetians built a fortress on the high ground here. It was followed by a port in this large, exceptionally well-protected natural basin. A town grew up around the harbor, and also around the oldest building in the town, St. Martin's Church, dating from the 15th century.

Lošinj Island became a popular resort in the 19th century at a time when the Habsburgs were busy discovering new winter spa destinations. Many old villas, like those in the popular bay of ★**Čikat** ③, lined with huge pines, have survived from those times. The sub-tropical park of Mali Lošinj was established by Archduke Karl Stephan von Habsburg himself. But ocean trade and shipbuilding were also important to the Habsburgs, and they encouraged both vigorously. At the beginning of the 19th century, therefore, there were several dockyards here, where excellent sailing ships were built. But the switch to steamships, which were built elsewhere, spelled ruin for the docks. Today, yachting tourism flourishes here, and there is a modern marina.

One of the most beautiful walks on the Adriatic follows the east coast down to neighboring ★**Veli Lošinj** ②. This town is older than Mali Lošinj, and it was once the main settlement on the island. But it had a far smaller natural harbor and was therefore put out of business in the 19th century by Mali Lošinj.

Veli Lošinj occupies the nicer location, however, with a picturesque old **harbor basin** lined with cafés and restaurants, and **St. Anthony's Church**. It also offers hikers a better starting point for trips around the southern tip of the island. You will find the quietest and pleasantest bays for swimming south of Veli Lošinj; **Vinikova Bay**, for instance, where you can drop all your clothes without a second thought.

Travel agents organize trips to the sandy island of **Susak** ③, to the "flower island" of **Ilovik** ④, where sailors like to put up for the night, and to the green, carfree island of **Unije** ⑤, an attractive destination for nature lovers who like quiet places. But you won't live entirely like Robinson Crusoe on these islands: they boast several pretty fishing villages with good, simple restaurants and rooms to rent.

RIJEKA (051)

ⓘ Užarska 14/II, tel. 335882, fax. 333909.

▦ ⊜⊜⊜ **Hotel Bonavia**, Dolac 4, tel. 333744, fax. 335969, central, casino, nightclub. ⊜⊜ **Hotel Jadran**, Šetalište 13, divizije 46, tel. 216230, fax. 217667, central; **Hotel Kontinental**, Šetalište Kačića Miosića 1, tel. 216477, fax. 216495. ⊜ **Hotel Neboder**, Strossmayerova 1, tel. 217355, fax. 216592. *CAMPING:* **Preluk**, tel./fax. 621913, well-tended campsites with pine trees, boat dock.

✕ **Restaurant Sokol**, Ulica Obitelj Duiz 4, tel. 515650, cozy place with pizzeria and terrace, centrally located; **Restaurant Tri Palme**, Ivan Zajca 24, tel. 25096, fish and international food.

▥ **History and Maritime Museum** (Povjesni i pomorski muzej), Pomerio 18, tel. 213578, daily 9 a.m.-2 p.m., Sat. 9 a.m.-1 p.m.

▣ **Ivan Zajc National Theater**, Verdieva, tel. 37680, 211268, tickets: 37114.

▰ The over 500-step climb up the Trsat is strenuous, but the view from the castle is excellent. Hikers will find a recreational center and winter resort on the Platak, tel. 515650.

FERRIES: Rijeka is one of the most important harbors for passenger ships on the Adriatic. The **Jadrolinija** shipping line has its headquarters here. Most connections and cross passages through the Dalmatian islands start out from this point. Information in the main building directly on the quay (Riva 16, tel. 30899, fax. 213116).

KRK ISLAND (051)

BASKA

ⓘ Zvonimira 11, tel./fax. 856544.

▦ ⊜⊜ **Hotel Corinthia II and III**, outside of the town center, tel. 856651, 856824, fax. 856584, big complex with shops, beach, horse-back riding, 15 tennis courts, windsurfing, dancing in the evenings; **Corinthia I**, "Zvonimir," tel. 856824, fax. 856584. *CAMPING:* **Bunculuka**, tel. 856806, fax. 856895, nudist autocampground, sports.

KRK TOWN

ⓘ Trg Sv. Krivina 1, tel./fax. 221359.

▦ ⊜⊜ **Hotel Koralj**, V. Tomašiča, tel. 221044, fax. 221137, beach, restaurant, self service-shop, sauna, solarium; **Hotel Dražica**, Ružmarinska, tel. 221022, beach, pool; **Hotel Marina**, Obala Hrv. Mornarice, tel. 221128, fax. 221137, attractive city hotel.

✕: **Frankopan**, tel. 221437; **Grota**, tel. 221511; **Anex**, tel. 221112, pizza, pasta.

MALINSKA

i Obala 43, tel./fax. 859207.

Hotel Palace, Haludovo. 859111, fax. 859330, beach, pool, best hotel in Malinska. **Hotel Tamaris**, Haludovo, tel. 859111, fax. 859330, beach, tennis, restaurant with vegetarian menu; **Hotel Ribarsko selo**, Haludovo, tel. 859111, fax. 859330, hotel with annexes, beach, sports; **Hotel Slavija-Marina**, tel. 859122, fax. 859330, beach, sports. CAMPING: **Glavotok**, tel. 227240, open year-round, in the forest.

NJIVICE

Restaurant Konoba Rivica, tel. 0532/846101, fish and lamb specialities.

OMIŠALJ

Hotel Omišalj, tel. 842126, just a few kilometers away from the Krk Bridge, large hotel complex with restaurants, bars, discotheque, sports center, and a private beach.

PUNAT

i Obala 72, tel./fax. 854970.

Hotel Park, in the city center, tel./fax. 854103, near the beach. CAMPING: **Pila**, tel. 854020, fax. 854101, sports.

MARINA: Marina Punat, tel. 854030, the best-equipped Marina on the island with 800 berths.

CRES ISLAND (051)

FERRIES: Brestova (Istria) – Porozina every 30 min., July-Aug. also at night. Valbiska (Krk) – Merag, 30 minutes, several times per day.

BELI

CAMPING: Autocamp Brajdi, tel. 840522, simple, but with shade.

CRES TOWN

i Cons 11, at the harbor, tel./fax. 571535.

Hotel Kimen, tel. 571161, fax. 571163, beach, extensive recreational activities, restaurant (vegetarian food), inexpensive. **Hotel Cres**, tel./fax. 571108. CAMPING: **Kovačine**, tel. 571423, on partly shady peninsula, sports activities, Apr-Oct.

Amfora, Trg Frane Petrić 5; **Riva**, Riva Creskih Kopetana 13. Both at the harbor, fish specialties.

MARINA: Marina Cres, tel. 571622, 460 berths, restaurant, tennis.

LOZNATI

Konoba Bukaleta, cozy village inn, tel. 571606.

MARTINIŠĆICA

CAMPING: **Autocamp Slatina**, tel. 571439.

OSOR

i Tourist office on the main square, tel./fax. 237007.

Buffet Osor, fish specialties, beautiful garden, reservations recommended, tel. 237167.

PUNTA KRIŽA

CAMPING: **Baldarin**, tel. 231518, with nudist area, pine trees, rocky bay.

VALUN

i Tourist office at the harbor, tel. 535084.

CAMPING: Mmall campground with pebble beach, very simple, not accessible by car, tel. 535050, fax. 535085. Private rooms are arranged by the tourist office at the harbor, tel. 535084.

Konoba Toš Juna, cozy restaurant in a former oil mill at the harbor.

LOŠINJ ISLAND (051)

FERRIES: From Pula (Monday, Tuesday, Friday, Saturday) and from Zadar (daily during the Summer) to Mali Lošinj.

MALI LOŠINJ

i Tel. 231884, fax. 231547.

Hotel Alhambra, tel. 232022, fax. 231904, beach, restaurant, a good value; **Hotel Bellevue**, tel. 231222, restaurant, nightclub, beach, indoor swimming pool. CAMPING: **Čikat**, tel. 232125, shady place with lots of recreational activities, mid April to October.

Restaurant Marina, tel. 231232, all typical dishes are deliciously prepared here.

Yacht Club Mali Lošinj, with marina, tel. 231077, fax. 231611, 120 berths for boats up to 20 meters long. Diving schools offer diving classes, sailing schools offer one week boat license courses, for example, at **Pro-Sailing Academy**, tel./fax. 232800, or **Harbor Bureau**, Mali Lošinj, tel./fax. 231438.

SIGHTSEEING FLIGHTS: From Lošinj Airport, tel. 231666.

VELI LOŠINJ

Hotel Punta, tel. 231022, fax. 236301, in the middle of a pine forest, seafood restaurant with terrace, bar, disco, beach, swimming pool, sports, activity program for children.

NEREZINE

Restaurant Televrin, tel. 237121.

VINODOL, VELEBIT, RAB AND PAG

VINODOL
SENJ
PLITVICE LAKES
VELEBIT
RAB ISLAND
PAG ISLAND

Vinodol, Velebit, Rab and Pag

VINODOL

South of **Kraljevica**, parallel to the coast, runs the 25-kilometer-long **Vinodol** (Wine Valley), a stretch of land almost untouched by the huge streams of tourists struggling their way south on the coastal Magistrala.

This valley is separated from the sea by an over two-kilometer-wide and 300-meter-high range of hills. It was first mentioned in a 12th-century chronicle under the name of *Vallis Vinearia*. But it is known that in Roman times there was already a road running along this valley connecting Aquileia with *Senia*, today called Senj.

In the year 1225, the Croatian-Hungarian king gave the Vinodol to the Frankopans of Krk as a feudal tenure. Towards the end of the 13th century, the new lords had a legal code developed which was supposed to set out the relationship between them and their vassals. This "Vinodol Law," written in Croatian and in Glagolithic, contains criminal, civil and constitutional clauses, and is the first known legal code of the Croats – indeed, of any of the Slav peoples.

Preceding pages: A long way from home in the barren Velebit landscape. Left: In Plitvice Lakes National Park.

With the arrival of the Turks, the Frankopans lost their unchallenged authority over the area, and the Croatian-Hungarian House of the Counts Zrinski gained control of Vinodol and later over the Kvarner, too. Reminders of the Frankopans still survive in the form of a few castle ruins. The Zrinskis, meanwhile, have been immortalized in the name given to a very strong brandy which lulls many Croatians into the arms of Morpheus for an evening.

Those who arrive in the valley today will miss the vineyards that gave the name *Vinearia* to the area. Many of the houses are deserted, the population having found work either abroad or on the coast. A journey here will be a nostalgic foray into earlier, greater times.

Drivenik

Driving from Kraljevica inland through Vinodol, travelers will soon encounter **Drivenik ❶**, one of the places mentioned in the legal code. The settlement is still dominated by the ruins of a **castle** of the Frankopans and the Zrinskis. In 1978, in the yard of the primary school in the center of the village, a **monument** to an earlier inhabitant of the valley was erected. This story alone is worth a little detour:

The monument – created by Zvonko Car – stands in honor of Julije Klović, a Croatian Renaissance painter of miniatures. He was born in 1498 in the town of Grižane and went to Venice at the age of 18, where he worked as a medallion maker. Later, he traveled to Mantua where he studied painting with the famous Gulio Romano.

This is where he painted his first miniatures. He worked in the court of the Hungarian king Louis II for some time (until the year 1526). He also painted for the Pope, as well as for Cosimo Medici. His admirers, of whom there were quite a few, called him the Michelangelo of the miniature.

He was, in fact, a friend of Michelangelo, Vasari and Brueghel. Klović, known to art historians as Gulio Clovio, died in 1578 in Rome, and was interred in the Church of San Pietro in Vincoli, a privileged burial place.

Above: A little rain never hurt anyone – especially in southern climes.

★Crikvenica

Passing the ruins of the fortress of **Badanj ❷**, the road returns to the sea and leads to **Crikvenica ❸**, the largest town on the Vinodol coast. Its name dates back to a church (*crkva*) built in the 14th century at the mouth of the Dubracina River. In 1412, a Frankopan built a **castle** here, which he donated to the Paulines.

The Paulines in those days had a strong presence in Croatia (207 monasteries, 127 of them in the Croatian-Hungarian kingdom). They maintained schools in their monasteries, and thus played a role in spreading the Croatian language. In 1786, this monastery was dissolved, and the local community gave it to Archduke Joseph of Austria, who later converted it into a sanatorium for officers. Tourism followed shortly afterwards.

Crikvenica is still considered a spa for chronic rheumatic diseases, slipped discs, bronchitis and asthma. The former castle-monastery is today the **Hotel Kaštel**, and incorporates the erstwhile cells of the monks. Young people congregate on Crikvenica's over two-kilometer-long beach to play volleyball. In the evening, you can take walks under pretty laurel trees on the promenade enlivened by countless bars, ice-cream parlors and restaurants. Southeast of Crikvenica is **Selce ❹**, a small harbor with a promenade, and the Church of St. Catherine dating from 1498.

Bribir

The road from Selce to **Bribir ❺** passes through Jargovo. Until the beginning of the 19th century, Bribir was surrounded by a wall, and **castle ruins** show that this must have been an important place in the Vinodol. The Church of St. Peter and St. Paul once had the most valuable interior of the region; even today it has fine paintings, such as the *Washing of the Feet* by Palma the Younger.

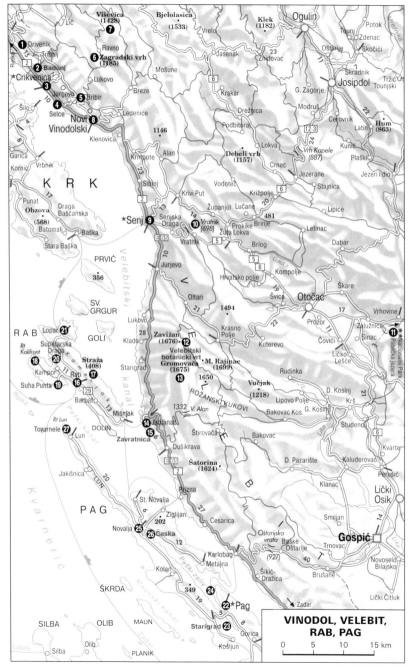

Bribir is especially interesting for nature lovers, being the gateway to the plateaus of the coastal uplands. A relatively poor road leads from here to the village of **Mokro**, behind Lukovo and Ravno. An approximately one-hour walk to the **Zagradski vrh** ❻ (1,185 meters) starts from the Poli Vagabundi Inn. But note: The higher you climb, the steeper the path, and toward the end there is no recognizable track at all. Those who want to climb up to the **Viševica** ❼ (1,428 meters) have to reckon on about two hours. After following the marked trail behind the inn for about 15 minutes, the path leads into a forest. The view from the top stretches to the Risnjak Mountains and over Rijeka Bay.

Novi Vinodolski

At the end of the Vinodol Valley, on a little hill, you will find **Novi Vinodolski**

Above: Novi Vinodolski. Right: The rocky coast always has a nook for good sunbathing.

❽. Behind it, the valley opens toward the sea. The Romans built the fortress of *Lopar* here. It is said that Novi Vinodolski and the valley were also protected by a castle under the Frankopans. It was during their rule that, on January 6, 1288, the Statute of Vinodol – the first Croatian law – was passed.

Over the centuries, the town was often pillaged, both by the Uskoks of Senj and the Turks. In 1493, Croats and Turks fought a battle in Lika, ending in a terrible defeat for the Croats. In order to secure the safe withdrawal of the survivors, Bishop Kristofor ordered that their horses should be shod with the horseshoes the wrong way round in order to lay false tracks. It is said that, thanks to this trick, everybody managed to escape the Turks. After having arrived back in Novi Vinodolski, the bishop had the Church of St. Philip and St. Jacob restored to show his gratitude. He was buried there in 1499. Since then, the church has had the status of a cathedral. In 1527, the Turks burned down the town.

Worth seeing is the ***old town**, built on a hill, with the **Filip i Jakov Cathedral**, the **Modrus Palace** and the remnants of the **castle** of the Frankopans, which today houses a library, a gallery and the **Narodni muzej** (National Museum). Following the harbor promenade you will reach **Lopar Beach**, a popular swimming spot with a flat sandy beach, and also pebble and rock beaches.

*SENJ

Senj ❾ is the gateway to the highest range of Croatia, the Velebit. Only 14 kilometers east of the town is **Vratnik ❿**, where the lowest pass between the sea and the hinterland breaks through at 698 meters.

This has been known since ancient times as the most important access route to the Balkans. Besides its strategically advantageous position, Senj also has special climatic characteristics: in winter, cold continental air will often sweep down here from the Vratnik to the Adriatic, and Senj is therefore the coldest town on the coast. The much-feared bora rages here, too. There is an old saying that the locals have: "The bora is born here, it lives in Rijeka and it dies in Trieste."

History

Throughout its existence, Senj has been the plaything of competing powers and it has often changed masters. But one group managed more than others to link its name with the town over a longer period, and they were the Uskoks. After the Hungarian king Matthias Corvinus captured Senj from the House of the Frankopans in the second half of the 15th century, he built a fortification marking the beginning of his *Vojna Krajina* (military border).

Senj became the most important base against Turkish attacks. In 1537, a stream of Croatian and Serb refugees flooded Senj, fleeing the Turks; they called themselves Uskoks (from *uskočiti*: escapees). Among them there were experienced and

talented fighters to whom the Habsburgs – the new local power brokers in the region – were happy to give asylum. The town and the military were put under the control of the Duke of Graz. But in time, the Uskoks grew in number and became more and more insolent. They didn't restrict their actions to fighting the Turks, but sailed their fleet on raids against the Venetians as well, especially when the Habsburgs were late in paying their troops.

Repeated demands by the Venetians failed to persuade Austria to control the Uskoks, so Venice entered into an alliance with the Ottoman Empire in 1613, and went on the offensive against the Uskoks. Senj was besieged by 85 ships, six galleys and 12,000 troops, supported by 4,000 Turkish cavalry, operating on the mainland. But even this effort did not

Above: The daunting Uskok fortress of Nehaj (16th century) in Senj. Right: The Plitvice Lakes, 16 bodies of water connected by 92 waterfalls.

manage to fully destroy the Uskoks, and the situation degenerated into an Austrian-Venetian war in 1615. The conflict was finally solved through the diplomatic intervention of the German emperor and the Spanish king, and the Uskoks were dispersed to other places.

Strolling around Senj

The **town wall**, with its many bastions mainly dating back to the 13th to 15th centuries, is testimony to the long military tradition of Senj. Most of the 13 bastions remaining today serve more profane purposes, housing bars and the tourist office.

The main attraction in the center of town is the **Čilnica**, actually named Marko Balen Square. It is one of the most beautiful Baroque squares on the Croatian coast, at the middle of which a fountain in classicist style bubbles away. On the eastern side is the **castle**, built in the 14th century as a residence of the Frankopans. On the western side are three

buildings that used to serve as salt offices. The southern side is marked by a little park. Around the corner is the **Katedrala Sveta Marija** (St. Mary's Cathedral), the oldest surviving building of the town. It is from this church that Glagolithic writing spread to other Slav countries due to the engagement of the local bishops.

Not far from the harbor is **Vukasovič Palace**, housing the **Municipal Museum** and its interesting archeological collection, plus a collection of documents and an exhibition on the flora and fauna of the Velebit.

The southern part of the town is dominated by the symbol of the Uskok resistance, the completly preserved ***Fortress of Nehaj**. Its creator, the town captain Ivan Lenkoci, did not consider the town walls strong enough, so he had Trbušnjak Hill completely cleared of all its buildings. His impressive square fortress was finished there in 1558. Today it houses a **museum** dedicated to the history of the Uskoks, showing, among other things, weapons and costumes.

****PLITVICE LAKES NATIONAL PARK**

A road leads from Senj inland over Vratnik and Otočac to the popular national park of **Plitvička jezera** ⑪ (Plitvice Lakes; 100 kilometers; two to three hours). Sixteen greenish-blue karstic lakes follow each other in a graduated progression over seven kilometers, connected by 92 waterfalls.

The lakes are in an area richly forested by beech, fir, pine and maple, and which has been declared a UNESCO World Heritage Site. The national park stretches over 20,000 hectares; about 200 hectares are taken up by the lakes and 14,000 hectares by the neighboring forest. The forest has the character of a jungle in places. The fauna is extremely varied: besides countless species of birds (including vultures) and small animals, there are deer, bears, wolves, wild boars and wildcats. The waters host species that are threatened by extinction in other areas, for example, the otter.

Into this deep valley, nature placed a series of lakes that cross a total difference in height of some 156 meters. This system was created by the erosion of the plateau of lime and dolomite by the Korana River. The river washed out the harder dolomite stone more sideways than downwards, thus creating the upper lakes. The deeper gorges were cut out of the softer limestone, and these formed the lower lakes. In this region, with its abundant rain, moss and lichen find an ideal habitat.

The sediment of calcium and magnesium carbonate in the water, together with the effect of certain kinds of moss and lichen, gave rise to the soft tufa rock, especially where there were natural barriers to hinder the water flow. Because of the permanent sedimentation, these deposit walls kept growing and formed the barriers between the lakes.

Meanwhile, the water pressure keeps breaking down these tufa barriers, so that the process never ends. The mineral sediment covers the bottom and the sides of the lakes with a white layer, adding to the special beauty of the water.

It is interesting to note that all objects that fall into the water – tree trunks, for instance – are also covered by the white sediment and eventually become petrified.

The entrance fee includes the use of a boat on Lake Kozjak, and travel on the panoramic train, with views across large areas of the park. It is worth getting ahold of a map before visiting because there are a great number of well-marked trails to chose from. Travel recommendations for drivers are also offered.

The devastation of the war, which started in this region at Eastertime in 1991 with the "ethnic cleansing" performed by the Serbs, did not affect the natural environment of the park, but the

Right: There is no lack of church spires in the townscape of Rab.

two Plitvice camping sites were destroyed along with many local homes.

*VELEBIT

Behind Senj rises the **Velebit** mountain range – the biggest Croatian massif and the longest of the Dinaric mountain ranges. From Vratnik in the northwest to the Zrmanja River in the southeast, the Velebit stretches for more than 150 kilometers.

Steep slopes scoured by the bora winds in winter, vast bare flanks on the coastal side and thickly overgrown terrain along the Lika Valley are the characteristic features of the karstic Velebit. The region has developed special flora, which can in part only be found here. Given that the average temperature for about 160 days of the year is close to the freezing point (with great differences between day- and nighttime temperatures), the summer months are best for exploration.

In 1966, a botanical garden was established on the Velebit, the **Velebitski botaniki vrt** ⑫, on the slopes of the 1,676-meter Mount Zavižan. From **Jurjevo** on the coast, a road leads into this mountain region. You turn off at **Oltari** (1,027 meters) and keep heading south until coming to the vicinity of the park, which is situated at an altitude of about 1,480 meters. There is a hostel here that has lodgings for the weary traveler. The true beauty of the garden unfolds during a walk among the plants, each individual variety of which is marked with a plaque bearing its name of species.

Another hiking trail leads from the hostel to a natural phenomenon, the so-called *Kukovi*. These are huge weird barren rock formations carved out of their surroundings by the wind and weather. One of these rocks, the **Gromovača** ⑬, at 1,675 meters, can be reached after two hours of trekking.

Further to the southeast are whole groups of these outcrops, like the

Map p. 125, Info p. 135

Hajdučki kukovi and the Rožanski kukovi. Over an area of about 18 square kilometers are more than 50 such rocks, rising to heights of more than 1,600 meters. You will come across almost all the phenomena characteristic of the karstic landscape. Only the nature park at Paklenica, near Starigrad, has more karstic features to show. The region is very isolated, so we recommend that only experienced climbers explore it.

Back on the coastal thoroughfare, the Magistrala, the panoramas that open up at every turn would be fabulous were it not for the fact that the traffic on this winding and difficult road is very dangerous. You must especially pay attention to the reckless overtaking by locals who trust in God enough to take the bends on the wrong side of the road. After it rains, the road can be rather slippery and especially dangerous.

One place that should not be missed is **Jablanac** ⑭, a small, pretty fishing village. It can be the starting point for tours into the Velebit Mountains, especially

into the **Alan** region (1,300-1,600 meters). Just about a kilometer further south is a part of the **Zavratnica Fjord** ⑮. The ferry crossing from Jablanac to the island of Rab takes only 15 minutes.

*RAB ISLAND

With its 93 square kilometers, **Rab** is the ninth biggest island in the Adriatic, and also one of the sunniest places in Europe, boasting a proud 2,500 hours of sunshine per year. The western side of the island facing the Adriatic does not suffer from the bora and the cold air coming down from the Velebit because of the ridges that run from north to south on Rab.

The 400-meter-plus **Kamenjak** mountain range is especially important for the protection of the communities on the sheltered side; the windswept east coast of the island is practically uninhabited.

The vegetation in the northeast is very sparce, consisting mainly of macchia, but the rest of the island is quite green. The

occasionally rich vegetation, wonderful beaches and idyllic bays have made Rab very popular with tourists.

The main settlement on the island is the town of **Rab ⑯**, at the foot of the Kamenjak. It was founded in the 2nd century B.C. by Roman soldiers for use as a military camp.

Its development into a civilian town started in A.D. 800, when Croatians settled here. Various Christian orders and the Venetians all left their architectural mark. Today Rab is listed among the most beautiful places on the Adriatic, and the flow of visitors during the day and also in the evenings is accordingly brisk. There are three bays (*padovas*) that are good for swimming in close to town.

Rab's famous townscape, with its characteristic four church spires, is very compact; this is mainly because of the thick

Above: Souvenirs and assorted wares being peddled at the foot of Rab's town wall. Right: The simple St. Mary's Cathedral in the town of Rab.

walls built against attacks by the Uskoks and Turks. In the alleyways of the **old town**, nestling on a narrow spit of land, you will encounter crowds of tourists armed with cameras busily clicking and videotaping the beautiful historic buildings.

The most impressive building in town is the **Katedrala Sveta Marija** (St. Mary's Cathedral), a three-naved basilica from the 11th century. It is said that it was consecrated in 1177 by Pope Alexander himself. The church was restored in the 15th century, and a **Pietà** was put above the main gate, executed by a Dalmatian, Petar Trogiranin, one of the best known stonecutters of the early Renaissance. The octagonal baptismal font in St. Peter's Chapel is also his work.

The **Reliquary of St. Christoforus** is of special value. It was presented to the bishopric in the year 923 by the Patriarch of Constantinople. In those days, Rab was already under Roman juristiction. Near the church is a 25-meter-high **bell tower**, also built in the 11th century. Its varied windows, reminiscent of the church of Pomposa by Ferrara, make it unique. What is especially fascinating about the entire old town is its uniformity and its palaces, the façades of which are often decorated with elaborate stone carvings. An especially beautiful example is the **Kneževdvor** (Rector's Palace) on Tito Square.

Outside the historic town center is beautiful **Komrčar Park**, laid out at the end of the 19th century. Walking through it you will reach the western shore of Eufemija Bay.

Those who want to climb the mountains of Rab must take the road to Lopar, and then turn right at the Sunga River and proceed into the uplands. You can enjoy an impressive panorama from the highest point of the Kamenjak, the **Straža** ⑰ (408 meters), reaching as far as the Velebit mountains.

Traffic is restricted on the wooded peninsulas of Frkanj and **Kalifront** ⑱, the latter having a road through the forest down to the idyllic **Gozinka Bay** (pebble beach, restaurant). Acknowledged centers of tourism are the settlement of **Suha Punta** ⑲ and the beaches of **Supetarska Draga** ⑳.

Lopar ㉑, at the north of the island, is not only a ferry harbor for boats from Baška (Krk Island), but is also a holiday resort with a dreamlike, almost two-kilometer-long sand beach, the **Paradiso**. It falls away gently towards the sea, and is especially popular with families with children.

Lopar has no special sights to offer, but there is a legend linking it to the founding of the tiny state of San Marino in Italy. It tells of St. Marinus, a stone mason from Lopar who lived in the 3rd century, who was involved in the building of the walls of the fortress in Rimini. He was a Christian, and therefore not very safe there – given that Emperor Diocletian hounded Christians mercilessly. To avoid persecution, Marinus retreated to Monte Tiano

and lived with other Christians there, building a church and later a little monastery: the beginnings of the state of San Marino, with which Rab has close links to this day.

PAG ISLAND

Along the Magistrala, at **Karlobag**, there is another opportunity to strike off into the mainland interior; to Gospić, for example, and the fertile Lika Plain. But you can also cross from Karlobag by ferry to Pag, the main settlement on the largely barren northern Dalmatian **Pag Island**. The road down Pag Island offers an alternate route to Zadar instead of the accident-prone E65 mainland coastal road. Pag and the smaller islands facing Zadar make up the northern Dalmatian island chain. The island has a surface area of 284 square kilometers and a length of about 60 kilometers.

Because of the bora's great squalls, Pag has very poor vegetation, though peasants and shepherds have built many

Vinodol, Velebit, Rab and Pag

kilometers of stone walls over the centuries as wind protection.

The Romans realized the strategic advantages of a location like Pag and occupied the island. The name Pag (*pagus* means "village") goes back to those times. In the Middle Ages, it was the bishops of Zadar and Rab who fought over Pag because of its rich salterns. The feud became so intense that at one point an attempt was made to partition the island. It was the Venetians who finally brought peace. After the old towns of *Cissa* and *Pagus* were destroyed by rebellions, Venice decided to build a new town and selected the famous architect Juraj Dalmatinac to be city planner.

The municipal area of the town of **★Pag ㉒** (population 2,500) has been preserved to our day. The first stone was laid for this ambitious architectural project on May 18, 1443. The street plan of Pag is built around a central square where two

Above: Hand-made lace – one of the nicest souvenirs from Pag.

main roads cross, following the examples of antiquity.

On the main square stands the **Parish Church of Sveta Marija**, a Gothic basilica with many Renaissance elements. The relief decorations of the façade are especially worth mentioning; the rosette inspired a specialty of the island, **Pag lace**. The motifs, mostly star shapes and rosettes, are famous all over the world. They compare favorably with Brussels and Venetian *Reticella* lace and are popular souvenirs. The center of manufacturing is at the lace-bobbin school.

By the saltern south of Pag town are the ruins of old *Pagus* (**Starigrad ㉓**), where only the remains of the basilica are to be seen. While in the old days the people of Pag made a living by refining salt, today they make their money in the restuarant business.

Viticulture is highly developed, though, unfortunately, the local quality wine, *Žutica*, is grown only in limited areas. Other specialties are olives, lamb and sheep's cheese. This cheese, called *paški sir*, has a special taste because it is made from the milk of sheep fed on spicy salt herbs.

Great faith is placed in the future of tourism. The eleven-kilometer-long **Paški zaliv ㉔** (Pag Bay) features sand beaches, and there are six hotels on the island. Nudist beaches and a camping site can be found near the fishing village of **Novalja ㉕**.

The once important settlement of *Cissa* – **Časka ㉖** in Croatian – enjoyed its heyday until the end of the 14th century, when marauding soldiers from Zadar destroyed it. Many ruins date back to Roman times. Because the coast sank here, some of the remains are under water. Near the harbor mole is a little beach for swimming.

On the narrow Lun Peninsula, a road runs north to **Lun**. The road comes to and end at the neighboring fishing village of **Tovarnele ㉗**.

CRIKVENICA (051)

Turistička zajednica, Crikvenica, tel. 241249.

Hotel Therapia, tel. 241511, fax. 241612, indoor and outdoor swimming pool, restaurant with vegetarian menu, the best and most traditional place in the area.

Hotel Kaštel, tel. 241044, fax. 241490, nice ambiance, the former Paulaner convent has been converted into a hotel, beach; **Hotel Ad Turres**, tel. 241022, simple hotel, beach, affordable; **Hotel Esplanade**, tel. 241133, fax. 241795, well-kept hotel on the edge of town, affordable, live music in summer; **Hotel Crikvenica**, tel. 241199, fax. 241833, simple, with restaurant; **Hotel Omorika**, tel./fax. 241211, located on a wooded slope, beach, children welcome.

Private rooms available through the tourist office.

CAMPING: **Kačjak**, tel. 242262, fax. 241262, with marina, open May-Aug.

Restaurant Riba, Šetalište Strossmajerevo 4 (pedestrian zone), tel. 241730, fish and grilled food; **Bistro Burin**, Dr. I. Konstrenčiča 10 a, tel. 242490, well-known for fish specialties.

From Crikvenica, the valley of Vinodol has hiking. On the Zagradski vrh and the Viševica in the Dinaric coastal mountain range the trails are marked; great panoramic view.

NOVI VINODOLSKI (051)

Hotel Lišanj, tel. 244002, fax. 244329, private beach, pool, sauna, sports (tennis and basketball courts), restaurant, bar.

TS Zagori, tel. 244122, fax. 244622, wide range of activities offered, this is a very big hotel with over 630 rooms; **TS Povile**, tel. 244135, has private beach and tennis courts.

CAMPING: **Zagori**, tel. 244644, rentals for apartments, tents and cabins, sports facilities, open May 1 to September 30.

PLITVICE LAKES (053)

Tel. 774015, fax. 774013.

Hotel Plitvice, tel. 774333, newly built; **Hotel Jezero**, tel. 751400, fax. 756160, 300 meters above the lakes in a national park, large complex, good furnishings, indoor pool, sauna, terrace, sports facilities and opportunities; **Hotel Bellevue**, tel. 751700, fax. 751965, also above the lakes, restaurants, shop, sports facilities and opportunities.

Lička Kuća, Specialties: lamb on a spit; first-class wine selection.

NATIONAL PARKS: The main street runs directly past both national parks. The signposts are good. It is recommended to head for the north entrance and begin your tour there, taking the trail along the ocean to the south end of the park. On the way back you can board the panorama bus, included in the entrance fee.

RAB ISLAND (051)

FERRIES: Baška (Krk) – Lopar, 1 hour 15 minutes, Jablanac – Mišnjak (Rab) 15 minutes, Rijeka – Rab (Rab) 3 hours 15 minutes. Ferry line **Rapska plovidba**, Stjepana Radića 3, tel. 724122, fax. 724108 (connection to the mainland and to Krk Island). **Harbormaster Rab**, Trg Municipium Arba, tel. 724023.

MARINAS: **ACI Supetarska Draga**, tel. 776268, fax. 776222, 280 berths and 150 dry dock spaces, all important facilities. **ACI Rab**, tel. 724023, fax. 724229, 150 berths, also for 15-meter yachts. Nicely located next to the old town.

RAB TOWN

Donja ulica 2, tel./fax. 724064.

Hotel Padova, tel. 724444, fax. 724418, across from the old part of town, private beach, comfortable rooms; **Hotel Imperial**, tel. 724522, fax. 724126, private beach and nice tavern; **Hotel International**, tel. 724266, fax. 724206, indoor swimming pool, nightclub, restaurant with vegetarian menu.

LOPAR

Hotel San Marino, tel. 775144, a favorite hotel, restaurant, currency exchange, café, sports. Paradise Beach is located directly in front of the hotel.

SUHA PUNTA

Hotel Carolina, tel. 724133, modern hotel, restaurant, salt-water pool with sun terrace, sports, private harbor, gravel-lined inlet for swimming; **Hotel Eva**, tel. 724233, fax. 724345, restaurant, bar, sports, pool in Hotel Carolina can also be used. Gravel-lined inlet for swimming and nudist beach nearby.

PAG ISLAND (053)

Pagus, Pag, tel. 611310, fax. 611101; **Bellevue**, Pag, tel. 891122, fax. 891015; **Biser**, Pag, tel. 611333, fax. 611444.

Smokva, Pag, tel. 611095; **Dubrava**, Pag, tel. 611317.

CAR FERRY: Prizna – Žigljan 15 min, Karlobag – Pag 75 min.

PASSENGER FERRY: Rab – Pag 2 hours.

Vinodol, Velebit, Rab and Pag

ZADAR
AND THE ISLANDS OF
NORTHERN
DALMATIA

NIN / ZADAR
NORTHERN
DALMATIAN ISLANDS
FROM BIOGRAD TO MURTER

Zadar

NIN

The Magistrala continues from Karlo-bag to the southeast and, after 44 kilo-meters, reaches the town of **Starigrad ❶**, which was known as *Argyruntum* in Ro-man days. About four kilometers behind Starigrad is the **Paklenica National Park ❷**. Its two deep gorges, **★Velika Pak-lenica** (with the Manita Peć stalactite cave), and **Mala Paklenica** (behind Seline), are worth a detour. The highest point in the park is the 1,758-meter **Vaganski vhr ❸**, which can be taken in on a good day's climb.

At **Maslenica ❹**, the **Novigradsko Sea** begins to widen. This is a large inland sea connected by a natural channel to the Velebitski *kanal* and thence to the Adri-atic. Even large vessels can navigate this narrow channel to reach the industrial harbor of Novigrad. Previously, one could cross the channel on a 300-meter bridge and continue to Zadar, 19 kilo-meters away. But the original viaduct was destroyed by the Yugoslav army during the recent war (one of the war's cause celèbre), and was finally replaced by a modern road bridge in 1997.

Preceding pages: A folkloric group gathers at the port of Jezera on Murter Island. Left: My pride and joy!

For those interested in history, it is worth making a detour to **Nin ❺** on the way to Zadar. Croatian history was writ-ten here. Today's small town of Nin, at the end of a bay of the same name, incor-porates the ruins of the historic town, which is on an island in the bay and is linked to the mainland by two bridges.

The tribe of the Liburnians built one of their more important settlements here. With its over 100 surviving Liburnian graves, Nin is a major archeological site in Dalmatia. When the Romans ruled here, they did a lot for the town – which they called *Aenona* – by giving it the sta-tus of a municipium. Aenona had a fo-rum, an amphitheater, an aqueduct and town walls. It also had a temple of monu-mental dimensions; the biggest in Dalmatia.

Nin could not cope with the attacks of both the Avars and the Slavs in the 7th century, but its total destruction also meant a new beginning. The Croats built their political, religious and cultural cen-ter here.

Around the year A.D. 800, Franconian missionaries arrived and started to con-vert people to Christianity. Until the 11th century, the Croatian rulers had no per-manent capital, and so they often stayed in Nin and occasionally staged their coro-nations here. After the Venetians con-

quered the town in 1570, the Serenissima, as Venice also known, had its fortifications and part of the town destroyed in order to stop the Turks from using it as a shelter. Though this did happen briefly in the 17th century. In the 18th and 19th centuries, Nin was rebuilt, but it never again achieved its former importance.

Nin's Old Town

In the middle of the old town, which is still partly surrounded by a wall, stands **★Sveti Križ**, the Holy Cross Church, a most significant piece of old Croatian architecture. It dates from the year 800 and has survived without any changes. With a circumference of only 36 paces, it is probably the smallest cathedral in the world – it is called a cathedral because it is assumed that it was the seat of a bishopric. Above the entrance is an inscription

Above: The entrance to Paklenica National Park – a terrific place to investigate the karst on foot or by mountain bike.

identifying Župan Godežav (Prince Godežav) as its founder. This is the oldest known reference to the name of a Croatian prince. For many years, the building was an enigma to scholars. On the one hand, they were struck by the perfection of its proportions; on the other hand, they couldn't find essential architectural elements they thought should be there. The riddle was solved by a painter from Dubrovnik, Mladen Pejakovič. He realized that the dimensions and the elements of the building were set out according to the position of the sun throughout the year; of the winter and summer solstices and the equinoxes. Thus a building was created that served as a clock, a calender and a place of worship.

Not far from the Church of the Holy Cross is the **Parish Church of Sveti Anselmus**. In addition to its few Romanesque and Gothic architectural elements, it is mainly the treasury that is worth visiting here. It houses excellent examples of metalwork in silver and gold, testifying to Nin's blooming culture in the early

Middle Ages. Among them are two reliquaries, works of Carolingian masters from the 8th and 9th centuries, and a ring of Pope Pius II (15th century). Near the road leading to the upper town gate is a **statue of Bishop Grgur Ninski**, the work of the sculptor Ivan Meštrović, who here recreated a smaller copy of the sculpture in Split.

On the road to Zadar, just about one kilometer south of Nin, you will see in **Prahulje** the **Church of Sveti Nikola** from the 11th century. The cupola was replaced later by an octagonal defence tower serving as an observation point against possible Turkish attacks. This area abounds in two- to three-meter-high burial mounds which go back to prehistoric times.

When passing Bokanjac, you might be lucky and see the intermittent lake **Bokanjačko blato**, which in rainy weather can swell to a surface area of up to five square kilometers. Eels reach the sea from here through underground channels.

**ZADAR

Zadar ❻, with its 70,000 inhabitants, is the cultural and economic center of northern Dalmatia. For a while, it was even the capital of the whole of the Dalmatian region. Here the Liburnians, the Illyrian tribe who settled in northern Dalmatia, founded the town of *Jadera*.

Then the Romans arrived, conquered the Liburnians, and introduced a layout of the town which is still apparent today. Within the fortified walls they built a capitol, a forum, a theater and thermal baths, and there was, of course, also sewerage. Under Emperor Trajan, a 35-kilometer-long aqueduct was built reaching up to Lake Vransko, south of Zadar.

During the period of the great migrations, Zadar was the only settlement in the region able to withstand the attacks of the Avars. But the Slavic tribes settled in the fertile hinterland of the town, and it was not long before Zadar became a Croatian-Roman settlement. Officially, it was part of the Byzantine Empire – but only on paper. Beginning in the 11th century, various powers fought over Zadar, among them the Croatian kings and the Venetians.

The "Great Assembly," the forum of the people of Zadar, meanwhile agitated for autonomy. At the beginning of the 13th century, the republic of the Doges demanded that, as "payment" for the use of Venetian ships, the crusaders destroy Zadar (Zadar had been the most bitter adversary of Venice of all the Dalmatian towns). In 1202, Doge Dandolo and an army of French crusaders conquered the town. In 1358, it fell to Hungary.

In 1409, Venice had reason to celebrate. The Hungarian King Zsigmond of Luxemburg sold Zadar and the neighboring coastline to the Doge Republic for 100,000 ducats. *Zara*, as the Venetians called it, became the seat of the *provveditore* (governor) of Dalmatia and Albania. Agriculture developed in the hinterland while crafts flourished in the town. But most of the profit from all this activity went to Venice. Trade was supposed to be exclusively with Venice, and occasional foreign imports attracted a double customs fee. It was forbidden for the inhabitants to keep provisions for more than four days. The Venetians, meanwhile, made Zara into the strongest bastion against the attacks of the Turks in the eastern Adriatic.

The town came under Austrian rule in 1797. Between 1917 and the end of the Second World War, Zadar was Italian. More than 8,000 inhabitants left the town during that time and their place was taken by thousands of Italians. During the Second World War, Zadar was heavily damaged by bombing. It was rebuilt under Tito, and the renovation of most of the historic monuments was completed during this period.

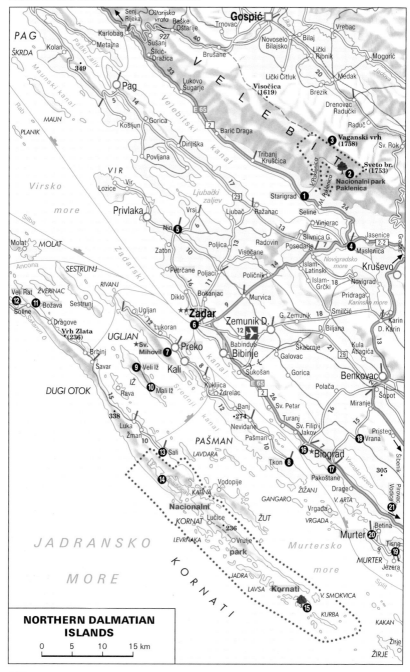

Visiting the Old Town of Zadar

The historic center of Zadar lies on a narrow peninsula. Of the original four town gates, only two have survived: the Sea Gate on the harbor side and the Land Gate to the east, through which you must go in order to access to the rest of the peninsula.

Sightseers generally begin their tour at the ★**Kopnena vrata** ❶ (Land Gate). It was built in 1543 based on plans by the Italian Renaissance master Michele Sanmicheli. Above the main arch, the coat of arms of the town (St. Chrysogonus on horseback) and the Lion of Saint Mark are carved in stone. To the left of the gate is the little harbor of **Foša** ❷; initially, it was part of the moat surrounding the town walls built by the Venetians. The moat was filled in, with the exception of this bit next to the sea.

Behind this little harbor stand the remains of the walls of a former citadel. The area around this destroyed fortress has been transformed into a park.

After passing through the Land Gate, you will find on your right the old **arsenal** of the Venetians. The next right turn leads to **Trg Petra Zoranića** ❸. The square's center is marked by a **Roman column**, used by the Venetians as a pillory. At the eastern end of the square is the medieval tower **Bablja Kula**. This is all that remains of the old town walls. The **five fountains** are also of interest: before the water conduit was built in 1838, they were the main source of water for the inhabitants.

The northeast corner of the square is occupied by **Sveti Šimun** ❹ (St. Simeon's Church). The church was once dedicated to St. Stephen, and was built on the site of a previous building dating from the 5th or 6th century. It has since been rebuilt several times. In 1632, the relics of St. Simeon were reinterred here, the church was rededicated to him, and a new Baroque façade was added.

The late Romanesque ★**sarcophagus of St. Simeon** in front of the choir is a remarkable example of the silversmith's craft. This masterpiece was created between 1377 and 1380 by Francesco da Sesto, a goldsmith from Milan, along with his assistants from Zadar. It was commissioned by Queen Elisabeth, the wife of the Hungarian-Croatian King Louis I from the House of Anjou.

On the sarcophagus, which is 1.92 meters long, 80 centimeters wide and 1.27 meters high, scenes from the life of the saint and other contemporary events can be seen, one of them being, for example, the splendid entry of Louis I into Zadar on the occasion when he returned the relics that had been stolen by the Venetians.

Every year on October 8, the saint's day, the shrine is opened and its interior, filled with valuable votive gifts, is exhibited to the public. Louis I wanted to win over Zadar with this valuable gift because he needed a connecting element beween his southern Italian and his Polish, Croatian and Hungarian possessions. This favorite saint of the town, Simeon, had the task of securing these ties. But it was all to no avail; in his struggle for the Hungarian crown, Louis lost out to his rival Sigismund. Inside St. Simeon's Church, on the north wall, Gothic frescos have survived.

The former **Decumanus** begins near St. Simeon's Church and is still the main east-west axis, though today it is called Kotromanić and Široka ulica (Broad Street). A walk down the Kotromanić to the west leads past the building of the former **town guard**. With its powerful late Renaissance style and its 19th-century clock tower, it cannot be overlooked. It houses the **Etnografski muzej** ❺ (Ethnography Museum), with a collection of traditional costumes, old household objects, instruments and folk art.

★**Narodni trg** ❻ (National Square) lies in front of the old guardhouse. This has been the center of public life in the town

Zadar

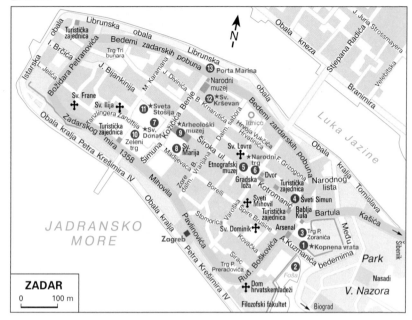

since the Middle Ages. On its northeast side, opposite the town guard, is the **Gradska loža** (loggia), built in the 13th century, rebuilt by Sanmicheli in 1565, and now glassed in. Right next to it is the old **Dvor** (Town Hall), considerably younger than the loggia, given that it was built in 1936. Right behind the Town Hall and easily reached through a gate is the Romanesque **Church of Sveti Lovro** from the 10th or 11th century. This served as a prison in the 18th century.

Following Široka ulica further to the west, one reaches the religious hub of Zadar: two churches and a monastery stand in great proximity to one another. The most prominent sight is the weighty rotunda of the ★**Church of Sveti Donat** ❼, which was started in the 9th century. It overpowers the free space around it, which was once the ancient forum, and is the most representative piece of old Cro-

Right: Classical music has a particular feel to it when played within the hallowed walls of the Church of Sveti Donat in Zadar.

atian architecture. It was commissioned by Bishop Donatus. Some time at the beginning of the 9th century, he headed a delegation of the Dalmatian towns to Byzantium and to Charlemagne's court. The visit to Aachen probably explains the similarity of this church to the court chapel there.

The 27-meter-high building makes a stark, monumental impression from the outside. The interior has a circular, two-storied middle hall with a passage around it, screened off by a row of columns. Three apses in the east served for the liturgy. A second floor accommodated additional believers. Almost all the material used to build the church originates from Roman times. Fragments of mosaics, gravestones and bits of columns are still recognizable. Today, the building is a concert hall.

Opposite the church, you can see the Renaissance façade of the **Church of Sveta Marija** ❽, belonging to the neighboring Benedictine abbey and dating back to the 11th century. It was the sister of the Croatian King Krešimir IV who promoted this project in the royal court. In the 16th century, the church was rebuilt and obtained its present form, looking very much like the cathedral of Šibenik. It was restored after the Second World War and the monastery was partly transformed into a museum of religious art. On the forum, near Sveta Marija, is the ★**Arheološki muzej**  (Archeology Museum). Its most valuable exhibits are the finds from Liburnian settlements and the graves of northern Dalmatia shown on the second floor. Other collections document Roman times and the early Middle Ages.

To the west of the former monastery, on **Zeleni trg** ⑩, or Green Square, is a 15-meter-tall **marble column**, on whose capitol one can recognize a relief of the Lion of St. Mark, slightly damaged by bullets. The column is part of the Roman forum, once 90 meters long and 45 meters wide. A few of its pavement stones have recently been exposed.

Not far away is ★**Sveta Stošija** ⑪ (St. Anastasia's Cathedral), one of the most monumental Romanesque basilicas of the eastern Adriatic. When, in 1202, the town was pillaged by crusaders, the cathedral suffered badly and had to be restored. This work lasted until 1324. The façade was marvelously decorated with three portals, and blind arcades on the upper floor which frame two rosettes. In the tympanum above the central portal is the Virgin Mary on the throne with two saints at her side, St. Zoilus and St. Anastasia. The two sides of the portal are guarded by figures of apostles.

The interior of the church is subdivided by two rows of alternating pilasters and round columns into a central nave and two aisles. In the nave, remnants of a mosaic floor dating from the 10th century can be seen. Artful triforia decorate the high walls of the arcade. The main altar is surrounded by early Gothic columns supporting a canopy. The choir stalls from

Zadar

the 15th century are also impressive. Under the main altar is a three-aisled crypt; the altar in the left aisle holds the shrine of St. Anastasia.

It is best to walk back from here to the site of the forum, and then turn left at the next crossing onto Šimuna Kožičića Benje (the main north-south axis, formerly called Cardo). Soon you will reach ★**Sveti Krševan** ⑫ (Church of St. Chrysogonus, 12th century) on the right. Behind the façade, with its three portals, is a nave and two aisles, divided by ancient columns with Corinthian capitals. The apses show frescos of John the Baptist, St. Chrysogonus, St. Anastasia and Christ dating from the 13th and 14th centuries.

But it is the outsides of the apses that are considered to be the greatest attraction. The structure of the walls, with the blind arcades and the column arcade of the main apse, are strongly reminiscent of examples from Lombardy. There is a little **café** here, from which you can admire at leisure this masterpiece of Dalmatian Romanesque style.

After all these visits to churches, we advise you to take a walk along the quays surrounding the whole of the old town. It is best to return to Šimuna Kožičića Benje and then turn right. Your attention will immediately be caught by the **Porta Marina** ⑬ (Sea Gate), the old entrance into the town from the harbor. The gate was built in 1560, and eleven years later a tablet was mounted in honor of the sailors from Zadar returning from the recent victory of a coalition of Austrian, Venetian and other Christian forces over the Turks in the historically-critical naval battle of Lepanto.

On the other side of the harbor is the new town of Zadar and the yacht marina. Along the quays, the tour and ferry boats to the nearby islands of Ugljan, Pašman, Dugi Otok and the whole of the northern Dalmatian archipelago are moored.

Above: The Roman forum provided building materials for the Church of Sveti Donat. Right: How many have taken a break here over the centuries?

NORTHERN DALMATIAN ISLANDS

For centuries, ruinous timber exploitation was carried out on the many northern Dalmatian islands. As a consequence of the systematic cutting of whole forests for shipbuilding, the earth was exposed to the strong winds, especially in winter. The meadows, meanwhile, offered less and less food for sheep and goats, as they were being spoiled by the salty sea air. The grazing animals pulled out the plants by their roots, thus destroying the remaining vegetation.

Whatever little agricultural activity survived is now confined to terraces and fields protected against wind and weather by stone walls. With the exception of Ugljan, Pašman and Iž, most of the islands here are almost completely karstic. Because of these conditions, the population emigrated to the mainland or went abroad. Today, only a few islands are inhabited, but there are some surprising exceptions, like the island of Iž.

Zadar

Ugljan   Pašman

Until 1887, Ugljan and Pašman formed one continuous island; but then a narrow, four-meter-deep channel was cut to ease the passage of vessels between the mainland and the other islands.

Ugljan is the most densely populated island. Many people from Zadar have holiday homes here. The green and fertile 55-square-kilometer island is a popular weekend destination. A real attraction for visitors is ***Sveti Mihovil** ❼, St. Michael's Fortress, above **Preko**, the largest settlement on Ugljan. You can reach the fortress, which was built by the Venetians in the 13th century, following a path starting at the sand beach of Preko near the *Jaz* restaurant. It takes about an hour to reach the top of the hill, which is at 265 meters. The effort is rewarded by a beautiful view over the Velebit, Pag Island and the Kornats to the southeast. For another plunge into local history, a visit to the Franciscan monastery of Ugljan is highly recommended.

Pašman Island, like Ugljan, is a popular weekend place. It is mainly people from Biograd who come here, because it is closer to them than to Zadar. All settlements on the 60-square-kilometer island are on the coast facing the mainland. In **Tkon** ❽, it is not only the sand and pebble beaches that are worth a visit, but also the **Kuzma i Damjan Monastery** dating from the 12th century.

Pašman also has olive groves in places, and vineyards as well, but its hinterland drops steeply toward the western coast, and has less opulent vegetation to show than Uglan.

*Iž

Between Ugljan and Dugi Otok lies the small island of **Iž**, which is well-protected from storms and surrounded by ten further tiny islands. In prehistoric times the Liburnians settled here, and agriculture has been pursued on the island ever since. Local pottery also has a long tradition. Popular tourist places are the old harbor towns of **Veli Iž** ❾ and **Mali Iž** ❿, while the east coast beckons with several sand beaches.

Dugi Otok

The name **Dugi Otok** means "long island." This one stretches for more than 45 kilometers. It is approximately four kilometers wide and reaches a height of 338 meters. Dugi Otok protects the whole archipelago in front of Zadar and Biograd from the storms of the Adriatic. The northern half of the island is richer in vegetation than the southern; there are vineyards, orchards and extensive pastures full of sheep.

The island used to belong to the rich monasteries of Zadar. It was with the beginning of the Turkish attacks that more and more people settled here. There is no fresh water source on the island, so in summer tankers have to deliver drinking water. Cars are a rarity, and until 1986 there were not even any paved roads. A modest center for tourism is **Božava** ⓫, situated in a partly forested bay with rock, pebble and sand beaches. On the northeast peninsula, one kilometer south of the village of Soline, is **Sakarun**, the most beautiful sandy bay on the island. A footpath leads from this beach to the nearby settlement of **Veli Rat** ⓬. To the northwest of the settlement, in a small forest, is the tallest lighthouse on the Adriatic (41 meters).

The capital of the island is the fishing village of **Sali** ⓭, numbering 900 inhabitants. The name points to the medieval salt-gathering activities of the area. At the southeastern end of the island the well-protected *Telašćica Bay ⓮ forms a big inlet. It counts among the biggest and most beautiful island bays in the Adriatic.

Right: Deep blue waters and stony karstic landscapes – the Kornats.

The salt lake of **Mir** lies at the end of a five-minute walk from the end of the road on the southwestern tip of the island. It is connected to the sea through karstic conduits and this leads to the noticeable phenomenon of its water level changing with the tides, albeit with some delay.

*The Kornats

The **Kornats** ⓯ make up the southeastern conclusion of the northern Dalmatian archipelago. This collection of more than 140 islands is spread over 300 square kilometers and boasts innumerable recondite coves with crystal clear water where swimming is sublime. Most of this island group has been turned into a national park, and there are daily inspections to catch divers and fishermen without permits. There are boat trips into the area from Dugi Otok, Biograd and Zadar, and various tour organizers have the Kornats on their program. A visit to the national park costs about US $6, organized day tours about US $30.

The national park is spread out over at least 109 islands, of which 72 are mere dots less than a hectare in size. Eighty-five percent of the land is barren rock; only five percent is cultivated. These grey-green sand-colored islands rising up from an ink-blue sea have the least vegetation in the whole Adriatic. But it is exactly this barrenness that is responsible for the special charm people find in the Kornats. That the vegetation of the Kornats is largely destroyed is partly due to the folly of earlier shepherds who thought that by clearing their pastures with fire they would achieve better growth of the grass.

The land flora of the archipelago may be poor, but underwater it is rich. In earlier times, the waters of the Kornats were known to be full of fish, and neighboring powers often fought for access. It seems the fishermen of nearby Sali, on Dugi Otok, usually managed to stay ahead of

Zadar

their rivals, and eventually the Venetian authorities gave them monopoly rights to fish these waters. Some fishermen amassed great fortunes during these years. But bit by bit the fishing areas were exhausted, and eventually the shoals disappeared altogether. The fish-processing industry, which was introduced at the beginning of this century in Sali, works today with imported fish. Sponge fishing, once very profitable, had to be given up because the grounds were plundered bare. Corals and underwater plants survived, however, and there are now even some fish again.

The Kornats evolved from the sinking of the coast about one meter every 1,000 years, with the sea flooding the former valleys. Two thousand years ago, the biggest island of the archipelago, Kornat, formed one stretch of land together with Katina and Dugi Otok. Some buildings from those times are today just below the surface of the water. The effects of surf and erosion were to carve 80 meter cliffs out of the partly vertically folded rock

strata. Although sailors find superb areas of sea here, some of the waters can be very dangerous. The island of **Taljurič**, for example, measuring only 70 by 50 meters, is often submerged and therefore easy to overlook.

FROM BIOGRAD TO MURTER

*Biograd ⑯ was the coronation place of the Croatian kings and is therefore one of the most significant towns in Croatian history. The Venetians destroyed it in 1125. By the 17th century, the rebuilt Biograd was serving as a border post. After Pasha Ibrahim leveled it to the ground in 1646, it was rebuilt, but it never achieved its former glory. In the Museum of Local History are archeological exhibits and old Croatian finds, and also a special "Treasures of the Sea" feature.

Today, Biograd's good tourist infrastructure earns it a place as one of the most popular spots along the Adriatic. You can book trips to the Kornats from here.

A short way after Biograd, the Magistrala leads to the holiday resort of **Pakoštane** ⓱. Here, on a beautiful beach, the **Club Med** has settled with its Polynesian-style straw huts.

The **Vransko jezero** lake in the hinterland is only two meters deep, but with its surface area of about 3,000 hectares it is the biggest inland lake in Croatia. Its brackish water is rich in fish. A little road leads from Pakoštane along the lake to **Vrana** ⓲. This small town developed around a Benedictine abbey which later became the property of the Order of St. John of Jerusalem. This same order built the fortress that was reduced to ruins by the Turks in 1538. The **Maškovića han** hostel is worth seeing. It was built in 1644 by Jusuf Maškovič as a caravanserai. It is a rare and valuable example of Ottoman architecture in Croatia.

Back again on the coast, you will pass the harbor and holiday resort of **Pirovac**.

Above: The Club Med in Pakoštane keeps its guests active with all kinds of aquatic sports.

before reaching **Tisno** ⓳ (Croatian for "narrow"). The small old town stretches on both sides of a swing bridge, built in 1832, that leads to the island of Murter.

*Murter is a 19-square-kilometer island belonging to the Šibenik Islands. Its only road leads to the former capital of the island, **Murter**, a picturesque place, though not one offering the usual sights. The center of the new **Murter** ⓴, situated along a broad bay, is a marketplace mainly for souvenirs. The town is also a supply point for campers and yachters. The island has good camping sites and beautiful sand beaches near Murter, Betina and Slanica, for example. All kinds of water sports are on offer. During the summer months, yachts and windsurfers dominate the landscape.

A modern ACY marina and countless restaurants have settled in 15th-century **Vodice** ㉑. The hotels are situated in the countryside. A trip to the fishing village of **Tribunj** (three kilometers to the west; map p. 156) should be combined with a walk up **Sv. Nikola Hill** (lovely views).

STARIGRAD (023)

Hotel Alan, tel. 369236, fax. 369203, on Paklenica Beach, restaurant, shops, sports (four tennis courts), playground; **Hotel Vicko**, tel./fax. 369304, on the Magistrala along the Adriatic, family hotel.
CAMPING: **Paklenica**, tel. 369245, fax. 369255.
Close to Starigrad-Paklenica is the **Paklenica National Park**, with impressive ravines. The Velebit range is well suited for mountain hikes – not for the unexperienced, because the climb is 1,400 meters; good hiking boots are essential. Info: Turistička zajednica Karlobag, tel. 694060.

ZADAR (023)

Turistička zajednica Zadar, tel. 25948, fax. 23841.
Hotel Kolovare, B. Peričiča 14, tel. 433022, fax. 433618, beach, vegetarian food, casino; **Hotelkomplex Borik**, tel. 206 309, 206407, fax. 332065, four km from Zadar, six hotels, beach, pool, marina, sports. **Hotel Punta Skala**, V. Paljetka 2, tel. 22748, fax. 430343; **Hotel Zagreb**, on south shore promenade, Obala P. Krešimira 9, tel. 211973, fax. 430153, typical city hotel; **Hotel Pinija**, Petrčane (twelve km north of Zadar), tel. 364222, fax. 312750, beautifully located in a pine forest, somewhat secluded.
CAMPING: **Borik**, Zadar, tel. 206406, fax. 332065, shady areas, beach, May-Oct; **Zaton**, tel. 264444, fax. 264225, with all camping amenities, resort complex attached.
Sax, Obala P. Krešimira 4 (waterfront promenade), tel. 443035, fish, grilled food; **Riblja konoba**, R. Boškovića 2, tel. 22021, fish, seafood.
Ethnography Museum, tel. 433239 (8 a.m.-2 p.m.); **Archeology Museum**, tel. 23950 (8:30 a.m.-2:30 p.m., Sat. & Sun. 9 a.m.-1 p.m.).
MARINAS: **Borik**, Kneza Demagoja 1, tel./fax. 331018, 200 berths, 100 dry dock spaces, well protected, all facilities; **Marina Zadar**, Ivana Meštrovića 2, tel. 430430, fax. 312500, across from the old town, 300 berths, all facilities.
EXCURSIONS from Zadar to **Kornats** are an impressive experience. Island excursions to **Iž**, with a visit to a pottery workshop.

BIOGRAD (023)

Turistička zajednica Biograd, tel. 383123.
Hotel Adriatic, tel. 383042, fax. 384564, beach, tennis; **Hotel Ilirija**, tel. 383556, fax. 384564, beach, sports area, vegetarian food; **Hotel Crvena Luka**, tel. 381616, fax. 312750, beach, tennis court.

CAMPING: **Crvena Luka**, tel. 383106, fax. 312750, partly shady area, tennis, surfing center, marina.
MARINA: **Biograd Marina Kornati**, tel. 383800, fax. 384500, 600 berths.

PAKOŠTANE

Club Med, tel. 37381000, fax. 37381610, judo, tennis, archery, various water sports, excursions, discotheque and club for kids.

NORTHERN DALMATIAN ISLANDS

IŽ (023)

Hotel Korinjak, Veli Iž, tel. 88324.
MARINA: **Veli Iž**, tel. 884486.

DUGI OTOK (023)

Hotel Božava, Božava, tel. 377619, several categories are combined here, beach, sports area, berths.
Hotel Sali, Sali, tel. 377048, beach.
For diving trips you will need a permit, it is best to go through a diving school.
FERRIES: From Zadar to Sali (1.5 hours) and Brbinj.

MURTER (022)

Colentum, Slanica, tel. 45208, fax. 45237.
CAMPING: **Jažina**, Tisno, tel. 48241, fax. 48920, partly shady place, tennis, marina; **Koširina**, Betina, tel. 45268, fax. 44498; **Plitka Vala**, Betina, tel. 45268, beach, tennis, partly shady; **Slanica**, Murter, tel. 45255, fax. 45237, partly shady place, marina, tennis.
MARINAS: **Murter-Hramina**, tel. 434411, fax. 435242; **Betina Murter**, tel. 434497, fax. 434498

PAŠMAN (023)

CAMPING: **Lučina**, tel. 691173, small, shady place with crane for small boats, May to mid-Sept; **Sovinje**, Tkon, tel. 85838, fax. 85719, tennis, nudism, rental caravans.
FERRIES: Biograd – Tkon.

UGLJAN (023)

Hotel Zelena Punta, Kukljica, tel. 373337, large, simple hotel in pine forest, tennis, mini-golf, surfing; **Hotel Zadranka**, tel. 88004, fax. 312750, reasonably priced, with annexes, beach.
Hotel Stari dvor; simple, spacious rooms, well-run pension with good food.
FERRIES: Zadar – Preko.
Hiking along **St. Michael's Fortress** above the town of Preko.

Zadar

ŠIBENIK AND TROGIR

ŠIBENIK
THE ISLANDS OFF ŠIBENIK
TROGIR
THE ROAD OF CASTLES

**ŠIBENIK

Unlike such towns as Split, Zadar and Trogir, **Šibenik ❶** has no Roman roots; it is a Croatian settlement, and, at the same time, is the oldest Slavic town on the Adriatic. It was first mentioned in 1066 in connection with the sojourn there of a Croatian king. The Venetians called the town Sebenico and granted its inhabitants a great degree of freedom, which they promptly applied to conducting a flourishing trade. The locals managed to strike peaceful deals even with the Turks when Ottoman control spread through the port's hinterland.

Šibenik experienced its best days in the 15th century. In competition with Zadar and Split, the people of Šibenik created some quite imposing buildings. More recently, after Croatia declared its independence from Yugoslavia, Šibenik was the scene of bitter fighting. Many Serbs had settled there in the years after the Second World War.

For those arriving from the north over the Krka Bridge, the town is immediately visible on the far bank of the river. Nes-

Preceding pages: Mass being held in St. Lawrence's Cathedral in Trogir. Left: Italian influences are not only to be seen in Šibenik's Venetian architecture.

tled against a mountain slope, its three fortresses dominate the winding Krka estuary before the river flows into the Adriatic. The main road runs through Šibenik above the old town.

The center of the ***old town**, which has been closed to traffic, is next to the harbor. The harbor promenade, called **Obala palih omladinaca**, with the former Bishop's Palace and the Ducal Palace from the 15th century, is dominated by ***Katedrala Sveti Jakov** (St. James' Cathedral), the most significant piece of Renaissance architecture in Croatia. It was built between 1431 and 1536. The work was supervised until 1447 by Juraj Dalmatinac, who was called in from Venice to take on this task. Initially, it was supposed to be a simple church with one nave, but the town leaders soon expressed a wish for a more representative building. So Dalmatinac changed the plans, adding transepts and apses. Further additions were a sanctuary and an underground baptismal chapel. The exterior apse walls show a frieze of 74 portraits. Each head is a study in character, and Dalmatinac, it is thought, probably used contemporaries for his models. He was certainly mocking some of them.

The cathedral was built entirely of limestone and marble, the latter of which came from the island of Brač. There are

Šibenik and Trogir

FROM SIBENIK TO SPLIT

0   5   10 km

16 Kaštel Štafilić
17 Kaštel Novi
18 Kaštel Stari
19 Kaštel Kambelovac
20 ★Kaštel Gomilica
21 Kaštel Sućurac

clearly two building phases to be discerned: the lower part is still indebted to late Gothic style, while the cupola and the dome are built and decorated in Renaissance style.

Dalmatinac also created the grand ★**baptistery**, which can by reached by way of a staircase to the right of the altar. The ceiling of the baptismal chapel is a single monolith, and its rich decoration is considered to be a sculptural masterpiece, as are the four apses and the baptismal font supported by angels. The stone leaves of the blind capitals at the edge of the apses have an extraordinary feature: if you play them like a xylophone, each of them gives a different tone – the question is for the student of architecture: is it an accident or a work of genius?

Beginning in 1477, three years after the death of Dalmatinac, his pupil Nikola Fiorentinac (Niccolò Fiorentino, also a

Right: St. James' Cathedral in Šibenik is one of the most important Renaissance monuments in Croatia.

former pupil of Donatello) took over the completion of the cathedral. He had proved his knowledge and expertise in Trogir, where he designed the Ursini Chapel of the cathedral.

In Šibenik he wanted to outdo his earlier work. He designed the galleries, the ceiling of the nave and the cupola, all of them done in barrel vaulting, with the vaulting of the apses clad in stone panels. There was hardly any wood used in the cathedral because the fear of fire was so great at the time. The cathedral has no bell tower – its function was taken over by the tower of the former town wall standing nearby.

Also worth seeing is the **Main Portal**, which depicts the Twelve Apostles being sent out into the world and the Last Judgement, as well as the **Lion Portal** on the north side, which depicts the beginnings of mankind (through Adam and Eve) and the origins of the Church (through Peter and Paul).

A **bronze monument** by Ivan Meštrović on the square in front of the ca-

Šibenik and Trogir

thedral recalls the great master builder, Juraj Dalmatinac.

On the north side of the cathedral is Republic Square, with a typical Venetian *loggia, a reminder of the rule of the great Italian city-state. The building was designed by Sanmicheli in 1532-42 and was once the Town Hall.

Any visitor prepared to take a stroll would find the streets of this old town inviting. Ulica Jurija Dalmatinca starts on the northwest side of Republic Square. You will soon reach the **Palazzo Orsini** on the left side of the road, built in 1455. The famous sculptor Giorgio Orsini lived here in the 15th century. The maze of alleyways around the Dalmatinca stretching up to the castle hill is called Bordo di Mare. Here is **Sveti Lovro** (St. Lawrence's Church), a pretty Baroque building from 1697. If you continue to the left behind the church, you will climb the hill and reach the oldest of Šibenik's three fortresses, **Sveta Ana**. If you choose to continue to the southeast from St. Lawrence's Church, you will reach the old

town pedestrian zone, Zagrebačka, which leads directly onto the main square, Poljana maršala Tita, and to the city theater.

**Krka National Park

The **Krka River**, which follows a very irregular channel through jagged karstic terrain, is the principal feature of Šibenik's hinterland. It is interrupted here and there by waterfalls and rapids, and marks the border between northern and central Dalmatia. The whole 75-kilometer zig-zag course of the river has been declared the Krka National Park. Its most interesting section is the *Skradinski buk Waterfall ❷, about twelve kilometers from Šibenik. Over a distance of 400 meters, the river tumbles down 17 cascades, each of them about 100 meters wide. The height difference is about 45 meters. The volume of water rushing down into **Prokljansko jezero ❸** lake is subject to seasonal variation; in winter it is almost 43 cubic meters per

second. The water sometimes floods nearby woodlands, and ridges of white limestone sediment are left behind. This part of the park is generally frequented on weekends by visitors from Šibenik and its surroundings. Near the biggest waterfall is a tourist center with a pleasant terrace.

Drniš and Otavice

The **Dalmatinska Zagora** is a plateau behind Šibenik. The main town is **Drniš** ❹, which is situated at an altitude of 300 meters. The ruins of the **Turski kaštel** (Turkish Castle) offer a marvelous view along the valley of Petrovo Polje, towards the Promina Mountains in the north and to the gorge of Čikole. The Turks occupied this castle for 200 years and used it as a base to threaten Šibenik. Drniš and the castle were finally captured with Venetian help in 1683. Even today, remnants of Ottoman architecture can be seen

Above: Bubbling cascades in the Krka National Park.

in the town. Drniš is known for its excellent ham, and is a good starting point if you want to visit the Krka waterfalls.

Nine kilometers east of Drniš is the village of **Otavice** ❺. In 1883, the famous Croatian sculptor Ivan Meštrović was born here. He was influenced by Michelangelo and Rodin, among others. He emigrated to the U.S. in 1942. There is a Meštrović mausoleum in the village, but his most significant sculptures are exhibited elsewhere – in various coastal towns of Croatia, in Zagreb and in South Bend, Indiana.

*Primošten

About 30 kilometers southeast of Šibenik is a picturesque coastal settlement which looks surprisingly similar to the town of Rovinj in Istria. **Primošten** ❻ is the biggest tourist center on the Magistrala before you reach Trogir and Split. It was an island until the narrow passage separating it from the mainland was filled in. The name still reminds one of those earlier times, *Primošten* meaning "over the bridge."

The strong fortifications of the settlement, built on the town that rises up in the shape of a cone, go back to the time of the Turkish wars. The majority of the population in those days were poor refugees and Uskoks. They built modest houses for themselves, and their church – which dominates the view from all around – was very humbly executed, too. It is thanks to tourism that this little town is blooming now; rock and pebble beaches beckon, there are various water sports facilities, and the bay of **Marina Lučica** is very popular among nudists.

THE ISLANDS OFF ŠIBENIK

Off the coast, directly before Šibenik, are many small islands, of which Žirje, Kaprije, Prvić and Zlarin are the biggest. There are regular ferry connections to the islands from Šibenik and from Vodice, further along the coast.

Prvić Island

The island of **Prvić ❼** is closest to the mainland and has a surface area of a mere 2.3 square kilometers. No wonder that cars never became popular here, nor indeed on any of the other islands described below. The two main villages, Šepurine and Prvić Luka, are connected by a kilometer-long path. Walking and swimming are the most popular pursuits on this island.

Prvić is fertile: grapes are grown here and the slopes are covered in olive trees. In the past, the island belonged to rich patrician families from Šibenik. The tenants lived from fishing and from raising animals; they would simply take their sheep and goats onto neighboring islands leaving them to roam around freely. Today, the main source of income is tourism. There aren't many fish in the sea here, at least not close to the coast.

The biggest village on Prvić is **Šepurine**. Its natural stone houses are lined up in a picturesque row along the harbor. If it weren't for the ugly modern post office and the supermarket, you might think time had stopped here. This impression is even stronger late in the season, when mainly locals are to be seen in the streets.

Prvić Luka is the second most important village, stretching along Luka Bay. The village itself makes a very friendly impression because the facades of the houses are decorated with colorful shutters contrasting pleasantly with the strict gray of the stone walls. In the 15th century, Franciscan monks settled here, but, unfortunately, their monastery was destroyed by fire; it was rebuilt in 1884, in order to give a new home in the Šibenik area to the Glagolithic movement.

Krapanj Island

Krapanj ❽ is the smallest and at the same time the most densely populated island of the group off Šibenik. More than 1,500 people live on an area of just over two-fifths of a square kilometer. In earlier times, they earned their living diving for coral and sponge. In the house of diver Jerko Tanfara you will be introduced to the tradition of sponge diving. This trade was taught to the locals by the Franciscan monks who settled here in the 16th century.

*Zlarin Island

Zlarin Island ❾ (population 400) lies directly at the mouth of the Krka estuary. It has been praised for the beauty of its terrain, and in earlier times was also called the "Golden Island" (*zlato* means "gold"). Compared with the other islands of the archipelago, Zlarin has the largest variety of tourist facilities.

The town of **Zlarin** developed beside a deep bay; along the quay runs a pretty

Šibenik and Trogir

promenade adorned by palm trees and houses in late Gothic style. The only hotel, near the harbor basin, is called Hotel Koralj. Its name points to the special characteristic of the island: Zlarin was the only island in this region which was surroanded by waters rich in coral. Unfortunately, not much is left of this splendor. Only the **Koraljski muzej** (Coral Museum) shows the magnificence of what once was, although it looks more like a souvenir shop. Zlarin is the destination of many excursion boats.

Kaprije Island

Kaprije ❿, with its ten square kilometers, counts as one of the bigger islands off the Šibenik coast. Its name comes from the caper bush; caper buds preserved in vinegar are used in the local cuisine. Near the biggest bay on the south

Above: Trogir. Right: Detail of the Romanesque portal of St. Lawrence's Cathedral in Trogir, a masterpiece by Radovan (1240).

of the island is the village of Kaprije, the only settlement on the island. From the two hillocks near the village (132 and 122 meters), you can enjoy a lovely view of the neighboring islands. At the same time, you can choose from here your own personal bay in which to go for a swim.

Žirje Island

The biggest island of the archipelago, Žirje, is also the farthest away from the mainland. Its 15 square kilometers offer ample opportunities for long walks, and its coast has lots of beautiful coves where swimming and sunbathing are especially delightful. Two parallel rows of hills run along Žirje Island with a fertile valley stretched between them. Grapevines, olives and fruit grow in abandance. The name of the island originates from *žir* (acorn), indicating that the island probably used to be covered in oak forests.

The ferry docks in **Murna**, on the north side of the island. A footpath leads from there up to the higher-lying village of

Žirje ⓫, which was probably inhabited as early as prehistoric times. Near **Velika Stupica**, in the east of the island, the remains of a fortress from late antiquity were found. A road running along the valley connects Žirje and Velika Stupica. By foot, this takes 45 minutes. Near Velika Stupica, pretty rock and pebble beaches and untouched bays beckon, with only the occasional boat to distract you.

**TROGIR

After traveling 61 kilometers down the road from Šibenik to Split, you will reach **Trogir** ⓬. This is one of the most typical small Mediterranean towns on the Adriatic, in addition to being one of the most rewarding destinations for visitors – Trogir has rightly been declared a UNESCO World Cultural Heritage site.

At the end of the 3rd century B.C., Greeks from Issa (Vis Island) founded a settlement here and called it *Tragurion* (Goat Island). After Roman and Byzantine interludes, the Middle Ages brought eventful times to Trogir. Conflicts broke out constantly between the locals and the feudal lords from the mainland, whether Croatian, Venetian or Ottoman. But feuding among the town's patricians themselves was also permanently on the agenda. Still, the centuries before 1420, when Venice annexed the town, count as its best years.

You can see this even today, given that Trogir has kept its medieval appearance. The winding alleys, often roofed over, with their Gothic houses and Renaissance palaces, form an ensemble of special architectural value. The old town, on a small island, is connected to the mainland by a bridge and is constituted of two parts. The eastern part is the actual old town, while the western part, called Pasike, formed the town outskirts where land laborers lived. Both these areas, however, were protected by the former town walls.

The **Kopnena vrata** (Land Gate) ❶ was built in Renaissance style and is decorated by a statue of St. Lawrence. After walking through it, turn left, take the second right, and you will be on Torgir's main square, **Trg Ivana Pavla II** ❷. The northern side of the square is taken up by ****Sveti Lovro Cathedral** ❸ (St. Lawrence's), a highlight of Dalmatian art history. The entrance under the spacious vestibule, with its ribbed cross vaulting, is decorated by a Romanesque ***portal** built in 1240 by local master Radovan.

The stonemasonry of the portal shows mainly biblical scenes, but there are also some aspects of everyday life in the Middle Ages depicted. Adam and Eve riding on lions flank the entrance; the arches are decorated by episodes from the life of Christ, with the Crucifixion in the center. The half-columns are decorated by scenes symbolizing the months of the year, showing the typical work of farmers, for example, grape harvesting in September. To the left of the vestibule is the **baptismal chapel**, its interior decorated

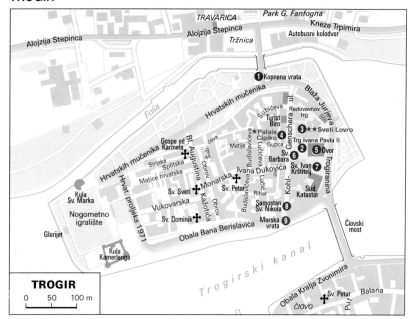

TROGIR

0   50   100 m

fully in Renaissance style, with a paneled ceiling, cherubs and garlands. It is the work of the Albanian master, Andrija Aleši, who was a pupil of Juraj Dalmatinac.

The interior of the church is partitioned by two rows of four heavy columns into a three-naved basilica. In the center of the left aisle is the ★★**Orsini Chapel**, a highlight of Dalmatian Renaissance work, built between 1468 and 1497 by Nikola Fiorentinac. The chapel is dedicated to the bishop of Trogir, John Orsinus, who in the 11th century was elevated to the position of the town's second patron. The chapel's ceiling is Fiorentinac's masterpiece, given that it was the first time since antiquity that a vault was put together without supports or horizontal beams, but only out of stones cut in the shape of wedges along their edges. The panels are decorated with angels' heads; in the middle you can see God the Father, with an orb in his hand representing the world. The niches show the figures of the Twelve Apostles and John the Baptist,

and are the work of local artists. The main altar in the chancel apse is also of some significance: the high canopy, the monumental pulpit and the Gothic stalls count among the best Romanesque-Gothic ecclesiastic interior architecture in Dalmatia.

Opposite the western façade of the cathedral stands **Čipiko Palace ❹**, built for a rich merchant family in Venetian Gothic style with Renaissance elements. It represents an extraordinary example of Dalmatian civic architecture. The southern side of the square is taken up by the airy **loggia**, a building with many functions which used to serve mainly as a courtroom. The reliefs on the stone table in the middle of the main room were carved by Fiorentinac. On the clock tower next to it you can still see the chains to which people who had been sentenced were fastened and exposed to the scorn of their fellow citizens.

The **Dvor ❺** (Town Hall), which was built during the 14th and 15th centuries, concludes the attractions on the square.

The edifice was most probably designed by Venetian architects and is not dissimilar to the northern Italian fortress-style public building, complete with an atmospheric interior courtyard.

Close to the main square are several churches. Right behind the loggia, for instance, is **Sveta Barbara** ⑥, the oldest church in Trogir, and **Sveta Marija**. To the south of the Town Hall is **Sveti Ivan Krštitelj** ⑦ (Church of St. John the Baptist). It dates back to the 13th century and used to belong to the Benedictines, the predominant order in Trogir.

The road continues south to another Benedictine establishment, **Samostan Sveti Nikola** ⑧ (St. Nicholas' Monastery). A testament to the times of antiquity is kept behind the walls of the old monastery: a Hellenic relief showing the god Kairo. The Greeks worshipped him as the god of the right moment or of the right opportunity – something which had to be taken advantage of when it occurred. Near the monastery, the road makes a turn and leads past St. Nicholas' Church to the **Morska vrata** (Sea Gate) ⑨ and the fish hall next to it. In this part of the town big sections of the **city wall** have survived.

From the coastal promenade you can see across to **Čiovo Island** ⑬, which today is a kind of suburb linked to Trogir by a bridge. In the Middle Ages, however, this was the place to which people suffering from leprosy were banished, and where they were looked after by monks. Today, holiday-makers arrive here in search of a less harrowing time. In the north, more and more summer houses are being built, but the south has so far managed to keep its original features.

The island has been inhabited since prehistoric times. The Romans used to exile heretics and political offenders here. Then, beginning in the 5th century, monks started arriving and soon built a monastery. Čiovo began its career as a safe haven for sick people and for refugees fleeing the Turks. Since the 15-kilometer-long island almost reaches to the cape of Split, it forms something resembling a natural harbor for the so-called "Bay of Castles."

The Franciscan monastery **Sveti Ante**, on Mount Drid on the east side of Čiovo, is the oldest on the island and was built above a former hermit's cave. Worth seeing here is a painting by Palma the Younger depicting the two "desert saints," Anthony and Paul. The nearby **Bay of Saldun** has been covered by newly-built holiday houses, so that today the old fishing village of Gornji Okrug seems to be more of a scattered settlement. On the eastern side of the island, in the direction of Slatine, is Arbanija, with the pretty Dominican monastery of **Sveti Križ**, dating from the 15th century. The chapel houses a miraculous crucifix. In Slatine, the last settlement on the eastern shore, there are rows and rows of modern houses on the slopes leading to the sea. Lying off the headland southwest of Trogir are the islands of **Mali Drvenik** ⑭ and **Veli Drvenik** ⑮, known in antiquity as the double island of Tarion. The islands were probably covered originally in forests, because their name comes from the Croatian word *drvo* (wood). After the forests were cut down for houses and shipbuilding, olives, figs and grapevines were planted. Both islands are quite untouched by tourism; only yachts anchor occasionally in the bays, some of which have beautiful sand beaches.

THE ROAD OF CASTLES

The "Road of Castles" runs parallel to the Magistrala on the coastal side and connects Trogir with Split. When, in the 16th century, the Ottoman Empire managed to expand up to the fringes of Split and the Kozjak Mountains, the nobility and the Church realized that their possessions were in danger. Patricians and bishops of the Split area had countless castles

Šibenik and Trogir

tifications occupy the northern part. Around the castle a village came into being. It was the setting for the Dalmatian version of Romeo and Juliet, called *Mijenko and Dobrila*. The grave of the two lovers is in the Church of St. John the Baptist. The story of the star-crossed lovers was first written down and published in 1833 by an author from Trogir.

If you drive about two kilometers, you will reach **Kaštel Novi ⑰** (New Castle), built in 1515 by Pavao Čipiko, also from Trogir. **Kaštel Stari ⑱** (Old Castle) is the oldest piece of architecture on the bay. It goes back to an earlier relative of Čipiko, the humanist Koriolan Čipiko. In 1476, he had a castle built, the southern side of which looks like a summer palace. Over time, a village developed in front of the castle. Two kilometers further is **Kaštel Kambelovac ⑲**, a cylindrical defense tower from 1566.

*Kaštel Gomilica ⑳ on Gomile Island, which once housed a Benedictine nunnery, fires the imagination – one can well imagine how the settlement would have looked in earlier times. Within the castle walls the local people built 30 houses. On the other side of the bridge linking the castle to the mainland another village sprang up, which was also surrounded by defensive walls against potential attacking enemies. Three kilometers further is **Kaštel Sućurac ㉑**, built by the bishops of Split in 1483. Further inland rises the **Kozjak**, which stretches for more than ten kilometers from east to west. Its highest peak towers at 780 meters; its southern wall is really rocky with slopes descending practically vertically. About ten kilometers above Kaštel Stari on the road inland to Drniš is the mountain hut **Malačka ㉒**, at a height of 552 meters. You can walk from there (90 minutes) to the peak of the Biranj (661 meters), to the **Church of Sveti Ivan Krštitelj** (St. John the Baptist). There is a marked trail. Every year, on July 26, there is a pilgrimage to the church.

built along the coast which were meant not only to defend the crops but also served as dwellings. In times of danger, help could also be expected from the sea. The serfs and tenants soon started building their own houses in the immediate vicinity of the castles. In time, whole villages came into being, with a fortress or a fortified tower in their middle. Industrialization of the coast between Trogir and Split unfortunately caused severe damage to the environment in this area. The Bay of Kaštela is one of the great ecological problem zones of the Adriatic coast.

Near the seaside resort of **Resnik** stands a small Venetian fortress from the 16th century, which is unfortunately far less often visited than the local beach. Nearby is Split airport. Stjepan Štafileo, from Trogir, had a fortified palace, **Kaštel Štafilić ⑯**, built here around the year 1500. The dwellings are situated in the southern wing of the complex, the for-

Above: Kaštel Gomilica, on the "Road of Castles," still has its moat.

ŠIBENIK (022)

Hotelkomplex Solaris, tel. 363999, fax. 361801 (for the entire complex), located to the southwest of Šibenik, is made up of four hotels: **Hotel Andreja**, **Hotel Ivan**, **Hotel Jure** and **Hotel Niko**, private beach, pools, extensive sports activities, restaurants, bars, shops.

CAMPING: **Solaris**, tel. 363999, fax. 361801, partly shady area, private marina and separate nudist area, open from May through September, tennis, rental cars, bungalows; **Zablaòe**, tel. 363999, fax. 361801, tennis, rental cars, bungalows; **Martinska**, tel. 28460, fax. 29160, tennis, bungalows and car rentals.

ZLARIN ISLAND: **Hotel Koralj**, tel. 53621, this small hotel is the only one on the island, no private beach.

Restaurant Zlatna Ribica, K. Spuzava 46, Brodarica, tel. 50300, very good fish restaurant, grilled specialties, wine cellar; **Restaurant Vila Velebita**, Srednja Magistrala 1, tel. 24410; **Restaurant Konoba Stari Dvori**, V. Nazor, Betina, a favorite spot with locals, fish dishes; **Steakhouse Barum**, Podsloarsko 66, tel. 50666, steaks, fish; **Uzorita**, B. Jelačiča 58, tel. 23660, seafood, meat dishes, wine.

Diving Center Jastog, Obala, Osloboenja 4, Šibenik, tel./fax. 29096.

MARINA: **ACI Marina Skradin**, tel. 71165, fax. 71163, located at the end of the Krka Falls, 210 places, open year-round.

EXCURSIONS: A visit to the **Krka Falls** should not be missed if you are in the area. The national park (142 sq km) is suitable for long walks. The karst river Krka runs through a ravine for several kilometers.There are some beautiful places for swimming.

The biggest waterfall in the national park is the **Skradinski buk**, about 15 kilometers away from Šibenik. Ferries to the coastal islands leave from the harbor in Šibenik. Hiking there is especially good because there are no cars.

There is a nice trail on **Prvić Island**, connecting two traditional picturesque villages and taking you through wonderful cultural landscapes, going from Šepurine to Prvić Luka.

Hiking on the island of **Žirje** is also recommended. In the meantime, mountain bikers have also discovered beautiful parts of the island to practice their sport in.

PRIMOŠTEN (022)

Hotel Zora / Slava, tel. 570066, private beach, very touristy, sports facilities.

Hotel Raduća, tel. 70399, private beach and sports area.

CAMPING: **Adriatic**, tel. 70022, fax. 70317, smaller campground, open from May through October, tennis.

Taverna Dalmacija, tel. 70009, serving excellent seafood.

TROGIR (021)

Hotel Concordia, Obala bana Berislavića 22, tel. 885400, fax. 885401, small, comfortable hotel on palm-lined promenade.

Hotel Medena, tel. 880588, fax. 880019, large modern apartment complex with its own private marina, beach, sports, two kilometers from the city; **Hotel Jadran**, tel. 880401, two kilometers from the city in a pine forest, this is a nice no-frills place with a private beach.

CAMPING: **Rožac**, tel. 881105, the campground is beautifully located on a peninsula in the shade of a small forest; **Vranjica-Belvedere**, Trogir-Seget Vranjica, tel. 894141, fax. 894142, tennis courts and water sports facilities.

Cafe Restaurant Radovan, located right on the city square; **Restaurant Marijana**, old town, featuring fish and seafood dishes; **Restaurant Monika**, in the old town, nice courtyard.

In July and August in Trogir a **Summer Festival** is held, featuring, among other things, a lot of folklore and traditional music.

MARINAS: **ACY Trogir**, tel. 881226, fax. 881258, 200 berths, great location just across from the town square of Trogir, open year-round;

Agana Marina, ten kilometers from Trogir, tel. 889321, fax. 889010, 140 berths for yachts, 100 dry berths, 100 parking spaces, open year-round, all necessary facilities.

KAŠTEL STARI (021)

Hotel Palace, Obala Kralja Tomislava 82, tel. 230666, fax. 230852, big hotel with restaurants, conference room, dancing in the evening, lovely location on the sea.

CAMPING: **Bilus Marica**, tel. 230543, rental cars, bungalows, shady areas, open from June through October; **Bilus Josip**, tel. 230543, rental cars, bungalows; **Mini Camp**, tel. 231390, rental cars, bungalows.

On the "Road of Castles" there are numerous pizzerias and pleasantly-situated and cozy inns.

EXCURSIONS: All the other castles and towns on the "Road of Castles" are easily accessible from Kaštel Stari. You are really diving into the Middle Ages here, especially in **Kaštel Gomilica**, a Benedictine Monastery on a sea cliff.

SPLIT AND THE MAKARSKA RIVIERA

SPLIT

KLIS

SINJ

OMIŠ

THE MAKARSKA RIVIERA

Split and the Makarska Riviera

****SPLIT**

With a population of more than 200,000, **Split ❶** is the most prominent Dalmatian city. The most important harbor on the Dalmatian coast is here, as is extensive industry (shipyards, cement, chemical products). Split is also considered to be a stronghold for sports: the *Hajduk Split* soccer team is internationally known, and Split's basketball team plays at top European level. Many players from here are on teams in foreign countries; some, indeed, in the American National Basketball League.

The mountainous hinterland, combined with its location on the sea, gives Split a special character, with the old town having a special power of attraction: it stands with its narrow lanes on historic ground, squeezed into walls built by the Romans. Between the 4th and 3rd centuries B.C., Greeks from Issa founded a settlement they called *Aspalathos* on a bay south of the present day city. During the Roman epoch, nearby *Salona*, birthplace of the emperor Diocletian, was the capital of Dalmatia. When Diocletian ordered a palace to be built near his home

Preceding pages: The shore promenade of Split is inviting for an after-dinner stroll. Left: A good place to meet – Diocletian's Palace.

town in 295 B.C., he laid the cornerstone for the city of Split. After his death, this palace was never again used by an emperor. The city of Salona was destroyed by the Avars in the 7th century, and the populace fled to Diocletian's old palace, where the strong walls offered protection. It was more than a little ironic that the population by this time was made up mainly of Christians, whom the emperor had wanted to annihilate, and that these very Christians converted his mausoleum into a church (later the cathedral) and his main temple into a baptistery.

Split did not play a significant role in later history until Zadar, formerly the principal coastal city, was taken over by Italy in 1920. During the short-lived Kingdom of Serbia, Croatia and Slovenia (the so-called SHS State founded in 1918) and afterwards, under Tito, Split was developed into the second-largest harbor in the former Yugoslavia. Its immense importance in Dalmatia has been retained to this day.

On the Trail of Emperor Diocletian

The Roman emperor had a palace, ****Dioklecijanova palača ❶**, built directly on the sea to be used as his retirement home. Construction work lasted from 295 to 305 B.C. He laid the ground

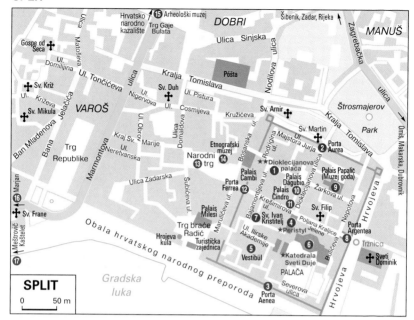

plan for a *castrum* with a north-south length of 215 meters and an east-west length of 180 meters. This massive bit of masonry was two meters thick and boasted no fewer than 16 towers. Building materials were shipped in from the island of Brač; some were even obtained from Egypt. The city gates each mark out the end points of the two main axes: Decumanus (east-west) and Cardo (north-south).

Even if the **Porta Aurea ②** (*Zlatna vrata*; Golden Gate) on the north side of the city, which opens toward Salona, is regarded as the main entrance to Diocletian's palace – note here the modern ★**monumental sculpture** of *Bishop Gregor of Nin* by Ivan Meštrović – a sightseeing tour of the **old town** is nevertheless best begun on the seaward side.

The dimensions of the palace can best be viewed from the palm-lined **shore**

Right: The peristyle of Diocletian's Palace in Split – a good spot for taking in the historic city, especially in the evening.

promenade: from here the gallery, which in antiquity gave this side of the palace its unmistakable façade, can be seen. The openings of the gallery were, however, walled up in the 18th century when residential housing was built here.

At the time of the palace's construction the sea came right up to the south wall, so that the southern gate, the **Porta Aenea ③** (*Mjedena vrata*; Bronze Gate), could only be used by supply ships. This gate led directly to the **cellar rooms**, which were used as storehouses, and above whose vaults the emperor's private quarters were situated. The upper floors were destroyed in World War Two air raids, but because of the arrangement of the cellar vaults it is possible to see where the emperor's rooms were actually located. Along the length of the cellar runs a wide corridor opening on to numerous rooms, as well as a large three-naved hall with an apse: it was right above here that the splendid hall for public ceremonies must have been located. These days, exhibitions are on display in the cellar vaults.

From the Porta Aenea, a passageway leads through the cellar to the *peristyle ④, a large courtyard surrounded by columns. This is the central point of the entire grounds, similar to a Roman forum, where the Cardo and Decumanus meet. To the side of the imperial suites, i.e., the south side, Diocletian had a monumental domed hall built, complete with a **vestibule ⑤**, which formed the main entrance and in which he sometimes appeared before his dignitaries. Four granite columns support the gable of the outer hall, in the middle of which there is an arched vault. The hall was formerly decorated with mosaics and dressed in marble.

Between the one-time arcades, which continue the architecture of the outer hall on either side, one can today settle down to a cup of coffee. In summer, the peristyle forms a stylish backdrop to theatrical productions.

To the east of the peristyle, Diocletian had his **mausoleum** erected. After limited reconstruction in the 7th century, the building was consecrated as *Katedrala

Sveti Duje ⑥. Going through the splendid tower, built from the 13th to the 17 century, a staircase leads to an octagonal room. Two **sphinxes** once flanked this entrance, one of which can today be seen in the outer hall of the emperor's rooms, the other of which is on display at the Temple of Jupiter. The cathedral's interior is in the form of a cross and is divided by a row of columns. On the friezes on these columns the motif *Eros on the Hunt*, can be seen, along with portraits of Diocletian and his consort Prisca. A brick cupola in the ceiling arches over the room.

The main altar is consecrated to St. Anastasius, a martyr from the era of Christian persecution. It has been adorned with an outstanding representation of the Scourging of Christ.

Across from the entrance to the mausoleum, a small lane leads to the one-time **Temple of Jupiter**. The temple, built upon a raised foundation, is entered through a richly-decorated portal. In the 7th century it was converted into the

Sveti Ivan Baptismal Chapel 7. A special characteristic of this uniquely well-preserved building is its wonderful compartmented clay vault. In the middle of the room stands the cross-shaped baptismal font. One of the slabs of stone forming the basin is decorated with a representation of Christ. In addition to the two prominent sarcophagi, which serve as the final resting place of famous bishops, it is the bronze figure of *John the Baptist* by Ivan Meštrović that really stand outs.

The eastern palace gate, the **Porta Argentea 8** (*Srebrna vrata*; Silver Gate), was once topped by two heavy octagonal towers. In the lanes before the gate and at the foot of St. Dominic's Church, a picturesque and colorful *mar-ket takes place daily.

In the course of time, as more and more people moved in, the palace developed into a lively city. Ancient buildings were

Above: The sphinx guarding the entrance has ancient rights.

reconstructed or else torn down to make room for modern houses. In this way, several valuable palaces came into being: the most attractive Gothic one is no doubt **Papalič Palace 9** in Papaličeva. The Municipal Museum, **Muzej grada Splita**, which is housed here, documents Split's history with documents, books and various historical artifacts.

Dágubio Palace 10 on the Cardo (today's Dioklecijanova ulica) is a building with characteristics of both Gothic and Renaissance styles, designed by Andrija Aleši. Even Baroque managed to make its way into Diocletian's Palace; going west towards the Porta Ferrea you will come across **Čindro Palace 11**, with its monumental decorated façade (corner of Dioklecijanova ulica and Krešimirova ulica).

Behind the double gate of the **Porta Ferrea 12** (*Željezna vrata*; Iron Gate) is **Narodni trg 13** (National Square), which from the 15th century on developed into the city's central square, whereby the Roman peristyle remained the church square. Of the row of public buildings along the north side of Narodni trg, only the 15th-century **Town Hall** has survived. Today the **Etnografski muzej** ⑭ (Ethnography Museum) is housed here, with its rich collection of folk costumes, textiles, household objects and jewelry from all over Dalmatia.

To the northwest of the old town, on Frankopanska ulica, is the **Arheološki muzej** ⑮ – the oldest archeology museum in Croatia – containing exceptional collections from prehistory, antiquity (especially from Salona) and the Middle Ages. Prominent among the items on exhibit here are magnificent works of glass and late-Roman sarcophagi, such as the Phaedra Hippolytos sarcophagus (the museum is expected to remain closed until early 1999).

Mount Marjan

Before the Romans built Diocletian's palace they had already built a temple to Diana atop 178-meter **Mount Marjan** ⑯. Today, Mount Marjan is the favorite outing destination of Split's residents. This mountain was of little interest before the 19th century, when 168 hectares of its cold, rocky slopes were successfully forested. By driving west along the harbor from the old town, you come to the **Muzej hrvatskih arheoloških spomenika** (Museum of Croatian Archeological Monuments). Here important pre-Roman and Roman sculptures are kept. There is an especially elaborate baptismal font by Višeslav of Nin from the early 9th century on display.

Just before the yacht harbor, a road to the right leads up Mount Marjan. Only a few hundred meters along the road, situated in a park, is ***Galerija Meštrović** ⑰: the summer residence of Croatia's famous modern sculptor. After being donated for public use, the villa was converted into a gallery in 1952, and now features a permanent exhibition of the

artist's work, with examples from every period of his creative life.

Not far away is **Meštrović Kaštelet**, a 17th-century villa complete with chapel, built by a rich family from Split and reconstructed by Meštrović in 1932. He also added a church and an atrium to the complex, which today is a museum.

Ivan Meštrović was born in Octivace, southeast of Šibenik, in 1883. After apprenticing with a stonecutter in Split, he moved to Vienna in 1900, where he was taken in by the painter Otto König. He studied at the Academy of Fine Arts, moving on to Paris in 1908, where he fell under the influence of Rodin, whom he had met in Vienna in 1902. The young artist was awarded many commissions early on, and later received commissions from the Yugoslav State: which is why many of his works of art can be seen in the larger cities of the successor states to the former Yugoslavia. From 1947 on, Meštrović lived in the United States, where he died in 1962.

Salona

The ancient archeological site of **Salona** ❷ lies somewhat outside Split in Solin, in the direction of Trogir. Thanks to its position on a river in a protected bay and with fertile land nearby, this was the most important Roman settlement in the area, until an Avar invasion in the 7th century left it in ruins.

The former importance of Salona can be easily judged from its ruins. The city contained, in addition to its many temples and seven Roman baths, an amphitheater with room for 20,000 spectators, in which even *naumachias* – simulated naval battles – could be staged. When Diocletian divided the administrative regions into eastern and western halves, Salona came to be located precisely in the middle, thereby becoming one of the most important cities in the Eastern Roman Empire. All the trade routes between the Orient

Split and the Makarska Riviera

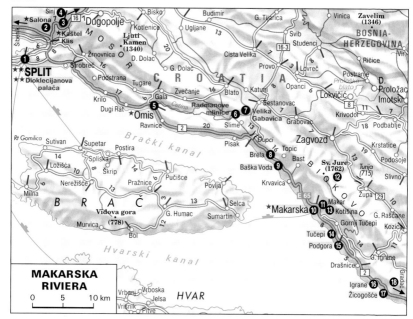

and Italy crossed through Salona. It is no wonder, then, that Diocletian had his retirement home built nearby: from here he could still keep an eye on things even after relinquishing his position and status. From the 4th century on, lively commerce from the western Orient took place here. Merchants brought not only wares with them but religion as well, and Salona soon developed into a center of Christianity; hence the numerous basilicas and the early Christian necropolis.

KLIS

Some nine kilometers outside of Split to the northeast, situated at a height of 340 meters, lies the original preserved fortress of ★Kaštel Klis ❸. An important pass road ran through here from the fertile plains around Split to the mountainous hinterland. When the Turks conquered Bosnia and Herzegovina, the way

Right: Donkeys are still a preferred means of transporting burdens out in the country.

to the Dalmatian coast was opened to them. Despite bold resistance, strategically-important Klis could not be held: in 1537, the fortress fell into Ottoman hands, and a period of continuous plundering took place. Fortified castles were erected at many settlements to protect the populace and the harvests. These fortifications can be seen today on the so-called "Road of Castles" (see previous chapter). Despite enormous effort, Venice could not recapture the fortress of Klis. It was only when the Turks withdrew from the Balkans entirely that Klis once again returned to Christian hands. Because the Venetians did not consider their position to be secure, they had the fortress further fortified. There is a magnificent view from the uppermost level.

The **Mosor**, a 25-kilometer-long mountain range, stretches from Klis to Cetina. Its peaks reach heights of up to 1,340 meters and offer clear views of the distance. The trails are clearly marked, and mountain huts are available to hikers in season.

SINJ

Sinj ❹ is situated in the Cetina Valley at the foot of the Dinaric Alps. Caves and the ruins of old fortified shelters are to be found in the surrounding area: evidence of early settlement. In the Middle Ages, Sinj was the capital of the administrative district of Cetina and recognized the sovereignty of the Croatian princes. When the Ottoman Empire expanded into the Balkans, Sinj, too, fell into Turkish hands. It was liberated again in 1699.

Of interest in the town is the **Franjevačka crkva** (Franciscan church), including its monastery. After the Franciscan monks of Rama fled to Herzegovina, they found refuge here and built a monastery. It is true that the monastery was destroyed in an invasion, and that it was damaged in an earthquake, but it was always rebuilt; for inside the monastery the marvelous picture of the Mother of God of Sinj, which was brought here by monks in the 17th century, is kept.

Above the town and the valley stands **Kamičac Fortress** which, in the 18th century, the Venetians laid out on a star-shaped ground plan. Every year since 1715, on the first Sunday in August, the ***Sinjska alka**, a knights' tournament, has taken place here, recalling the time when a troop of only 600 men managed to hold off a Turkish siege. During the tournament, the *alka*, a metal ring with two hoops, must be lanced at full gallop; preferably, of course, in the middle. People from all over the region pour into town for this festival dressed in traditional costumes.

*OMIŠ

Twenty-two kilometers along the Magistrala, past the beach town of Podstrana and at the mouth of the Cetina River on the Adriatic, lies **Omiš ❺**. Directly beyond the town rise the foothills of the Mosor, through which the Cetina cuts a path at this point. The island of Brač looms out of the sea to the south. Its

Split and the Makarska Riviera

favorable location helped Omiš to develop into a bustling harbor. The main occupation of the residents here was not, however, commerce, but rather piracy; whereby they brought the other Dalmatian cities into difficulty. And even though Omiš was brought to its knees in numerous wars, the people always returned to their old ways. It was only after the Venetians irrevocably conquered the city in 1444 that peace returned to the Dalmatian coast. The Omiš of today is a place marked by sand and pebble beaches with pine trees dispensing much-needed shade, and the cozy old town with its many cafés. However, because of several unpleasant industrial installations, Omiš has not been able to attract much tourism.

In the Priko neighborhood, on the right bank of the Cetina, stands the most important building in the city: the pre-Romanesque **Sveti Petar Church**. This single-naved edifice, with a cupola and

Above: The ruins of the fortress of Omiš. Right: The peaceful center of Makarska.

apse, was used in the 18th century as a Glagolithic seminary for novice priests.

A visit to the ★**Cetina Gorge** beyond Omiš is well worth the trip, especially to the destinations of **Radmanove mlinice** ❻ and the **Gabavica Waterfall** ❼.

THE MAKARSKA RIVIERA

Twenty-two kilometers beyond Omiš, on the coastal road that runs along the steep flanks of the Biokovo Massif, is one of the most beautiful stretches of beach on the entire Adriatic. A side road through the fragrant pine woods leads to the ★**white pebble beaches** (very crowded in summer) of **Brela** ❽. Around the town's idyllic center, quiet hotels, restaurants, and modern villas which rent out rooms and apartments are to be found.

The next seaside resort, popular for its long beach, turquiose-blue waters and large hotels, is ★**Baška Voda** ❾, four kilometers to the south. The best view of this former fishing and seafarers' village resting on a large bay is from the coastal road. A drink can be enjoyed in the shade of the trees at one of the cafés along the harbor promenade. Passing through vineyards and olive groves, the mountain villages of **Bast** and **Topic**, long ago constructed high on the slopes for protection, can be reached on foot from Baška Voda.

The touristic middle point of the 60-kilometer-long Riviera is the harbor town of ★**Makarska** ❿, located at the base of the highest peak of the Biokovo Mountains, Sveti Jure. The lively old town (with ferry ports for trips to Brač Island) stretches along the palm-lined **harbor promenade**, set between the peninsulas of Osejeva and Sveti Petar. Northwest of Sveti Petar (with its lighthouse), lies the nearly two-kilometer-long main beach of Makarska, Donja Luka, which made this place and the "Riviera" famous in the 1960s, and is where most of the hotels are located. Until it was aquired by Venice in 1699, Makarska was an important local

strategic point. From here, the much-feared "pirates" of Neretva made life along the middle Dalmatian coast unpleasant for the Venetians. Later it was the Turks who made use of this location.

These days, an illustrious international crowd fills the chic café-bars, music bars, ice cream parlours and restaurants along the promenade and tucked away in the lanes of the old town, as well as those on the central square, **Kačićev trg**.

From above the **monument** to the most famous local citizen, poet Andrija Kačić-Miošić (1704-69), created by the most important Dalmatian sculptor, Ivan Rendic, there is a good view of the 18th-century **Sveti Marko Parish Church**. At the **market**, everything from succulent Dalmatian figs to sweet Prošek dessert wine is on offer.

Those who have had enough of sand and sun might want to have a look at the **Franjevački samostan** (Franciscan monastery) on the east side of Makarska's harbor. The ***Malacology Museum** housed here has one of the fin-

est sea and snail shell collections in the world. Everything regarding the topic of shells is on display here; shells as money, as a source of color, as jewelry, etc.

There is a marked hiking trail leading from **Makar ⑪**, a village 233 meters above Makarska, to ***Sveti Jure ⑫**: at 1,762 meters this is the highest peak in the 36-kilometer-long and seven-kilometer-wide Biokovos. The climb takes about five hours. You don't have to hike to the top for the view, however, as the highest road in Croatia is located here on Croatia's "Holy Mountain." A side road leads to Makar's neighboring village of **Kotišina ⑬**, in which a **botanical garden**, featuring indigenous plants, herbs and medicinal plants, can be visited.

Above the village of **Gornji Tučepi**, beyond the Staza Pass, where, on the steep rocky slopes the **Biokovo Nature Preserve** begins (signposted, with parking area), an 18-kilometer-long paved toll road starts, which leads through the nature preserve to Sveti Jure. This is the highest road in Croatia, which, because

Split and the Makarska Riviera

of its many narrow, exposed curves, should only be attempted by very experienced drivers. From the Konoba Biokovo there is a wonderful view of the entire mid-Dalmation island and coastal world. Further in the distance stretch the karstic heights, perforated by many sinkholes. Chamois, mouflon and sheep are at home in this beautiful nature park.

From Makarska, traveling southwards, you encounter the small but lively seaside town of **Tučepi** ⑭, with its broad pebble beach and yacht harbor. From here it is just a half-hour hike to the old mountain village of **Gornji Tučepi**.

The fishing and resort village of **Podgora** ⑮ offers vacationers a bay lined with a pebble beach, with hotels and pensions on the sea. The shore promenade is closed to traffic on summer evenings and becomes a popular pedestrian area.

The island of Hvar seems so close to **Igrane** ⑯ that you can almost reach out

and touch it. The Old-Croatian St. Michael's Church, with its elegant bell tower, helps give Igrane its typical Dalmatian character. Ruins of the town walls and the "Turkish Tower" have been preserved. A broad pebble beach stretches south from here.

In **Živogošće** ⑰, which boasts a 17-century Franciscan monastery and a camping site in lush green Mediterranean surroundings, the most attractive section of the Riviera begins, with its many isolated bays and inlets. From little **Drvenik** a ferry takes you to the island of Hvar. **Zaostrog** is an especially popular destinatin for Croatian tourists.

The former fishing village of **Gradac** ⑱ has an enticing three-kilometer-long beach of fine pebbles, the longest on the Makarska Riviera. International tourism has long since returned to the hotel complex here.

Beyond Gradac the coastal road leaves the sea and runs right through the green hills to the Neretva Delta, passing by Lake Baćinska.

Oben: The Makarska Riviera – Tučepi Beach at the foot of the Biokovo Mountains.

SPLIT (021)

City Information: Trg Republike 2, tel. 342544, fax. 355358. Information for the region of Spit: Prilaz braće Kaliterna 10, tel./fax. 40853 or 362561.

Hotel Lav, eight km south in Podstrana, Galjevačka 29, tel. 304111, fax. 304531, private beach, sports; **Hotel Marjan**, Obala Kneza Branimira 8, tel. 342866, fax. 342930, large city hotel with indoor swimming pool; **Hotel Bellevue**, Ulica Bana Josipa Jelačiča 2, tel. 585655, fax. 362383, centrally located neo-Renaissance building.

Hotel Park, Hatzeov Perivoj 3, tel. 515411, fax. 591247.

Hotel Srebrena vrata, at the silver gate, tel. 46849, some rooms with shared bathrooms.

CAMPING: **Trstenik**, tel./fax. 303111, tennis.

PRIVATE ROOMS arranged through the tourist office.

Restaurant Diokletian, ship restaurant on the city harbor with a great view of the old town, fish, meat dishes; **Restaurant Crni mačak**, Skrade 22, in the old town, tel. 512721, fish, grilled specialties; **Restaurant Bogart**, D. Šimunovića 10, tel. 511765, trendy; **Restaurant Lijepa Dalmacija**, Hektorovića bb, tel. 522143, fish specialties, serves warm food until 1 a.m.!

Diocletian's Palace, 8 a.m. to 7 p.m.; the **Cathedral**, 8 a.m. to 1 p.m. and 3 p.m. to 6 p.m.; **Temple of Jupiter** , 8 a.m. to 1 p.m. and 3 p.m. to 6 p.m. **Ethnography Museum**, in the old Town Hall, 9 a.m. to 1 p.m.; **Archeology Museum** (closed until early 1999), 9 a.m. to 1 p.m.; **Papalič Palace** with the **Municipal Museum**, Tue-Fri 10 a.m. to 6 p.m., Sat 10 a.m. to noon; **Meštrovič Kaštelet**, 9 a.m. to 7 p.m. Some museums have different hours in winter; all are closed Mondays.

June 14-Aug 14: **Split Summer**, theater, opera, ballet and concerts; *July:* **Festival of Pop Music**; *mid-July to mid-August:* **Summer Festival**, with theater, music and dance along the Riviera; *first Sunday in August:* **Sinjska alka Knights Tournament**, in Sinj – the rehearsals on Friday and Saturday are also interesting.

For those interested in archeology, a visit to **Salona** is worthwhile. The excavated sites are the biggest in Croatia. The **Klis Fortress** is also worth stopping off to see.

For mountain-bikers and motorcyclists, the nearby **Kozjak Mountains** are interesting, with stretches of well-paved road (crushed limestone and tar). In the Mosor Mountains between Split and Omiš there is a trail that can be traversed by cross-country motorcycle, but it is difficult to find. Drive towards Stobreč, take the road towards Žrnovnica inland; behind the town, the road leads into the Mosor mountain range, and passes through Sitno and Dubrava to Gata and back to Omiš.

MARINA: **ACY Marina Split**, Uvala Baluni, tel. 355886, fax. 361310, also equipped for large yachts, 500 berths and all necessary facilities.

MAKARSKA RIVIERA (021)

BAŠKA VODA

Horizont, on the edge of town, tel. 604555, fax. 620699, tennis, pebble beach; **Slavija**, tel.620155, fax. 620740, on the promenade.

BRELA

Hotel Maestral, Brela, tel. 603666, fax. 603688, excellent hotel, private beach, sports; **Hotel Soline**, Brela, tel. 603222, fax. 620501, indoor pool, private beach. **Hotel Marina**, Brela, tel. 603666, fax. 603699, beach.

MAKARSKA

Trg Tina Ujevića 1, tel./fax. 612002.

Hotel Meteor, tel. 615344, fax. 611419, excellent hotel, beach, indoor/outdoor pools, bars, nightclub.

Hotel Dalmacija, tel. 615777, fax. 612211, private beach, pool, nightclub; **Hotel Biokovo**, tel. 615244, fax. 612073, comfortable, on palm-lined promenade.

Hotel Rivijera, tel. 616000, no beach, relatively large, not especially nice.

CAMPING: **Rivijera**, tel. 616000, fax. 611028, shady place with a dock, tennis.

Malacology Museum Makarska, mussels and snails, 11 a.m. to noon and 6 to 7 p.m.

Hiking to Vošac (1,451 meters) and **Sv. Jure** (1,762 meters). The Sv. Jure route is a one-lane road that is also interesting for mountain-bikers and motorcyclists. In addition, you have to go to Kozica and Vrgorac, during the course of which you will cross over the Staza Pass; from the pass, the street curves left.

OMIŠ

Hotel Ruskamen, tel. 862131. *CAMPING:* **Ribjnak**, tel. 862079, sports, shady areas, rental cars, June through Oct; **Lisičina**, tel. 861332, tennis.

A nice bike-tour takes you through the **Cetina Valley**. Just behind Omiš turn towards Kučiće, follow the river to Slime and the Dupci Pass (300 meters) and you come to the coast again, five kilometers before Brela.

PODGORA

Minerva, tel. 625303, on the promenade, beach, indoor pool. **Podgorka**, tel. 625100, centrally located, pebble beach, extensive recreational activities.

Split and the Makarska Riviera

179

THE CENTRAL DALMATIAN ISLANDS

BRAČ
ŠOLTA
VIS
HVAR
KORČULA

*BRAČ

The central Dalmatian islands of Brač, Šolta, Vis and Hvar extend along the coast of Split. Korčula, described in this chapter, belongs, strictly speaking, to southern Dalmatia. The closest island to the mainland, **Brač** – "the Stout One," as it is popularly known – is, with its 394 square kilometers, the third-largest island in the Adriatic and the largest in Dalmatia. It has a population of about 12,500. The island's northern side, which faces the coast, is more easily accessible than is its southern one, where the island's highest elevations, topped by 778-meter Vidova gora (Mount Vidova), make access difficult. The vegetation here is typically Mediterranean: the lanscape is marked by pine forests and low-growing, dense maquis; the barren, rocky hills are interspersed with ravines, stony bays and flat beaches.

The island dwellers make their living from farming and livestock: their traditional sources of income. The stone quarries of Brač also provide them with a good means of existence: the island is made of limestone, which as a building

Preceding pages: A solitary monastery on the island of Brač. Left: The "Golden Horn" of Bol changes its shape according to the currents.

material has become Brač's top export. As early as in Roman times, Brač served as a supplier not only of building stone, but of olives, wine and herbs as well. The white stone from Brač has been used in many famous buildings, including the White House in Washington, D.C., the Reichstag in Berlin, and the Parliament in Vienna.

As long as water supplies were limited to the island's few wells, Brač was able to maintain its rustic Mediterranean character. When water was piped in from the mainland, however, tourism began to really take off; so much so, in fact, that there is now even an airport 15 kilometers north of Bol. Sand beaches are found only on the north and south sides of the island; secluded bays, by comparison, are found all around Brač.

Supetar

The ferry boat from Split puts in at **Supetar ❶**, which is the administrative center of and the largest town on the island. The ancient settlement was situated on the small peninsula where today the cemetery is located. The cemetery's Oriental-style **Petrinovič Mausoleum**, a showpiece of Dalmatian stone-cutting work built in 1924 by sculptor Toma Rosandić, can be seen from the ferry.

A spacious holiday center with a hotel, a pool, and bicycle and boat rentals tends to the the wishes of summer visitors who crowd the sand and fine pebble beaches around Supetar.

Traveling west from Supetar, it is worth stopping off in the picturesque harbor town of **Sutivan** ❷. Situated on a protected bay on the north coast of the island, Sutivan was fortified by the Venetians in the 16th century. The parish church, a 17th-century castle, an old windmill, and a baroque palace with a park, now a hotel, help give the town its character. In the hilly interior south of Supetar lies the quiet village of **Nerežišća** ❸ (alt. 380 meters), once the administrative center of the island.

Milna

In the extreme west of Brač is **Milna** ❹, situated on the bay of the same name.

Above: White limestone from Brač is used the world over.

The original fishing village came into existence in the 17th century, when the aristocratic Cerinic family had a small church and a fortress built here. The rococo **Annunciation of Mary Parish Church** in the town center contains valuable art objects by local masters.

These days, tourism plays an important role in Milna: yacht captains call in gladly at the **marina**, which is open year-round. This is the only yacht harbor on the island, with 270 berths and dry docks.

Lovely pebble beaches lie to the west of the town, where they are easy to reach on foot. South of Milna are more alluring, isolated bays with crystal clear water.

The North Coast

Most of the island's villages lie on Brač's jagged, picturesque north coast east of Supetar, four kilometers from which you come to the sleepy village of **Splitska** ❺, an old harbor town near the oldest-known quarry on the east Adriatic. From this quarry the Romans shipped stone to Split for the construction of Diocletian's palace.

Nearby **Škrip** ❻, set in the bright landscape south of Splitska, is the oldest town on the island. Traces of Illyrian and Roman settlements can still be found here. An impressive **castle** with a tower and whitewashed roofs harks back to Venetian times. A small **museum** here houses an archeology and ethnology collection.

Taking the coastal road from Splitska, you reach **Postira** ❼, a small town with some lovely beaches nearby. The great Croatian writer Vladimir Nazor was born in a house on the harbor here, marked today by a plaque.

In **Pučišća** ❽, scenically situated at the end of a fjord-like bay, are the island's marble quarries. This town was often threatened by the Turks. Ruins of the 16th-century fortifications and the castle, with its defensive towers, are well preserved. Pučišća, and its surroundings are known as Dalmatia's stone-cutting center. In fact, this is where the only stonecutting school in Croatia is located. In a specialty shop located near the harbor hotel, a chunk of "Brač stone" can be purchased in the form of a vase or bowl.

The attractive town of **Povlja** ❾, situated on the northeast of the island, is especially popular for the excellent swimming in its craggy bays. Ferry boats from Makarska land at the small harbor town of **Sumartin** ❿ on the island's east coast.

A short trip inland leads to the mountain village of **Selca** ⓫. The parish church here is considered the most splendid marble structure on the island. In addition, busts of Leo Tolstoy, former German foreign minister Hans-Dietrich Genscher, who supported Croatian independence, and Pope John Paul II can be seen here.

Near **Gornji Humac** ⓬, known for its wine cellars and lamb specialties, the main east-west road intersects with the road south to Bol.

Bol

Because of its mounains, the south of Brač is not as populated as the north. The only large town on this side of the island is **Bol** ⓭ (population 1,100) – a popular swimming spot in summer – located at the coastal edge of the 778-meter-high mountain, Vidova gora. Looking out to sea, the mountains of Hvar can be made out.

Bol has always served as a supply center for seafarers. The Saracens destroyed the town completely in 827. When Bol was rebuilt, a fortress was planned which was to become the center of the town. From the 15th century onward, the Dominicans maintained a monastery here, the **Dominikanski samostan**, which today houses a **museum** with ancient artifacts, books and a painting from the school of Tintoretto.

To the west of Bol's harbor is ★★**Zlatni rat Beach** ⓮: the famous "Golden Horn." This beach is a phenomenon unique in the entire Adriatic: a 630-meter-long sandbar juts out around 300 meters into the water. Depending on the current, the "horn" points sometimes to the west and sometimes to the east. As the Golden Horn is the only large sand beach here, it is overcrowded during the peak season. However, there are beautiful pebble beaches nearby as well.

Hikes up **Vidova gora** ⓯ begin in Bol. The trail (about two hours) is marked; but don't forget to wear good hiking boots! From the peak there is a magnificent view of the mainland, Hvar Island and the Golden Horn.

Blaca

To the west of Bol is the village of **Murvica** ⓰, which can be reached on foot in about two hours. There are several monasteries and hermitages nearby. The **Samostan Blaca** ⓱ hermitage is especially worth seeing, although it is a fur-

The Central Dalmatian Islands

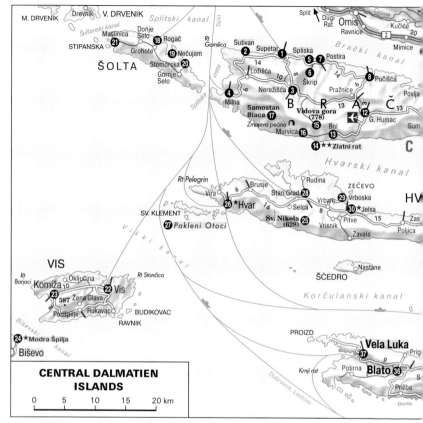

CENTRAL DALMATIEN ISLANDS

0 5 10 15 20 km

ther two-hour hike from Murvica. A Glagolithic community fleeing from the Turks came together in Blaca and settled here in the 16th century. After being destroyed by fire, the entire settlement was rebuilt in the 18th century. It has retained its appearance from that time.

The picturesque complex, which is nestled into the rockface, is a museum. Monastery life, which went on until 1963, is vividly documented in the museum's exibits. Above the monastery the trail continues on to the **Dragon's Cave** (one hour), which also served as a Glagolithic refuge. Various **reliefs** and engravings can be seen in the cave, in the western section, for example, are a dragon, a human head and a lion.

ŠOLTA

Šolta, with a surface area of 52 square kilometers, is one of the smallest of the central Dalmatian islands. In spite of its fertile fields and luxuriant maquis, its olive groves and vineyards, Šolta has no mass tourism, though it is a coveted destination for residents of Split. The tourist infrastructure here is comprised of only a few vacation apartments in the larger towns and three hotels. Šolta has been inhabited since antiquity. The island has been plundered often and had many different rulers over the centuries.

There is a road from the ferry harbor of **Rogač** ⑱ (swimming is possible beside the harbor basin) to the neighboring bay

VIS

Vis is the westernmost of the central Dalmatian islands. Another superlative: the town of Vis on the island is also the oldest settlement in Dalmatia. Vis – or *Issa*, as the city was known in antiquity – was founded in 397 B.C. by Dionysius the Elder, Tyrant of Syracuse (Sicily). Syracuse, at that time the most powerful city on the Mediterranean, erected its first colony in the eastern Adriatic here. From a base at Issa further colonies were founded in the region, for example, Trogir and Salona. In this way, the Greeks managed to create an excellent trade network and to gain enormous influence over the entire Adriatic.

When Rome later took over the island, a forum, a theater, temples and thermal baths were built. In the course of time, however, Issa became dependant on Salona. The city remained famous principally for its wine, praised by the 2nd-century Greek historian and geographer Agartharchid of Knidos.

After the Second World War, Vis was made naval staff headquarters and was thereby declared a prohibited area. It wasn't until 1989 that regulations were relaxed and part of the island was made accessible to tourists.

Vis has a viticultural area of some 700 hectares. Its best-known wines are the ruby-red *Plavac* and the golden-colored *Vugava*, which has a fragrant, honey-like aroma.

In the town of **Vis** ㉒, traces of the ancient theater can be seen near the **Gradina** Franciscan monastery. Otherwise, except for several imperial forts from the 19th century, not much stand out. In **Komiža** ㉓, on the island's western side, by contrast, there is a 16th-century Venetian fortress which is in excellent condition.

From Komiža there are boats available upon request to the small island of **Biševo**. There is a Blue Grotto here, simi-

of **Nečujam** ⑲. The only actual bastion of tourism on Šolta is located in this former fishing village; a bungalow development replete with tennis courts. The 100-meter-long pebble beach is therefore very crowded during the tourist season. Taxi boats shuttle to nearby islands.

The fishing village of **Stomorska** ⑳, somewhat further to the south, has a more typical character. The road to Stomorska leads through lush vegetation; carob, pine and fig trees, and lavender bushes. The town is on a lovely bay, picturesquely encircled by palm and cypress trees. There is a small camping site here. **Maslinica** ㉑, to the west, also offers visitors lodging; a Baroque 17th-century castle that has been converted into a hotel.

The Central Dalmatian Islands

lar to the one on Capri; the ***Modra spilja ㉔**. The best time to visit the grotto is from 11 a.m. to noon, as the sunlight at that time creates the most beautiful effects, producing silver, gold and violet colors.

****HVAR**

The island of **Hvar** – the " Long One" – is one of the most interesting, most beautiful and therefore most-visited of the Adriatic's islands. Hvar stretches 68 kilometers from east to west and is extremely mountainous. Its western end is up to eleven kilometers wide; though its average width is only about five kilometers. The island's larger towns are located on the craggy bays of its northern side, while there is hardly any population at all on the extremely steep southern

Above: Just the right temperature for an ice cream or a cold drink. Right: Sućuraj at the eastern tip of Hvar, a stone's throw from the mainland.

coast. The highest point on the island, and a rewarding destination for hikers, is 628-meter **Mount Sv. Nikola ㉕**, south of the city of Stari Grad.

Thanks to the mild winters and warm summers here, there is a luxuriant growth of maquis. In June, the island is dressed in a lilac-colored covering, for this is when the lavender blossoms. But other shrubs also grow amid this rich subtropical vegetation; in the spring, Hvar smells like a herbalist's shop. Besides the lavender, there is a rich palette of herbs which grow here, commanded by rosemary and followed by sage, marjoram and thyme. Some of these herbs were originally planted on Hvar centuries ago.

The Venetians promoted the cultivation of herbs here, primarily because they wanted to compensate for the disintegration of the spice trade with the Orient. The oils distilled from lavender and rosemary became hugely successful exports. In addition to the colorful flora, the island also offers pristine sections of coastline far from the tourist enclaves concentrated near the larger towns at Hvar's western end.

The Town of *Hvar

The island's main town, **Hvar ㉖**, is picturesquely located in a protected bay on the southwestern side of the island. Hvar experienced an unexpected boom in 1420 under Venetian rule, and developed into the richest community in Dalmatia. Every ship that was on its way to or from Venice called in here without exception. In 1571, a Turkish invasion completely destroyed the town; its historic buildings are essentially from the late 16th century.

Hvar has been known as a seaside and health resort since 1870. The heart of the city beats at the ***harbor**, where the most important sights are grouped together. The **arsenal**, directly on the jetty, was built in 1579 and was immense by contemporary standards. It is an enclosed dockyard in which even a complete war galley could find room to maneuver. The head of the city at the time, Pietro Semitecolo, however, wanted to outtrump even this superlative, and to that end had a theater, one of the oldest in Europe, built into the top floor of the arsenal. In addition to dramas, tragedies and comedies, pastoral so-called "Shepherd's Plays" were also put on here, after which participants retreated into intimate rooms where they could be alone with their "shepherd" or "shepherdess." Before this theater came into being, theatrical productions were staged in the area before the cathedral.

Across from the arsenal is the **loggia**. This lovely Renaissance building is credited to Sanmichele of Verona and masters from Korčula. At the end of the square stands **Sveti Stefan Cathedral**, which was built in the 16th century on the foundations of an earlier Benedictine monastery, and combines elements of Renaissance and Baroque architecture. The elegant **bell tower**, with its biforium,

triforium and quatriforium, was built by local masters. The altar in the cathedral's interior, bearing a 13th-century image of the Madonna, is one of the most valuable in Dalmatia. The carved seats in the choir section are from the year 1573. The neighboring **Bishop's Palace** houses the cathedral treasures. On the other side of the main square, which is, incidentally, the largest town square in Dalmatia, rises the belfry of the former St. Mark's Church, in whose ruins an archeology museum is now housed. The Palace Hotel, which was built into the ruins of the old town fortifications, is located nearby: the best view of the arsenal and the cathedral are from its terrace.

Outside of the city gate is the unfinished Gothic **Hektorovič Palace**, which is representative of the aristocratic living standard of the time. Behind the palace a picturesque quarter begins, which extends to the ***Spanjola** (Spanish Fortress). From the fortress, built under the Habsburg Charles V in 1551, there is a wonderful view of the harbor. There is

The Central Dalmatian Islands

also a restaurant for tired sightseers to catch their breath in.

Some distance away from the center, which can be overcrowded during the tourist season, on **Kriza Bay**, is the **Franjevački samostan** (Franciscan monastery), built in the mid-15th century. In the lunette of the monastery's portal a work by Nikola Firentinac (Niccolò Fiorentino), a *Madonna with Christ Child*, can be admired. Inside the monastery are a number of altar paintings, the works of Italian artists, which were originally votive offerings by wealthy citizens. Inside the one-time refectory, a **museum** and an art gallery are now installed.

From the harbor, taxi boats take off to the nearby "Hell's Islands," **Pakleni otoci ㉗**, to which Jerolim and Stipanska, amongs others, belong; popular bathing spots which also allow nudity. The is-

lands received their unusual name because of the resin extracted from pine trees here, which, once it was processed into black pitch (*paklina*), was used to repair boats and ships. The root word of *paklina, pakao*, means "hell."

Stari Grad

Only 20 kilometers away from Hvar is **Stari Grad ㉘** (Old Town), the former center of the island, called *Pharos* in antiquity. Stari Grad is another very popular tourist spot, with its huge number of wine cellars and comfortable taverns providing an extra attraction. Numerous noblemen, philosophers and writers – such as the Dalmatian poet-prince Hektorovič – had their summer villas built here.

There is still a number of palaces to be found in the eastern section of the city. The only relic from antiquity is a section of the nine-meter-thick Cyclops Wall, which can be seen at the Tadič Gramatorov House and on Ćiklopska ulica (Cyclops Street).

Above: In Stari Grad, the poet Hektorovič built himself a castle, Tvrdalj, in the 16th century. Right: Keeping the spirit alive with a procession in Korčula.

A visit to ***Tvrdalj Castle**, which the poet Hektorovič had built for himself in the middle of a park in the southwestern part of Stari Grad in 1520, is a special experience. The massive Renaissance structure is situated on the south side of a water basin surrounded by stone vaults. Many of the stones have quotes from Hektorovič's works in Croatian, Latin and Italian written on them. Inside the castle there is a small ethnographical collection, featuring the tools of Hvar's fishermen and vine growers.

An **archeology museum** is located inside the nearby 19th-century **Dominikanski samostan** (Dominican monastery), which also has an enormous church. Hvar's main vine-growing region stretches from Stari Grad to Vrboska. Wine has been made here since antiquity. Today, *Plavac* is the wine predominantly produced on Hvar.

Vrboska and Jelsa

Vrboska ㉙, situated at the end of a steeply-cut bay, was once a fishing village in which fish was mainly salted and preserved to be sold to the Venitians as ship's provisions. This brought the town a modest degree of prosperity. The invasion of the Turks in 1571 did not spare Vrboska, which is why, when the town was later rebuilt, a fortified church, **Sveta Marija**, consecrated to the Virgin Mary, was constructed here.

The most important collection of paintings on the island is located inside the baroque **Sveti Lovro Church** (St. Lawrence's), with works by the Venetians Veronese and Bassano, as well as the painter Medovic from Dubrovnik.

The area behind the contemplative harbor and bathing town of ***Jelsa** ㉚ – from here taxi boats set out to the nudist island of Zečevo – seems ever more deserted the further toward the east the only road here is taken. There are very few settlements in this region, and tourism plays only a minor role; some swimming areas can be reached from the road only by foot path. **Sućuraj** ㉛, a small ferry harbor, marks the eastern end of the island. Sućuraj is quite close to the mainland: the harbor of **Drvenik** on the Makarska Riviera is only six kilometers away.

*KORČULA

The southern Dalmatian island of **Korčula** stretches along a length of 47 kilometers and is on average between six and eight kilometers wide. Its backbone is formed by a mountain chain, the highest peak of which is the Klupca, at an elevation of 568 meters.

The ancient Greeks called the island *Kerkyra melaina* (Black Korčula), because it was completely covered by thick forests. According to legend, the first colony on Korčula was founded by the Trojan prince Antenor.

The Romans developed an interest in this fertile island as early as the 3rd century B.C., though it took until the year 35

The Central Dalmatian Islands

B.C. before the island was actually Romanized. Like all the central Dalmatian islands, Korčula, too, experienced a stormy history until the Venetians finally brought stability in 1420.

The Town of ★★Korčula

Ferries from Orebič, Split, Hvar and Dubrovnik land at the town of **Korčula** ㉜, whose historical center covers a conically-shaped peninsula. Because of its picturesque situation and its many medieval squares, churches and palaces, the city has also been given the nickname "Little Dubrovnik."

The town was completely reshaped in the 13th century when the streets were newly laid out, which the architects and city planners did very cleverly: with the exception of the north-south central axis, nearly every lane runs from west to east. This way the cold bora – the powerful and cold northeastern wind – has very little chance of blowing into the town, while the pleasant mistral manages to breeze in unhampered from the west. The streets end at the elongated Cathedral Square, which occupies the highest spot on the peninsula. Korčula was once enclosed by a ring wall, of which now only ruins and four bastions remain.

At the highest elevation in the old town, the late-Romanesque **★Sveti Marko Cathedral** (St. Mark's), the most important historical building here, stretches its tower into the blue sky. Construction on the three-naved basilica was begun in 1420, with principally local stonecutters, who had developed a good reputation all over the Adriatic, working on the project. However, the Venetian authorities could also afford to engage foreign masters, such as Bonino of Milan, who was responsible for creating the magnificent **portal** which is guarded by

Right: The old town of Korčula, designed to fend off the bora winds.

lions. St. Mark is depicted in the cathedral's lunette.

The interior of the cathedral has a host of figurative ornamentations, which spread out over the main as well as the side naves. The **ciborium** above the main altar deserves special attention: four slender columns support an octagonal, three-tiered roof which tapers into a pyramid. The Annunciation is represented on its fore side. The **altar painting** depicting Kočula's patron saints – Mark, Bartholomew and Jerome – has been attributed to Tintoretto.

The cathedral's fourth nave was actually planned to be a separate votive church (against the plague), however, no building site was available in the narrow city. When the plague raged over the island in 1529, it infected a majority of the city's population. The church was meant to offer protection to them from further epidemics, and it would have been consecrated to the saints Rocco, Cosmo and Damian. On the ground floor of the belfry beside the church there is a baptismal chapel, inside of which is a valuable bronze relief depicting the Resurrection of Christ.

Very near the cathedral, to the right of the campanile, stands the alleged **birth house of Marco Polo**, who is still famous today for his Asian journeys. This is according to legend, at any rate, as the name Marco Polo was quite common in Korčula at the time.

A Venetian subject, Marco Polo journeyed to China in 1271, together with his father and his uncle, visiting a world which up until that time had never seen a European. His journey lasted 25 years and when he returned, no one believed his charming and fantastic stories.

In 1298, a battle was fought in the sea off Korčula between the Genoese and the Venetians. The Genoese won the battle and took thousands of prisoners, among them Marco Polo. While imprisoned, his tales, which he dictated to a fellow pris-

oner from Pisa, were first set down on paper. After his release from prison, the Pisan published this now-famous book.

Examples of aristocratic architecture are found directly across from the church: the 16th-century **Gabrielli Palace**, adorned with magnificent windows and balconies, for example. Today, the **Gradski muzej** (Municipal Museum) is housed here, which, in addition to archeological displays, also contains exhibits about the stonecutter's art and ship-building, as well as documents from the city's past. The neighboring late-Gothic **Arneri Palace** is composed of several buildings with interesting façades arranged around a Baroque courtyard. In the southeastern corner of the old town stands **Svi Sveti Church** (All Saint's), which from 1301 on was the seat of the city's oldest brotherhood. The **icon collection** which is maintained here is especially worth seeing.

Every year in Korčula, in late July, ***traditional sword dances** are staged: the *Moreška* and the *Kumpanija*. The Moreška – which is derived from the Spanish word *Morisco*, meaning Moorish, and which has a 400-year tradition in Korčula – looks back to battles with the Moslems: the "good white" king faces off against the "evil black" king. *Kumpanija* dancers are clad in bright traditional costumes and stage a battle using sabres: a symbol of the fight for liberty.

Just beyond the harbor of Korčula is the island monastery of **Badija** ㉝, which can only be accessed by boat during the tourist season. This tiny island has a former Franciscan monastery that has been converted into a hotel. The landscape is thick with maquis and pine forests, and offers excellent places to swim, including a nudist beach.

Lumbarda

Six kilometers south of Korčula town is the seaside resort of **Lumbarda** ㉞, which has lovely sand beaches and an excellent tourist infrastructure. The attractive village also has lovely Gothic and

The Central Dalmatian Islands

Renaissance summer villas, which wealthy citizens had built here. From the vineyards on the slopes around Lumbarda comes *Grk* (Greek), a well-known, heavy white wine which is popularly drunk with seafood in Dalmatia. Grapes have been grown here since antiquity. The island of Vrnik can be seen from Lumbarda

On the Way to Vela Luka

Beautiful bays for swimming are spread out all along the route to Vela Luka, the second main town on Korčula, accessible generally by gravel roads. The best-known is **Pupnatska Luka** ㉟, which is fairly tough to get to.

There was a time when **Blato** ㊱ (just before Vela Luka) was the largest and most affluent town on the island, to which old palaces, churches and the Municipal Museum still attest. Vinyards are located

Above: The traditional Moreška sword dance, now a spectacle for tourists performed every July 29 in Korčula.

on the surrounding hills, which are the region's main source of income. A vine blight destroyed the island's vines after the Second World War, suddenly leaving residents with no means of income. Many emigrated; those who remained found work in shipbuilding and tourism. The *Kumpanija* saber dance is especially impressive when performed in Blato.

Vela Luka ㊲ forms the western end of the island. With its 4,400 residents it is the largest town on Korčula. The many archeological discoveries made in the area point to very early settlement by Illyrians and Greeks, though the town remained largely insignificant throughout antiquity. Vela Luka did not begin to grow until the 19th century, when a wharf and a fish processing factory were built here. Tourism is helping the town grow still further today. The many swimming areas in the bays around Vela Luka have attracted hotels, restaurants and rehabilitation centers. There is a therapy center in the Adria Hotel complex where arthritic illnesses are treated with local sea mud.

BRAČ (021)

FERRIES: Split – Supetar: 45 min., hourly departures in the peak season; Makarska – Sumartin.

BOL

i **Tourist Office**, tel. 635122, fax. 635638.

😊😊😊 **Hotel Bretanide**, tel. 635288, fax. 635120, three-story pavilions, pool, spacious area; **Hotel Elaphusa**, tel. 635288, fax. 635150, dance café, bowling alley and more.

😊😊 **Hotel Kaštel**, tel. 635140, fax. 635466, small hotel; **Hotel Borak**, tel. 306202, fax. 306215, beach, pool, surfing school, tennis.

❌ **Vidovica**, tel. 635120. **Dva Ferala**, tel. 635108.

SUPETAR

i Petra Jakišća 17, Tel./fax. 630551.

😊😊 **Hotel-Restaurant Villa Britanida**, tel./fax. 631038; **Hotel Kaktus**, tel. 631133, fax. 631130, beach, sports facilities.

CAMPING: **Supetar**, tel. 631066, fax. 630022, sports, nudism.

❌ **Dolac**, tel. 631230; **TS Palma**, tel. 631363.

MILNA

MARINA: Marina Milna, tel. 636306, fax. 636272, with 270 berths, dry docks, open all year.

ŠOLTA (058)

FERRIES: Car ferry Split – Rogač: five times daily, one hour.

😊😊 **Hotel Olint**, Stomorska, on the bay, reasonably priced.

😊 **Pension Avlija**, Maslinica, in the old castle.

CAMPING: **Mido**, Stomorska; small, simple, partly shady.

❌ **Krčma Komin**, Stomorska, on the pier, shady terrace, simple dishes.

VIS (021)

FERRIES: Rijeka – Vis: once a week, 16 hours, June 1-Dec 28; Dubrovnik – Vis: once a week, 7 hours, June 7-Sept 27; Split – Vis.H 😊😊😊 **Hotel Issa**, tel. 711124, near town center, wide range of sports.

HVAR (021)

i Tel./fax. 741059.

FERRIES: Drvenik – Sućuraj: 12 times daily in summer; Split – Stari Grad: 3 times daily, 2 hours; Split –

Hvar: 2 hours; Rijeka – Hvar: 4 times weekly; Ancona – Stari Grad: once weekly, 15 hours, June 1-Sept 28.

😊😊😊 **Hotel Amfora**, Hvar, tel. 741202, fax. 741711, indoor pool, private beach, one km from center; **Hotel Palace**, Hvar, tel. 741966, fax. 742 420, on the harbor, indoor pool; **Hotel Adriatic**, Hvar, tel. 741 024, private beach, pool.

😊😊 **Hotel Sirena**, Hvar, tel. 741144, pavilions, quiet, private beach; **Hotel Arkada**, Stari Grad, tel. 765555, hotel complex 1.5 km outside town; **Hotel Bodul**, Hvar, tel. 741744, simple, affordable; **Hotel Pharos**, Hvar, tel. 741028, private beach.

CAMPING: **Vira**, Hvar, tel. 741059, rental caravans, marina, shady, June 1-Sept 15.

❌ **Gostionica Eremitaž**, Stari Grad, on the shore promenade, nice terrace, good fish dishes.

MARINAS: Marina Vrboska, tel. 774018, fax. 774144, about 100 berths, well equipped (crane, showers, etc.); **Marina Jelsa**, no major installations.

Interesting off-road tracks for **mountain-bikers** on the eastern side of the island. **Hiking** opportunities to Sv. Nikola (621 meters) from Selca.

KORČULA (020)

FERRIES: Rijeka – Korčula (town): 6 times weekly, 14 hours; Hvar – Korčula; Orebić (Pelješac) – Korčula; Split – Vela Luka: once a day in peak season; Ancona – Vela Luka: once a week, June 1-September 28.

KORČULA TOWN

i Tel. 715701, fax. 711710.

😊😊😊 **Hotel Liburna**, Korčula, tel. 711006, fax. 711746, small hotel, pool, private beach, tennis.

😊😊 **ACI Marina**, Korčula, tel. 711661, fax. 711748, apartments on the harbor, clean, affordable; **Hotel Korčula**, Korčula, tel. 711746, small neo-Renaissance house; **Hotel Marko Polo**, Korčula, tel. 711100, sports.

😊 Villas, apartments, tel. 711067.

❌ **Marco Polo**, old town; **Stari Grad**, affordable; **Adio Mare**, excellent fish; **Pizzeria Anfora**, center; **Farula Ice Cream Parlor**, center.

MARINAS: ACY Korčula, tel. 711661, fax. 711748, 200 berths, 50 dry docks, boat rentals, all the usual important amenities, open year-round; **Marina Lumbarda**, tel. 712730, fax. 712755, 170 berths, not completely finished yet.

VELA LUKA

😊😊 **Hotel Adria**, tel. 812700, fax. 812044, health center, pool; **Hotel Poseidon**, tel. 812226, fax. 812044.

CAMPING: **Mindel**, Vela Luka, tel. 812494, open year-round, wide range of sports, hardly any shade.

The Central Dalmatian Islands

BOSNIA
AND
HERCEGOVINA

CROATIA

Šibenik
Split
Brač
Makarska
Hvar
Korčula
Mljet
Dubrovnik

Sarajevo
Mostar

MONTE-
NEGRO

Podgorica

ADRIATIC

Herceg
Novi

SEA

ITALY

Ulcinij

SOUTHERN DALMATIA

PELJEŠAC
DUBROVNIK
MLJET
CAVTAT

Further south on the coastal Magistrala, passing by the **Baćinska Lakes** in their solitary setting, is the city of **Ploče ❶**; one of the largest harbors on the Dalmatian coast. Ploče was constructed after World War II on the northern edge of the Neretva Delta, and was intended to provide access to the sea for the then-socialist republic of Bosnia-Herzigovina. The name of the town was later changed to Kardeljevo; today, however, it is again called Ploče and is Croatian. From here the ferries start out for Trpanj and the Pelješac Peninsula, and there is a railroad that runs to Mostar and Sarajevo.

Beyond Ploče stretches the **Neretva Delta**, formed by the confluence of its twelve tributaries. The Neretva originates in the Bosnian mountains and at 218 kilometers is the longest river to empty into the Croatian Adriatic. It is navigable by ships with a limited draft (2.2 meters) as far as the town of Metković in Bosnia, after which a marshland begins. This is where the center of the Narentans was located, a people who controlled the borderlands between the Cetina and Neretva rivers, and who made a name for themselves mainly from piracy.

Preceding pages: Dubrovnik, on UNESCO's World Heritage List. Left: Prijeko awaits its guests every evening.

To the south of the delta is the border with **Bosnia-Herzegovina**, which has a six-kilometer-wide access to the Adriatic. The main town in this narrow section of Bosnia-Herzegovina is **Neum ❷**, a modern seaside resort. The transfer of goods, however, takes place in Ploče, as this is the only port in the area with suitable capacity. Only four kilometers beyond Neum you are back in Croatia again, in the region of Dubrovnik.

THE PELJEŠAC PENINSULA

The ferries that operate between the cities of Korčula and Orebić connect the island of Korčula with the **Pelješac Peninsula**. There is, in addition, a ferry route to the mainland between Ploče and Trpanj. Drivers normally take the coast road through Ston to the peninsula.

The Pelješac Peninsula is 65 kilometers long and between three and seven kilometers wide, with a total surface area of 355 square kilometers. The peninsula is known for its wine from the vinyards that grow and thrive on the terraced slopes of the rising hills here, which climb to a height of 961 meters at Mount Sv. Ilija. Two wines that must be sampled here are *dingač* and *postup*. Both have a high alcohol content of 14-15%. *Dingač* won a gold medal in Paris in 1910 and

Southern Dalmatia

Above: Vegetable fields in the Neretva Delta.
Right: Mali Ston offers fresh oysters.

was the first Dalmatian wine ever to have its name protected.

Despite the streams of tourists that cross the peninsula on their way to and from Korčula, very little has changed here over the years. The residents live from fishing, raising oysters and producing wine. Many locals have, however, left the peninsula in search of employment in Dubrovnik or abroad. The Pelješac Peninsula is a place of natural beauty, with lovely pine forests, rocky heights and picturesque farming villages.

*Ston

Beginning at the coastal Magistrala, the town of **Ston ❸** forms the gateway to the Pelješac Peninsula. It is made up of two fortified quarters located on two separate, unconnected bays. On the northern coast, on the Neretvanski Canal, lies Mali Ston; on the Stonski Canal to the south lies Veliki Ston. The Romans erected a small settlement on this location. Sea salt has been extracted in the area around Ston since antiquity.

In the late Middle Ages this region was ruled by various Slav principalities, such as the Duklja and the Serb Nemandjids. Ston and the Pelsješac Peninsula later became part of an expanding Dubrovnik when the city bought the area from King Dušan. The new rulers considered whether or not they should completely isolate the peninsula from the mainland by digging a canal, though they seemed to find it more effective to construct defensive walls.

From the 14th century on, a system of fortifications was erected around Ston comparable to any in Europe; for Ston possessed a valuable salt works of more than 400 square kilometers – the richest in the entire Adriatic. The city-state of Dubrovnik relied on the salt trade for a good third of its revenues, and this source of income had to be protected from enemies. Famous architects, such as Michel-

ozzo Michelozzi, Bernadin of Parma and Juraj Dalmatinac were hired to work on the fortifications. A 5.5-kilometer ***defensive wall** was constructed, with 40 towers and seven bastions. Five kilometers of wall and 20 towers have been preserved. The walls simultaneously formed the foundation for the city of Ston, which was laid out in the form of a pentagon. The streets were likewise geometrically planned: three streets each in a north-to-south and an east-to-west layout divide the town into 15 equal sections, in each of which ten houses were to be built. Interestingly, residential buildings were constructed in the town's center, while public buildings were relegated to the edge of town. Only two gates allowed access to Ston. Construction on water and sewage systems was begun as early as 1581. Of interest in Ston are the **Knežev dvor** (Rector's Palace), the **Bishop's Palace** and **Franjevački samostan** (Franciscan monastery); all of which are attractive buildings from the 14th and 15th centuries.

Oysters are harvested in the small harbor bay of **Mali Ston**, which can be obtained on the spot with white bread and lemon. The **Koruna fortress ruins** (Veliki kastio) dominate the town and provide a marvelous panoramic view.

*Orebić

There are endless vineyards to be seen along the road to Orebić. But fig, pine and cypress trees, as well as thick maqui, also adorn the slopes. Early in the 16th century the ferry harbor of **Orebić** ❹ was still known as Trstenica; until the year 1516, when the Orebić family commissioned a castle to be built here. The present-day city is situated within the original castle walls. Orebić was regarded as an important maritime center; the Republic of Dubrovnik, for example, recruited most of its sea captains from here – or at least from the Pelješac Peninsula.

The **Pomorski musej** (Maritime Museum), located on the quay, provides visitors with a look into the eventful history

Southern Dalmatia

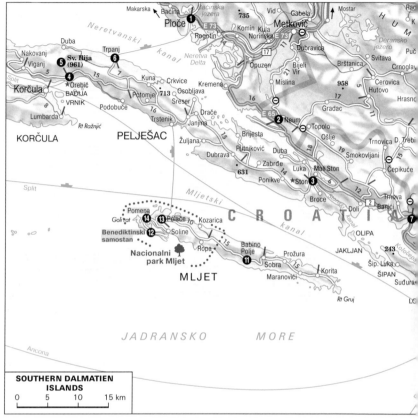

SOUTHERN DALMATIEN ISLANDS

0   5   10   15 km

of Orebić: navigational instruments, sea maps and pictures of old schooners are on display here. Numerous former captains' houses in the town are a reminder of Orebić's seafaring tradition.

West of the town center is the Franciscan **Gospa od Andela Church** (Our Lady of the Angel). For centuries this was the most important sanctuary for local sailors. From the church there is a good view of the narrow, busy channel which separates the Pelješac Peninsula from Korčula. Numerous votive offerings from seafarers are kept inside the church, as are art objects that sea captains brought back with them from their journeys abroad. Orebić was predestined to become a seaside resort, thanks as much to

its pine-shaded sand, pebble and stone beaches as to its little island (which is reserved exclusively for nude bathers).

Above Orebić and the Franciscan monastery looms 961 meter **★Mount Sv. Ilija** ❺, which requires a four- to five-hour hike to reach its summit. There are no marked hiking trails through this wild, romantic, natural area, and good hiking boots are an absolute must: if for no other reason than as protection against the poisonous sand vipers found here (that is where the Italian name for these hills – the *Vipera* mountains – comes from). The vine-growing and fishing village of **Trpanj** ❻, located on the northern coast and built upon Roman foundations, is a great place for excursions. A glass of the

Dubrovnik ❾ (Italian: *Ragusa*; population 44,000). Its unique location, on a peninsula at the foot of a limestone mountain chain surrounded by subtropical vegetation, combined with its historical buildings, makes a stay in Dubrovik – a city that for centuries rivaled Venice as a sea trading port – an incomparable experience. The impressive history of Dubrovnik can be seen on every corner of this famous city, which has been declared a World Heritage Site by UNESCO. Palaces, churches and squares make a wonderful backdrop to the annual **Libertas Festival** which takes place here. The car-free old town boasts the largest pedestrian zone in Europe and offers visitors the opportunity of delving into the animated life of the historical town center without having to worry about being bothered by traffic. Since the earthquake of 1667, Dubrovnik has had predominately Renaissance and Baroque features.

History

In antiquity, *Epidauros* (today Cavtat), further to the south, which was founded by the Greeks, was the most important settlment in the region. Under the Romans the town became *Epidaurum*, one of the most important trading centers in the southern Adriatic. When Epidaurum was destroyed during the great migrations, the residents of the town relocated to the north in the 7th century, settling in the fishing village of *Ragusium*. Later, Slavs settled in the hinterland, and within a short time the two communities melded together. Over time, a thriving city came into being; a city which, since 1919, has been called Dubrovnik, from the Slavic *dubrava* (oak forest).

In the 9th century, Arabs occupied the growing town. In the year 1000, the Venetians came for the first time, and, in 1081, the Normans under Robert Giuscard conquered affluent Ragusium. The Normans did not remain long, however,

deep red *Dingač* wine can be tasted directly at the vintner's.

Leaving the peninsula toward Dubrovnik, the Magistrala bypasses the attractive bay of **Slano ❼**, with its lush green vegetation, and goes on to **Trsteno ❽**. This village, with its expressly Mediterranean character, has its own **arboretum**, which stems from the Renaissance and contains rare trees and plants. **Gučetič Villa**, in the center of the grounds, has a collection of furniture, as well as a lapidarium.

★★DUBROVNIK

The capital city and pulsating center of southern Dalmatia is without question

Southern Dalmatia

and the Byzantine Empire once again became the city's protecting power.

Because of its political – as well as its territorial – isolation within the southern Dalmatian sphere, the urge for autonomy took root in Dubrovnik. For this reason, the citizens of Ragusa signed treaties of assistance with neighboring kingdoms in order to be prepared to defend themselves against expansionist Venice. The small city-state, which by now had managed to build up an impressive fleet of its own, even made a pact with the pirates of Omiš. A document from the 12th century verifies the existence of a free state with an elected president as its leader. In its position as mediator between the Balkan lands and the Middle States, Dubrovnik experienced a strong economic boom.

The threat to Dubrovnik by Venice remained a continual problem. Treaties with other important cities of the Adriatic

Above: Sundown over Dubrovnik's offshore islands. Right: You can walk around the entire city on Dubrovnik's old walls.

region were concluded, as, for example, with Molfetta, Ravenna, Bari, Ancona and, most importantly of all, Venice's arch-rival Pisa. After Constaninople fell into the hands of the Venetians, it took no longer than 1358 until Dubrovnik, too, became dependent upon Venice. There was, however, no interruption in business. Quite the contrary: Dubrovnik's economic and political power actually strengthened.

When Venice lost Dalmatia to the Croatian-Hungarian kings in 1358, Dubrovnik acknowledged the supremacy of Hungary while continuing to expand as an independent aristocratic republic. A Large and a Small Council, composed of the city's noblemen, elected a so-called Rector for a specific length of time, but provided him only with limited powers of authority. In this way abuses of power were almost completely eliminated.

When the Ottoman Empire expanded its power base into the Balkan region, Dubrovnik concluded trade agreements with the Turks and later also paid tributes

Southern Dalmatia

to them. In order to avoid a common border with Venice – the masters of Dalmatia – a small corridor (including the town of Neum) was ceded to the Ottomans. Dubrovnik reached the apex of its power and wealth in the 15th and 16th centuries, despite a severe earthquake in 1520. The Republic's fleet of 200 ships sailed all the world's seas and was, based on its storage capacity, the third largest fleet in the world. Its monopoly in the salt trade and mining interests in neighboring Bosnia in particular insured Dubrovnik's prosperity and advanced the local trades.

When sea trade fell into crisis, the city-state's fleet shrank porportionately. The hardest blow of all, however, was the devastating earthquake of 1667. In order not to fall victim to Venice during this period of weakness, an agreement of protection was forged with Austria. When a revival in sea trade came about in the 18th century, though, Dubrovnik once again recovered and managed to surpass even its age-old rival Venice. The enormous activity of the Dubrovnik fleet awakened

the displeasure of a new power, however; namely that of Napoleonic France. The European economic blockade against Great Britain brought an end to Dubrovnik's navigation, and thereby an end to the aristocratic republic, which was dissolved by the French in 1808. After the final defeat of Napoleon in 1815, Dubrovnik went first to Austria and then, in 1919, to Yugoslavia, which developed the city into one of the most important economic centers on its southern coast.

More decisive yet for the fate of Dubrovnik was its development as the most important tourist center of Dalmatia. The town's citizenry enjoyed the wealth brought in by this trade. When Croatia broke away from Yugoslavia, it was hoped that the revenues generated by the city would no longer be used for the regional compensation allocated to benefit economically weak areas, such as Kosovo, Macedonia and Bosnia, and that Dubrovnik's income would remain in Dubrovnik. Golden times were envisioned for the future of the city; but the

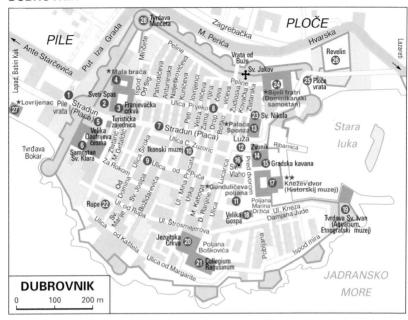

Labeled map featuring:

PILE · PLOČE · Tvrđava Minčeta (28) · Zagrebačka · M. Perića · Hvarska · Lazareti · Put Iza Grada · Ante Starčevića · Lapad, Babin Kuk · Peline · Minčete · Vrata od Buže · Sv. Jakov · Revelin (26) · Mala braća (4) · Palmotićeva · Antuninska · Naljeskovićeva · Kunićeva · Lovrijenci · Miličeva · Njina · Zama · Drop · Ploče vrata (25) · Bijeli fratri (Dominikanski samostan) (24) · Sveti Spas (1) · Ispod Od Sig. · Ulica Prijeko · Peti · Vetra · Čeva · Viteva · Žudioska · Kovačka · Zlatarska · Sv. Nikola (23) · Lovrijenac (27) · Pile vrata · Stradun (Plača) (2) · Franjevačka crkva (3) · Turistička zajednica (5) · Boško · Palača Sponza (13) · Stara luka · Velika Onofrijeva česma (6) · Stradun (Plača) (7) · Ulica C. Zuzorić (8) · Luža · Ribarnica · Tvrđava Bokar · Samostan Sv. Klara (9) · Zlatarić · M. Getaldić · Za Rokom · Ikonski muzej (10) · Ulica Siroka · Zvonik (12) · Gradska kavana (15) · Od Domina · Sv. Josipa · Božidarevića · Ulica od Puča · Ulica Mha Pracata · Uska · Ratanje · Sv. Vlaho (16) · Pred dvorom (14) · Knežev dvor (Historijski muzej) (17) · Rupe (22) · Ul. od Rupa · Sv. Marije · R. Ranjine · D. Bunića · Ulica · Gundulićeva poljana (11) · Poljana Marina Držića · Ul. Kneza Damjana Jude · Tvrđava Sv. Ivan (Aquarium, Etnografski muzej) (19) · Velika Gospa (18) · Ulica od Kaštela · Ul. Strosmajerova · Jezujtska Crkva (20) · Poljana Boškovića · Pobijana · Ispod mira · Collegium Ragusinum (21) · Ulica od Margarite · JADRANSKO MORE

DUBROVNIK

0   100   200 m

reality of the situation turned out to be completely different. Although there was never any doubt that Dubrovnik belonged both culturally and historically much more to Dalmatia – and therefore to Croatia – than it did to Bosnia, Serbian military units, out of blind hatred for this thriving, open, multi-cultural community, attacked the city with grenade launchers from the hinterlands (the border is less than ten kilometers away) and destroyed the surrounding area completely. Many grenades hit the historic old town; on the famous Stradun, the main street, the number of grenades was precisely 36. Numerous buildings were damaged, and tourism – along with all other branches of the economy which were more-or-less dependent upon tourism – completely collapsed.

Damage to the historical section of the city has since been cleared away, thanks to the assistance of UNESCO, and the

Right: Dubrovnik – a city that lives and breathes history.

city has been rebuilt and restored to its former glory. Once again foreign visitors can experience the Dubrovnik of old.

A Stroll through Dubrovnik's Old Town

Although diplomatic Dubrovnik managed to avoid armed conflict during the Middle Ages, the city fathers took great care in providing the town with **fortifications** in order to be prepared against any eventuality. This system of fortifications, which has existed since the 13th century, is considered to be one of the most massive and impressive in all Europe. The ****city wall** (*Gradske zidine*), up to 25 meters high and six meters thick in places, surrounds the entire core of Dubrovnik. The landward side is further fortified by an outer wall, as well as by nine small bastions. In addition, in order to protect the harbor and access to the sea, further especially-resistant fortifications, such as **Lovrijenac** in the west, **Revelin** in the east, the **Sv. Ivan Harbor Fortress**

Southern Dalmatia

and the powerful **Minčeta Tower**, which has long since become a hallmark of the city, on the northwest corner, were also constructed.

Two gates – Pile vrata (Pile Gate) in the west and Ploče vrata (Ploče Gate) in the northeast – are the only means of entry into the historic city center. The coast road passes by the modern suburbs of Gruž, with its harbor, and Lapad, on the peninsula across from Gruž, and leads to the western entrance of **Pile vrata ❶** (14th-16th century). The gateway arch is adorned by a statue of the city's patron saint Sv. Vlaho (St. Blasius), which was created by Ivan Meštrović in 1922. A three-arched bridge from the 15th century leads to a small park, the one-time moat, and to the Pile Gate. Caricaturists, portrait painters and street performers usually wait here for customers.

Directly behind the Pile Gate, on the left, is the small **Sveti Spas ❷** (Church of the Redeemer). One of the staircases to top the of the city wall is also located here. The over two-kilometer-long city wall tour should preferably be made either during the morning hours or else during the late afternoon, as there is no shade anywhere on the battlements.

Next to the Church of the Redeemer stands **Franjevačka ckrva ❸** (St. Francis' Church). In the tympanum of the south portal is a representation of Mary with the body of Christ, above which God the Father watches over. To the left and right, St. James and John the Baptist are depicted. This portal is regarded as the finest example of Dubrovnik's sculptures. The grave of Dubrovnik poet Ivan Gundulič (1588-1638) is located inside the single-naved building. Directly beside the church is the ***Mala braća ❹** Franciscan monastery, which was built in the 14th and 15th centuries and altered after the earthquake of 1520. The oldest section of the building is the magnificent **choir** from 1317: it shows a ribbed vault and an open hexaforium, upon which a rich assortment of mask, animal and plant motifs can be seen. Directly in front of the choir is the **Farmacia**, for which an entry

fee is charged. It contains numerous fascinating old objects. This ancient pharmacy was established in 1317 and is still in use today.

Across from the Pile Gate is the monumental **Velika Onofrijeva česma** (Large Onofrio Fountain), erected in 1444, which stands at the end of a twelve-kilometer water line. It was named after its Neapolitan builder, Onofrio della Cava. During his stay in Dubrovnik, from 1436 until 1444, he laid out the city's water supply system.

To the right of the fountain is the **Samostan Sveta Klara** (Monastery of St. Clare), built at the end of the 13th century and reconstructed after the earthquake of 1667. The daughters of noble families and rich citizens were raised here. Still others were forced to join the order because their dowries were too small. An orphanage – one of the first in Europe – was added in the 15th century.

Above: The Large Onofrio Fountain. Right: Evening on the Stradun.

Today a restaurant is located in the choir of the former monastery. Public administrative offices are located in the other buildings. A cinema has also made its way into the one-time monastery.

From the Pile Gate, the ★**Stradun** – also known as *Placa* – stretches for more than 200 meters to the clock tower at the entrance to the harbor on the other end of the old town. Stradun was once a marsh which separated Slavic *Dubrava* from Roman *Ragusa*. Today, it unites the population, which shows itself here every evening, well-dressed, sociable and, of course, flirtatious. This admission-free performance begins every evening at 7 p.m. During dinner time the street temporarily quiets down, but then it picks up again later with: "Where did you eat and how did it taste? Have you been to that new restaurant at the end of Prijeko? Is there anything new on at the cinema...?"

The patricians' houses along Stradun were all built in the years following the earthquake of 1667. There are still shops located on the ground floors, just as

things were planned hundreds of years ago. Living and dining rooms used to be situated on the first floor and bedrooms on the second; the attic contained the kitchen and rooms for storage.

There are two streets running parallel to the Stradun and which are almost as important: Ulica od Puča in the south and Prijeko in the north. Each has a character of its own. Over the years, **Prijeko** ❽ has evolved into one long, continuous restaurant: one place is connected to the next which is connected to the next and so on. These restaurants often change not only their decor, but ownership as well: competition here is fierce. *Burek* shops (snack bars), cafés, specialty restaurants and unpretentious wine bars wait along Prijeko for the much-desired customer.

In contrast to the Prijeko, **Ulica od Puča** ❾ has more the feeling of a shopping center, although the shops here tend not to have much in the way of necessities to offer: from the square surrounding the Large Onofrio Fountain on out there is an almost endless row of jewelry stores of-

fering gold and silver filigreed baubles and bangles. The trade in silver and gold here has always been in the hands of Christian Albanian families. The dealers know each other well and are generally good friends; there isn't a trace of competition amongst them. It isn't uncommon for one of them to call on another to go out for a coffee or a small snack. Then they simply close up their shops.

Further along, toward the center of the old town, galeries and souvenir shops dominate the scene. And then, suddenly, you find yourself standing in front of a 19th-century Serbian church. Beside the church is the **Ikonski muzej** ❿ (Icon Museum), which has a valuable collection of icons by Byzantine, Cretan-Venetian, Russian and local artists from various epochs on display.

At the east end of Ulica od Puča is ***Gunduličeva poljana** ⓫ – the market square. During the morning, fruit, vegetables and fish from the region can be bought from the colorful market stalls, which are set up at the feet of the great

Southern Dalmatia

poet of the city, Ivan Dživo Gundulič; a bronze statue of whom, created by local master Rendrič in 1893, occupies a spot in the middle of the square. There is also a square at the east end of the Stradun, **Luža** ⑫, the impressive Loggia Square, where most of the objects of interest are concentrated. Public buildings, such as the Customs Office, the Rector's Palace and the cathedral, stand here not far from the harbor. In the midst of the square looms **Roland's Column**, a stone pillar with a sculpture of the medieval warrior and knight Roland, created by the Milanese Bonino in 1418. Roland's Columns symbolize, here as in other European cities – especially in harbor towns – the sovereign jurisdiction of a free city-state. The length of Roland's right forearm is also the yardstick for an important Dubrovnik unit of measure, the *ell*, which is carved into the pillar's pedestal.

Above: Opening of the Libertas Festival at the Sponza Palace. Right: The arcade of the Rector's Palace provides a bit of shade.

The *****Palača Sponza** ⑬ (Sponza Palace) on the north of Luža, also known as Fondik, was constructed in the 16th century and formerly served as the customs office. The building's outstanding stonework was carried out by master stonecutters from Korčula. Inside the elegant atrium, which is adorned with arcades, the original bronze figures from the bell tower are kept on display. Above the loggia is a Latin inscription with the text: *Fallere nostra vetant et falli pondera / meque pondero dum merces / ponderant ipse deus* (Cheating is forbidden and it is wrong to falsely weigh; when I weigh goods, God weighs them with me). Dubrovnik's prosperity depended upon well-functioning commerce: the precise gauging of weights and measures and the value of money formed the basis for a sound trade relationship. Inside the palace, therefore, the city's mint and the office of the market watchman – who was responsible for controlling commerce – were also housed. Today, Sponza Palace serves as a museum for Dubrovnik writings. In the evenings, the interior courtyard is converted into a stage for performances of chamber music. In summer, the Libertas Festival is opened here.

In 1480, the Republic erected the **clock tower** with its **bell loggia**. The tower's chimes were used as an alarm and at the same time as signals. Mostly they were used to call the city council members to meetings. The clock showed not only the time of day, but the phases of the moon as well. Two male figures made of bronze hit the bell on the hour. In the course of time, oxidation caused the bronze figures to turn green, which is why they came to be known as *Zelenci* (The Green Ones). The tower began to tilt dramatically as a result of the severe earthquakes here. It was pulled down as a protective measure in 1902 and reconstructed in its original form in 1929. From beneath the clock tower the path to the left leads to the Dominican monastery, and the path to the right to the harbor. A second staircase to the top of the city wall is also here.

The **Mala Onofrijeva česma** (Small Onofrio Fountain) bubbles away on Luža Square. This fountain apparently was built not by Onofrio della Cava, but by the Milanese Pietro di Martino, and is ornamented with symbolic figures. The fountain is set into a niche of the **Palace of the Great Council** ⓮, which is mentioned in a document as early as 1303. The building burned down in 1817 and was rebuilt in 1864 in the neo-Renaissance style of Lombardy. Today the palace is used by the city council to hold meetings and also houses a theater. A section of it is used by the Municipal Café.

Behind the Council Palace the **arsenal** was orignially located, in the huge spaces of which the largest galleys of the day could find room. A large section of the arsenal was torn down in 1863 in order to make room for a new theater building. The wide arcades which open to the harbor, and which now belong to the **Gradska kavana** ⓯ (Municipal Café),

are part of the old arsenal. The best view of the harbor is from the café: you can see fishing boats and barques, the Sv. Ivan and Revelin fortifications, and the ferries that run to the resort island of Lokrum.

The character of the southern end of the square is formed by the richly-adorned Baroque **Sveti Vlaho Church** ⓰ (St. Blasius'), constructed in the early 18th century from plans by a Venetian architect. The church is dedicated to the city's patron saint Blasius, images of whom can be seen on nearly every coat of arms and emblem of Dubrovnik, as well as of city enterprises. The famous **St. Blasius Statue** is to be found on the church's main altar and is a masterpiece by the goldsmiths of Dubrovnik, who made the statue out of gilded silver in the 15th century. In his left hand the saint holds a model of the city as it looked before the earthquake of 1667.

From Luža Square we turn to the south (the walk to the north will be mentioned later). Between St. Blasius' Church and the Municipal Café, Pred dvorom leads to

Southern Dalmatia

the ****Knežev dvor** 🔟 (Rector's Palace), one of the most beautiful buildings in the city. The original palace, which was destroyed by a gunpowder explosion, was replaced by a second palace, built by Onofrio della Cava in late-Gothic style, in 1435. The second palace burned down some 30 years later and was reconstructed in part in Renaissance style. This building, too, was severely damaged: namely by the earthquake of 1667. The present palace, restored with the help of della Cava's original plans, dates from 1739.

In the ***Atrium**, an impressive example of Onofrio's architecture, the only bust of a deserving citizen ever put up by the city-state can bee seen: that of Michele Prazato (Miho Pracat), a ship-owner and banker who bequeathed his entire fortune of 200,000 ducats to the city. The bronze bust is the work of P.P. Giocometti from 1638. Two entrances

Above: Young life in old streets. Right: The St. Blasius reliquary, a masterpiece in gold.

lead to the inner courtyard. One, the State Gate, was only opened on special occasions. The richly-decorated columns in the Atrium date to the 15th century. A lovely Baroque **balustrade staircase** leads to the upper story where, above the doorframe of the portal to the Councilors' Hall, an inscription can be seen which states: *Obliti Privatorum Publica Curate* (Forget the personal and take care of the public things!). The palace also served as the residence of the rector, who was always elected for one month and spent this time basically interned inside, away from his family, and was only allowed to leave on official business. In this way it was hoped that the rector would be able to concentrate completely on his duties. He was elected from the aristocracy, who through this system were by no means the first ones to come up with the idea of quarreling over public offices and prebends, since the new rector could change everything anyway. The palace also houses the **Historijski muzej** (History Museum), which has exhibitions of furniture, paintings, clothing and documents from the city's rich history.

In a corner of the secular center of the city stands a spiritual work of art: the **Velika Gospa** 🔞 (Assumption of Mary Cathedral). According to legend, Richard the Lion-Hearted suffered a shipwreck on his return from the Third Crusade in 1192 and managed to save himself on the island of Lokrum. A generous donation by the king made possible the erection of a church on this site. This Romanesque church is supposed to have been one of the wealthiest in Europe. It was so heavily damaged by earthquakes and fire, however, that it was replaced between 1671 and 1713 by the present structure. The architect Paolo Andreotti furnished the design for the building, for which he used examples of Roman architecture as his inspiration. In the church's interior there are numerous art treasures by local masters, as well as by Italian artists, to be

212 **City Map p. 206, Info p. 217**

seen. Titian's **Assumption of Mary**, from about 1552, is the highlight of the main altar. To the right of the choir is the entrance to the ***treasure chamber**, with, among other things, the gold, siver and filigree **Reliquary of St. Blasius**.

In the east end of the cathedral – undisturbed by all the earthquakes – is the impressive Renaissance-style **Bishop's Palace**. Following Ulica Kneza Damjana Jude along the city wall, which separates the harbor from the residential part of town, you come to **Tvrđava Sv. Ivan** ⑲ (St. John's Fortress), the present-day appearance of which dates back to the 16th century. Three museums are housed inside the fortress. The **Aquarium**, located on the ground floor, has displays of the vivid flora and fauna from the waters around Dubrovnik – and from the Adriatic in general. Upstairs is the **Ethnography Museum**, featuring traditional folk costumes, household articles, hand-crafted works and national folk instruments. In the **Maritime Museum**, Dubrovnik's seafaring tradition is docu-mented with model ships, navigational devices and maps.

To the south of the cathedral and to the south of the market square, a Roman-esque-inspired Baroque staircase leads to the **Jezuitska crkva** ⑳ (Jesuit church) of St. Ignatius. It is an early 18th-century Baroque building by Andrea Pozzo, an important architect and painter in his day, who was a Jesuit himself. The Jesuit Church of Dubrovnik also played its part in the anti-reformation; the defense of Catholic belief in Europe. Frescos here by the Spaniard Gaetano Garcia are among the earliest examples of Jesuit painting in Europe. Since the Jesuits took over all education in Dubrovnik, it is not too surprising that beside the church is the **Collegium Ragusianum** ㉑, where many respected members of the community completed their educations.

Following Ulica Štrosmajerova and further along its western extension, you come to the **Rupe** ㉒; the "Holes." This is actually the granary, which consists of 15 silos carved out of the rock. During the

16th century the city's grain supplies – 1,500 tons of cereals – were stored in the constant 17° C temperature of these vaults. Nowadays, archeological discoveries are kept in storage here.

Turning north from Luža Square, you will find **Sveti Nikola** ㉓ (St. Nicholas' Church) behind the Sponza Palace, at the end of the Prijeko. The 11th-century late-Romanesque building was given a Baroque façade in the 17th century.

A passageway on the left-hand side of the church leads to the ***Bijeli fratri** ㉔ Dominican monastery, one of the most striking architectural monuments in Dubrovnik, (early 14th century). Though the monastery's church was renovated several times during subsequent centuries, it has retained its early-Gothic appearance. The only Romanesque portal in Dubrovnik, the South Portal, was designed by Bonino da Milano in 1419 with a Gothic setting which fit in with the spirit of the times. Gothic as well as Renaissance elements are combined in the interesting 15th-century **choir**. Also worth seeing are the **chapter hall** and the **church treasury**, which contains works of gold and paintings by artists including Titian.

The second main entrance to the town, the ***Ploče vrata** ㉕ (Ploče Gate) and the tower that protects it, the Assimov Tower, both date back to the same era as the Domican monastery; the early 14th century. A bridge behind the Ploče Gate leads to one of Dubrovnik's three main fortresses, the **Revelin** ㉖, which was erected in the 16th century in order to protect the harbor from the north. The state treasury was once located within the Revelin's walls. Nowadays, concerts and traditional folk performances take place on the fortress' open terrace.

The street runs further east to the **Lazareti**. The self-reliant citizens of

Right: The island of Mljet, known for its expanses of pine woods.

Dubrovnik were very aware of their responsibilities toward the poor and the sick members of the community. But safety considerations also played a role in the building of this hospital: the trail of caravans from the hinterland ended near the Revelin, and to protect the city from illnesses or epidemics, new arrivals into Dubrovnik were first admitted into the Lazareti and put into quarantine. The city was especially susceptible because of its extensive trade relationships, and infractions against the quarantine regulations were dealt with very severely. These days, souvenir dealers, artists and a disco are found "in quarantine" here.

Dubrovnik's other large fortress, the ***Lovrijenac** ㉗, is situated on a 40-meter-high rock in the west of the town, and was the most important strategic point in the defense of the city. For this reason not even the soldiers and their officers who were stationed here were trusted as far as they could be thrown. What other reason could there have been for changing the garrison on a monthly basis; including the commanding officer, who came from the aristocracy? Their provisions weren't even sufficient to last a month. Today, theatrical performances are staged in the Lovrijenac. During the Libertas Festival they specialize particularly in performances of Hamlet.

On the northwest corner of the city wall, on the landward side, the **Minčeta Tower** ㉘ watches over the fortifications between the Pile and Ploče Gates. The best view of the old town can be enjoyed from here. At the foot of the immense round fortifications, in what was once the fortress moat, there is a street which connects the Pile and Ploče Towers.

In the **Ploče** quarter, to the north of the Revelin Fortress, is the lower station of the cable car, which was damaged in the war. It used to be go to the top of **Vrh Srđ** (Mt. Sergius): an altitude of 419 meters. During their occupation around 1810, the French selected the summit to set up their

Lokrum Island

Fort Impérial. The view of the old town and the Adriatic is marvelous. The Ploče quarter expands terrace-like along the slopes. The residents here have to be in good shape to carry their shopping up the endless stairs. The walk home is also exhausting for guests at the numerous pensions here. Another great sight is of the Sv. Ivan harbor fortress and Lokrum Island from Ploče's popular beach.

On the western side of Dubrovnik are the modern neighborhoods of **Lapad** and **Gruž**. The new harbor was constructed in the bay of Gruž. Wealthy merchants and aristocrats of the 15th and 16th centuries had their villas built here, the most impressive of which is lovely **Villa Sorkočevič** in Lapad. It dates back to 1521, and contains a Gothic triforium as well as an elegant Renaissance portal.

Behind Lapad, on a spit of land, is the **Babin Kuk** quarter. This neighborhood is compltely tuned in to tourism and contains hotels of various categories, pebble and rock beaches (including a nudist beach), and even an amusement park.

From the old harbor a ferry departs every half hour (starting around noon once an hour) to the resort island of **Lokrum** ❿, which has been declared a national park. Lovely trails lead through thick forests of laurel, pine, cypress, oak and oleander. Rock beaches with clear water (and showers) surround the small island. A section of beach is set aside for nudists. Vacationers can appease their hunger in the restaurant built into the old walls of a one-time monastery. A snack bar with a large terrace also invites visitors to linger awhile. Other rooms of the former monastery house the **Natural Science Museum**, with its ornithology collection and examples of flora and fauna.

*MLJET ISLAND

Ferries from Dubrovnik set out to **Mljet Island** several times per week during the tourist season. This is the southernmost of the large Adriatic islands,

Southern Dalmatia

with the most abundant forests. For nature lovers it is the most attractive island overall. Miljet claims to be *Ogygia*, the island of Calypso, the nymph who held Odysseus prisoner for seven years. In antiquity the Romans maintained large properties here. In the Middle Ages it fell to the principality of Zahumlje, whose rulers passed its possession on to the Benedictines of Monte Gargano in Apulia. It was the Benedictines who built the picturesque monastery here in the 12th century on St. Mary's Island in the middle of Lake Veliko.

The largest town on the island and its administrative center is **Babino Polje ⓫**. The town is located in a fertile hollow almost exactly in the middle of the island. On the island's western end **Mljet National Park** covers an area of 30 square kilometers. The salt-water **Lake Veliko**, which is actually a sea inlet, belongs to the park. The water for the lake is fed in

Above: Guzlas players – here in Čilipi – are quite rare these days.

over the isthmus of Soline. The originally Romanesque **Benediktinski samostan** (Benedictine monastery) on **Otok Sv. Marija** (St. Mary's Island), a popular spot for outings, was renovated into a two-story Renaissance building. The Benedictines abandoned the monastery in the 19th century. In 1961, it was converted into a hotel (at present only the restaurant is open).

Not far away is **Polače ⓭**, the largest and prettiest harbor on the island. In ancient times a magnificent **Roman villa** was located here, the remnants of which can be visited today. The only hotel on the island is found at the nearby Bay of **Pomena ⓮** (Hotel Odisej, tel. 020-744022, fax. 744042).

*★CAVTAT

A little way south of Dubrovnik lies a park on a bay with a lovely view of the city. About 14 kilometers further on, located on a green peninsula, is the seaside resort of **Cavtat ⓯**. Cavtat is ancient *Epidauros*, from which a busy center of trade developed with not one but two natural bays to serve as harbors. In the town's center are two patrician palaces that are worth seeing. In the so-called Rector's Palace – **Knežev dvor** – which dates from the 16th century, a **museum** has been installed. Besides displays of archeological finds, there is also a library containing drawings by Lucas Cranach and Italian masters, among others.

Present day Cavtat lives primarily from tourism. This branch of the economy was temporarily paralyzed by the civil war. The luxurius Hotel Croatia, a ten minute walk from the town center, is a comfortable place to stay.

After 20 kilometers, **Čilipi ⓰**, Dubrovnik's international airport, comes into view, and, after another 15 kilometers, you find yourself face to face with the border to Montenegro, a constituent state of Yugoslavia.

PELJEŠAC (020)

Hotel Ston, Ston, tel. 754001; **Hotel Faraon**, Trpanj, tel. 743422, beach; **Hotel Orsan**, Orebić, tel. 713026, beautiful beach, surfing and diving schools, boat and bike rentals.

Villas and apartments in Orebić, tel. 711067. *CAMPING:* **Prapratno**, Ston, tel. 754000, fax. 413922, pretty beach, sports, May 1-Oct 10; **Glavna plaža**, Orebić, tel. 713399, fax. 713390, beach, tennis; **Dubrava**, Putriković-Pelješac, tel. 756200, shade, beach, tennis.

Bota, in Mali Ston, freshly harvested oysters; **Gostiona Poseidon**, in Orebić right on the main street, excellent mousaka.

HIKING: On Mount Sv. Ilija (about 4-5 hours) starting in Orebić. To Koruna Castle above Ston. Visits to the salterns of Ston.

DUBROVNIK (020)

Turistička zajednica, Cvijete Zuzorić 1/2, tel. 426303, fax. 422480.

Hotel Argentina, Ploče, tel. 440555, fax. 432524, in a small park, rich in tradition, private access to the sea (rock beach), pool; **Hotel Excelsior**, F. Supila 20, tel. 414 222, fax. 414213, on the waterfront; **Hotel President**, Babin Kuk, tel. 441600, 448232/34, fax. 413265, all rooms with view of the sea, private nudist beach; **Grand Hotel Imperial**, Marijana Blažića 2, tel. 412675, fax. 4111340, dancing on the terrace evenings, no private beach; **Hotel Park**, tel. 414022, fax. 425640, private beach, pool, nightclub, sports facilities, sauna, fitness center, restaurant (also vegetarian food).

Hotel Villa Orsula, F. Supila 14, tel. 440555, fax. 432524, near the old town, nice view of the old harbor and Lokrum island, small charming hotel; **Hotel Lapad**, Lapadska Obala 37, Gruž harbor, tel. 432922, fax. 424782, pool and terrace restaurant, boat shuttle to the old harbor; **Hotel Libertas**, tel. 44 0555, fax. 432524, private beach, indoor pool, casino; **Hotel Minčeta**, Babin Kuk, tel. 447600, 448232/34, fax. 413819, affordable; **Hotel Sumratin**, Šetalište Kralja Zvonimira 31, tel. 431031, fax. 23581, in the center of Lapad, villa; **Hotel Zagreb**, Šetalište Kralja Zvonimira 27, tel. 431011, fax. 423581, on pedestrian zone in Lapad, nicely renovated villa, lively in the evening, garden, near a sand beach, tennis.

Private rooms are available through the tourist information office.
CAMPING: **Solitudo**, tel. 448166, fax. 427744, with private pier, tennis, windsurfing, caravan rentals, open year-round.

Aquarium (Sv. Ivan Fortress), 9 a.m. to 1 p.m.; **Maritime Museum**, 9 a.m. to 1 p.m.; **Rector's Palace**, 9 a.m. to noon. **City Walls** 9 a.m. to 7 p.m.

There are numerous specialty restaurants located on the Prijeko in the old town, for example: **Sebastian**, Prijeko 11, tel. 427540; **Restaurant Maestoso**, Kralja Tomislava 1, tel. 420986; **Ragusa**, Zamanija 12, tel. 422435, fax. 434727, 8 a.m. to 11 p.m., high-class restaurant.

Good medium- quality eateries in and around Dubrovnik include: **Restaurant Komin**, Babin Kuk, tel. 448613; **Restaurant Lapad**, Šetalište Kralja Zvonimira (Lapad pedestrian zone), tel. 425644; **Restaurant Amfora**, Obala S. Radića, tel. 433343; **Konoba Kamenice**, Gandulićeva Poljana (market square), tel. 422296, terrace, behind the cathedral; **Gradska kavarna**, Pred dvorom, tel. 426402, stylish coffeehouse with a terrace overlooking the old harbor.

Diskothek Mirage, in Hotel Adriatic, Masarykov put 9; **Arsenalclub**, near the old harbor, discotheque also featuring cabaret shows; **Diskothek Alcatraz**, in Hotel Libertas, Lapad.

MARINAS: **ACY Miho Pracat**, Mokosica, tel. 455020, fax. 455022, in protected bay with standard ACY equipment; **Marina Gruž**, tel. 417999, fax. 417944, yachts up to 20 meters.

SWIMMING: Large gravel beach near the hospital (fee); locals usually swim near Sv. Ivan Fortress. A road between Pile and Lapad leads past the Lovrijenac to the Cloister of St. Mary, behind which lies Danče beach. Taxi boats shuttle to the island of Lokrum, where there is some shade.

EXCURSIONS: Day-long boat trips can be made to **Mljet** and the **Elaphite Islands** of Sipan, Lopud and Koločep. **Lopud** has beautiful beaches for swimming. Special sights are the ruins of the Rector's Palace and the Pracatovič Villa.

FERRIES: June 1-Sept 30: Rijeka – Split – Korčula – Dubrovnik – Bari (I) – Igoumenitsa (GR) once a week; Aug-Sept additional weekend trips Bari – Dubrovnik; Dubrovnik – Igoumenitsa once a week.

June to September: **Libertas-Festival** with international artists from all branches; film festivalcl;assical and pop concerts; theater.

CAVTAT (020)

Croatia, tel. 478242, fax. 478213, private beach with nudist areas, pool, nightclub.
Epidaurus, tel. 478144, fax. 478156.
CAMPING: **Tiha**, tel. 478271, fax. 478156, shady spots, caravan rentals, tennis courts, open from June to October.

MONTENEGRO

MONTENEGRO

Montenegro is a constituent republic of Yugoslavia and runs from Nerceg-Novi on the border with Croatia to the Bojana River, which borders Albania. The republic's original name, *Crna Gora* (Black Mountain: *Monte Nero* in Italian; *Monte Negro* in Spanish), still accurately describes this pristine land, where wide forests and deep ravines offer scenes of rugged beauty, which the German writer Karl May used as the backdrop for his book *In den Schluchten des Balkan* ("In the Ravines of the Balkans").

But Montenegro also has another face: the heavily-populated 250-kilometer-long coastline, with historical centers such as the one-time principality and kingdom of Herceg-Novi, Kotor, Budva and Bar. It wasn't by chance that Cetinje was chosen as its capital. Its geographical location – in the mountains yet close to the coast – was intended to balance out the country's opposites.

The most important cultural impulses in this region all came from the coastline, which in antiquity was settled first by a number of Illyrian tribes, then by the Greeks, and later by the Romans. After

Left: Sveti Stefan, Montenegro's most picturesque island.

the decline of the Roman Empire and the acquisition of the land by the Slavs, Montenegro remained under Byzantine rule longer than did Dalmatia, falling in the 10th century to the independent principality of Zeta, which held it until the 12th century.

Under the founder of the Serb Empire, Stefan Nemanja, Kotor developed into the most important center for maritime trade and the second most important city in the empire. Kotor's influence on the Serbian royal court was considerable. After the death of the last and the mightiest Serb czar, Dušan, in 1355, Kotor placed itself, with its surrounding territories, under the protection of the Hungarian-Croatian King Ljudevit.

As political conditions in the Balkans became more and more unstable due to the expansion of the Ottoman Empire, the coast fell under Venetian dominion. It was in Montenegro that the long war between the Turks and the Venetians was most fiercely waged. It was only in a few cities, such as Kotor and Perast, for example, that Venice could maintain its dominancen. In the 16th cenutry, the Turks managed, at Herceg-Novi, at Bar and at Ulcinj, to gain access to the sea.

The continual changing of the ruling powers in Montenegro eventually led to a state of apathy in the populace; making it

Montenegro

all the more astonishing that Slavic nationalism and striving for independence actually got underway in this region. In the 19th century the influential prince-bishops, with Russian aid, succeeded in founding an independent state which was recognized by the Berlin Congress of 1878. In 1910, the Kindom of Montenegro was established under King Nicholas I. The two World Wars lead Montenegro again into a union with Serbia, with which it today forms the Federal Republic of Yugoslavia.

Before the conflict in Yugoslavia, tourism was the most important source of income in a country poor in mineral resources and industry. The collapse of the tourist economy in 1991 presented the Yugoslav government with massive unemployment and a weak infrastructure. Minister President Đukanovič's visit to the U.S. in April 1996 was solid evidence that the present situation does not look good at all: while there he asked for economic aid for Montenegro, also in regard to more autonomy vis-à-vis Serbia. In 1998, the first groups of package tourists began returning to Montenegro.

Coastal Cities, Mountain Roads and Sand Beaches

Montenegro's highlights include the coastal cities, with their Mediterranean character and their almost oriental bazaars, the high pass across Mount Lovčen (the famous Black Mountain, *Monte Negro*) above Kotor, which gives a very graphic image of the grandiose mountain world of this small country, and the kilometers-long sand beaches.

The popular beaches of Mogren and Slovenska plaža ("the Queen's Beach," once the summer residence of kings) near Budva , Miločer near Sveti Stefan and the four-kilometer-long sand beach of the nudist island Ada, on the mouth of the

Right: Budva's historic old town.

Bojana River (16 kilometers from Ulcinj), belong without any doubt to the prettiest beaches in Europe.

In **Igalo ❶**, just before Herceg-Novi, a health resort arose after the Second World War where Marshal Tito used to come to have his arthritis treated; the mud baths here are said to work wonders.

That Montenegro was once in Turkish hands can be felt in ***Herceg-Novi ❷**, where there are many charming oriental houses. From 1483 on, the city was the seat of a *sanjak*, an administrative region of the Ottoman Empire, and was an important harbor for the Turks, who could easily control access to the Bay of Kotor from here. It wasn't until 1687 that Venice was able to conquer the city. In addition to the fortress grounds, the Turkish **Salaat Kula** (clock tower) is of special interest. In one of the three churches of the nearby Serbian Orthodox **Savina Monastery** there are frescos from the 19th century and a valuable library that is open to visitors.

Perast ❸ is located on the shores of the Bay of Kotor, along which runs a beautiful coastal road. This town was awarded special privileges by the Venetians in their struggle against the Ottoman Turks for its unwavering loyalty. During the Baroque era, wealthy residents of the city, above all ship owners and captains, had their opulent palaces built upon the slopes of Mt. Ilijino. The **Municipal Museum**, containing historical documents, model ships, and collections of historical clothing and weapons, is located inside **Bujović Palace**, built in 1693. Of special interest is the war flag of the Russian fleet: it was awarded by Peter the Great to a Perast captain for his services in the battle against Sweden near Gangut in 1714.

A visit to the **Baroque church** on nearby **Gospa od Škrpjela Island ❹** is well worth making. The church's unusual tower is dotted with embrasures. In the interior of the church there are some 70 oil paintings by Peraster Baroque painter

Map p. 222, Info p. 223

Tripo Kokoljy, a student of Palma the Younger. Furthermore, some 2,500 silver votive plaques from Peraster's seafarers are also kept here; donated in gratitude for having been rescued at sea.

The port city of **★Kotor ❺** nestles on the rocks of the Lovčen Massif mountains, which tower almost vertically overhead. At the height of the city's medieval development, construction was begun on the **city wall**, which is still an impressive sight. The triangularly laid out city center and the 260-meter-high local mountain, **Sveti Ivan**, are surrounded by the five-kilometer-long, three- to 15-meter-thick and in some places up to 20-meter-high wall. The peak of Mount Sv. Ivan is crowned by a fortress.

Though the city may have been shaken by earthquakes on numerous occasions, it has been rebuilt each time. In the picturesque old town, which has retained its medieval appearance, is the 12th-century **Sveti Tripun Cathedral** (St. Tripun's). This is Kotor's most important object of interest.

The Romanesque building style was brought here by Benedictine monks. The Byzantine-Romanesque **Sveta Maria** (St. Mary's Church), from the 13th century, however, is also considered to be one of the most beautiful buildings on the entire coast. The **Maritime Museum** shows clearly that Kotor can look back on the longest sea-faring tradition on the entire coast (with its beginnings in the 9th century).

An overwhelming **mountain road**, said to be one of the most breathtaking in Europe, begins just behind Kotor. This serpentine road climbs up to the **Krstac Pass ❻**: a height of nearly 900 meters. At the level of the pass a paved road branches off to the 1,749-meter **Mount Lovčen ❼**, on the peak of which a mausoleum, created by Ivan Meštrović to the poet, bishop and ruler of Montenegro, Petar Petrović Njegoš (1813-1851) is located.

The city of **★Budva ❽**, which was founded by the Greeks, is, like Kotor and Perast, considered to be one of the jewels

Montenegro

of the Montenegrin coast. The fortress here was constructed on the ruins of a church and contains, therefore, something that is probably unique among fortresses: a frescoed wall. The old town was unfortunately heavily damaged by an earthquake in the 1980s.

On a rock formation south of Budva is the picturesque former fishing village of ****Sveti Stefan ❾**, connected to the mainland by a narrow sand bar. Thanks to tourism, the village has evolved more or less into a huge hotel, to which only guests have free access: everyone else has to pay an entrance fee. Sveti Stefan is the most luxurious vacation spot in all of Montenegro. The idyllic location and the comfortable facilities attract tourists now as before.

With **Stari Bar ❿**, Montenegro possesses a unique ghost town: when the Turks were driven out in 1878 the city was destroyed by powerful gunpowder blasts. Just over four kilometers away on a wooded bay, another town, **Novi Bar ⓫**, was founded. The ruins of Stari Bar were left to themselves.

The last Montenegrin city before the Albanian border is **Ulcinj ⓬**, the once-notorious base of the pirate Ulič Alija, whose men plundered ships – even Turkish ones!– in the southern Adriatic as far as Corfu and the Neretva Delta. Piracy was not eliminated here until the early 19th century. Many of the buildings in Ulcinj are from the Ottoman era, such as the Sinan Pasha Mosque, the *Hamam* (Turkish bath), the *Salaat Kula* (clock tower) and several *Türbe* (Turkish graves). The entire old town radiates an oriental atmosphere.

From Novi Bar and Ulcinj, scenic pass roads lead to famous **Skadarsko jezero ⓭** (Lake Scutari), which is the largest fresh-water lake in the southern Balkans (40 kilometers long, twelve kilometers wide and on average seven meters deep). Two-thirds of the lake are on the Montenegrin side of the border.

MONTENEGRO

ℹ️ Yugoslav embassies abroad: AUSTRALIA: Canberra, tel. (616) 295-1458; CANADA: Ottowa, tel. (613) 233-6289; U.K.: London, tel. (171) 370-6105; U.S.: New York, tel. (212) 879-8700, Washington, D.C., tel. (202) 462-6566. **Tourist information in Montenegro**: Tourist Office in Budva, tel. (086) 41814, Tourist Office in Ulcinj, tel. (085) 81608.

☎ The country code for Montenegro is 00381. To call from Montenegro to the U.S. or Canada dial 991, to the U.K. 9944, to Australia 9961. Phone calls can be made from post offices (in summer from 7 a.m. to 8 p.m.) and hotels.

📠 *GETTING THERE:* From Belgrad there are regular **domestic flights** to Tivat (Montenegro).

The **train route** from Belgrad to Bar is one of the most scenic in the entire Balkan region.

Between Ancona and Bari (Italy) und Bar (Montenegro), **car ferries** travel several times per week during the summer months. The express ferry line Rijeka (Croatia) – Igoumenitsa (Greece) is expected to be serving Bar in the near future.

🚗 *ENTRY REQUIREMENTS:* Travelers from EU and other Western countries require a visa and a passport valid for at least six months from date of entry for travel to Yugoslavia, and therefore to Montenegro. Children under the age of 16 must be entered in a parent's passport or else have their own passport. Visas can be obtained at Yugoslav consulates in many major cities; a few phone numbers for Yugoslav embassies are listed at the top of the page – they can be contacted for more precise information.

Accident insurance must be purchased at the border, the cost of which depends upon the duration of your stay.

Those who have booked a package tour must simply carry their passport with them. Entry cards must be filled out when flying, either in the airplane or at the airport; Montenegrin immigrations officers do not acknowlege passports.

According to the tourist office, the Croatian-Montenegrin border crossing at Debeli Brijeg, on the Adriatic Magistrala south of Dubrovnik, is open at the present time. Nonetheless, it is strongly advisable to obtain current travel requirements and information for the land route to Montenegro from a Yugoslav consulate prior to travel.

MONEY: The unit of currency is the Yugoslav New Dinar. 1 N Dinar = 100 Para; exchange rate: 1 US$ = ca. 5 N Dinar. Taking sufficient cash with you is recommended; traveler's checks and Eurochecks are only accepted to a maximum of around US$ 250 in banks, as a rule, and are exchanged only for N Dinar. Commissions are charged for the cashing of Eurochecks, or they may be exchanged at a bad rate. Credit cards are accepted only in some shops and restaurants.

Bank notes and coins in the local currency can be taken into or out of the country only up to a maximum of 30 N Dinar! There is no limit on the amount of foreign currency that may be brought into the country, though a customs declaration must be filled out.

HEALTH: There is no agreement between Yugoslavia and Western countries regarding health insurance coverage. All costs for medical treatment and medication are to be paid for privately on the spot. It is recommended that you obtain private medical travel insurance before going to Montenegro. These policies are often accompanied by theft and accident insurance.

LANGUAGE: The official language is Serb. Street signs and informational signs are written in Cyrillic, as are newspapers. English is spoken in many hotels, restaurants and shops.

LOCAL TIME: In summer, local time is CET (Central European Time) minus one hour.

CLIMATE / TRAVEL SEASON: The best time to travel here are the months from May to September. In July and August the temperature can reach 40° C. On average there are four rainy days per month. In June, July and August the sun shines for ten to twelve hours per day.

🛏️ *HOTELS:* ☺☺☺ **Sveti Stefan**, tel. (086) 68090, fax. 52145. This former island fishing village has been converted into the most luxurious accommodation on the Montenegrin coast, with coarse sand beaches, a restaurant with terrace overlooking the sea, a small swimming pool and spa. The rooms are stylish and elegant.

☺☺ **Avala**, in Budva, tel. (086) 51022, fax 51540, hotel at the edge of town, good place for swimming, breakfast buffet, shops, doctor, pool above the sea, water sports, five minutes from Mogren Beach; **Bellevue Cer**, in Ulcinj, tel. (085) 81711, in a pine park near the long sand beaches, bus connection to Ulcinj, simple rooms with balcony, restaurant with garden terrace.

Nudist Colony Bojana, Ada Island, tel. (085) 81351, rooms and apartments on the nature preserve island, long, quiet sand beaches, crystal-clear waters, restaurants, tennis courts, volleyball on the beach, possibilities of horseback riding and surfing.

🚗 *EXCURSIONS:* One-day trips are available from Budva to the largest fjord-like bay on the Adriatic, Kotor, which is listed as a UNESCO World Heritage Sight, and to Lovcen National Park.

A wonderful way to experience nature is to visit Lake Scutari (Skadarsko jezero) in the hinterland, where a number of rare species of birds, among them storks, herons and pelicans, can be observed in their natural habitat.

Montenegro

THE KARST

The wild romantic allure of the coastal landscape of Dalmatia, the smoothness of the hilly region of Istria, and the unique natural beauty of the Postojnska Jama, the Škocjanske Jame, the Krka Waterfalls and the Plitvice Lakes are all situated on the same geomorphological phenomenon: the karst.

The name originates from a barren mountain range dotted with white limestone blocks in the hinterland of Trieste, referred to by the Italians as *carso*, and the Slovenes and Croatians as *kras* (thin, rocky ground). It was within this small region that the natural phenomena and characteristics of this type of landscape were first examined closely. The name now applies to similar landscapes found throughout the world; whether in China, in Mexico, or in the United States.

Above and right: Mother nature really went to work here – the karst-born caverns of Postojna and Škocjan.

The Dinaric Alps and the backs of the Adriatic islands make up the largest connecting karst region in Europe. Rain is not lacking here, but, oddly enough, bodies of water, such as streams, rivers and lakes are missing; this is a typical karst phenomenon, because the precipitation seeps down beneath the limestone while the process of "karstation" is actually taking place. The purer the limestone, the more fissures it has and the higher the carbon dioxide content of the rainwater, the more intensive the process of corrosion. Over time, the seeping water loosens the stone more and more, thereby enlarging the existing fissures. As time goes on, cavities are created that soon become gaping holes. Karstation affects only the soluble stone, especially the Dinaric limestone.

Most noticeable in a karst region are the so-called *dolinas*. These are sinkholes or bowl-like cavities of from about two to 1,500 meters in diameter and up to 500 meters deep. Sinkholes exist at intersections of chasms where the corrosion is

more advanced until, finally, the crevice, which has existed for millions of years, caves in. The grandest one of all is the 400-meter-deep red dolina existing since 1942 on the northern edge of the Imotski Polje (about 20 kilometers northeast of Makarska).

Especially in Istria dolinas can often be seen along many of the roads. Besides these, there are also flat, bowl-like dolinas (*uvalas*) and potholes (*ponore*). The *poljes*, on the other hand, are huge sinkholes – depressions with jagged boundaries that can cover over 100 square kilometers.

Seeping rainwater often forms sharp-edged ridges and cracks in the bare limestone, which marks the high plateaus of most of the Dalmatian islands and coastal strips. In total, the karst covers more than 80 percent of the Croatian coast.

Karstic Caverns

The erosion process does not only have a lasting effect on the appearance of the landscape, it is also responsible for the formation of caves within the rock: through the transplantation process entire cave systems have been created.

The most glaring examples of this are the caves of Škocjan and Postojna. In a process that takes thousands of years, the water has managed to make its way through the limestone. Interestingly, it did not create a surface system, but rather a wide branching underground water system; the drought on the surface contrasts the abundant underground supply.

In the Kras Plateau region of Slovenia almost 6,000 underground caves have been discovered, many of which can even be explored on foot. A particularly impressive example of a karst cave is that which the Reka River (Timavo) created underground: this river, which dug out the Škocjan Grottos, disappears at the end of the cave in a karst channel, only to resurface for a mere 200 meters after 40 kilometers of underground travel before finally running off into the Adriatic by Duino.

Man's Ruinous Exploitation

If you drive on to Dalmatia after visiting the great karstic caves of Slovenia, you arrive at the Velebit Mountains. You cannot fail to notice the significant difference in the vegetation. The mountains of Dalmatia have all the features of a karstic region, but exhibit a noticeably sparser vegetation.

The differences here lie not only in the pronounced Mediterranean climate found around Rijeka and Senj, as opposed to the sub-alpine climate of Slovenia, but especially in the influence that the people have had on the landscape immediately surrounding them.

Karst regions do not necessarily have to be sparse in vegetation, even if this seems like a characteristic of the Adriatic coast. The so-called naked karst, that is, barren shards of rock that stick out of the

Above: Sheep and goats have accelerated the erosion process in the Kornats. Right: Maquis covers the ground in karst regions.

topsoil, came about thanks to the human touch. What was originally a thick covering of broad-leaved and coniferous trees is now a barren, desolate space: the islands of the Kvarner Gulf and the Kornats, the peaks of the Velebit and the Biokovo ranges are glaring examples of this starkness.

Through the wide ranging clearing of the forests – brought about for the most part by charcoal makers, who provided the area with one of its most important sources of energy – these regions revealed themselves as more and more susceptible to erosion. The surface soil was gradually opened to the elements and washed away by wind and rain. As the coastal region fell under Venetian dominance, the forests were almost completely cut down because of the need for timber in Venice, and for the construction of ships for its vast flotilla. Venice was built on thousands of stilts that came from Istria at the time.

The forests were unable to regenerate because of the presence of pasturing

sheep and goats; the loss due to the herds was just too great, the young saplings immediately fell prey to the goats. The progressive destruction of the trees ultimately led to complete and radical deforestation. Soon after, ground erosion set in, uncovering the rocks that make up the coastal mountains.

The powerful winds gusting in from the mountains during the winter months play an equally important role in the erosion process. The cold and fearsome bora from the northeastern inland regions hits almost the entire coast, the sea and the islands with hurricane-like gusts.

In the past, the dense forest covering the land absorbed much of the winds' force. Once the trees were cleared, however, soil erosion progressed unfettered, and eventually spread to the offshore islands of Krk, Rab and Pag. The vegetation on the sides facing the mainland is accordingly sparse.

The areas that were able to maintain their soil composition are the large karstic sinkholes such as the dolinas and the

related poljes, long elliptical depressions. In the winter, these troughs overflow when the underground channels and caverns fill with water, and the dolinas and poljes turn into veritable lakes. They often stay that way through all of spring and only drain in the early summer. The soaked loamy soil of some of the poljes are then used for agricultural purposes – a good example for this is the Čepić Polje in Istria (north of Labin).

In the meantime, maquis and smaller related shrubs have formed in many karst regions. In the highly karstic regions, the vegetation is dominated by low, frugal plants, tough survivors of the harsh climatic and soil conditions.

Despite the austerity, the flora here has its own special, subtle beauty: in summer the region is covered with aromatic herbs such as thyme, rosemary, sage and lavender. And in tiny crevices lovely little flowers, such as cyclamen, anemones, various kinds of daffodils, and lilies, among others, find adequate space and nourishment to survive.

Karst

227

WATER SPORTS ON THE CROATIAN COAST

The Croatian coastline may only be 530 kilometers long as the crow flies, but because of its many bays and inlets the total combined measurable coastline of the mainland and the islands is a mighty 5,800 kilometers.

The northwest to southeast layout of the coast and the Dinaric mountain range that runs parallel to the coastline provide for distinct climatic differences. In this regard, the regularly occurring local winds are also worth mentioning.

In winter, the average water temperature tends to be about 12° C, while in summer, temperatures of up to 26° C may be reached. The water temperature doesn't begin to sink again until about October.

Holiday makers who plan to take their own boats with them to Croatia should be

Above: The best way to explore the Dalmatian coast – in a two-master.

aware of certain regulations. First and foremeost: what exactly, according to the standards of the country, is a boat considered to be?

A boat can be an open speed boat, for example, a dinghy, a catamaran, an inflatable boat, or anything else that floats but does not have covered sleeping quarters on board. Any boat with a covered cabin is considered to be a yacht. The difference is important, as this qualification influences the basis of harbor tariffs and taxes.

The importation of boats by land – that is to say, by car or truck – is possible without any further formalities whatsoever: an oral declaration to customs officials is sufficient. Before a boat over three meters long or a motor boat can take to the water, however, harbor authorities must be notified. It is strongly advised to keep a copy of the boat's bill of sale on hand, so that payment of sales taxes can be verified to customs officials. Boats transported by trailer with a total length of over 18 meters require a special permit, the obtainment of which is coupled with a road-use tax.

For boats requiring permits, these are valid for one year from the date of registration. Registration fees are allocated for the safety of marine traffic and are used exclusively for the improvement of sea rescue operations along the Croatian coast. The tariffs for open boats and yachts are as follows: up to four meters, approx. US $37; four to five meters, approx. US $49; yachts up to seven meters, approx. US $108; and yachts from nine to ten meters, approx. US $160.

If you live aboard a yacht, you are required to register with the police; this can be done directly at the marina, at a tourist office or at a police station nearby. The registration card should be kept in a safe place. Should an operator's permit be necessary for certain classes of boat, the regulations in Croatia in this regard are similar to those in many other European contries.

The Croatian coast is a true El Dorado for hobby sailors and yachters. The extremely interesting coastline and the nearby islands offer a myriad of bays that are ideal for boating: that you can sometimes have a beautiful, isolated bay all to yourself only increases the pleasure. The supply network for all classes of boats for fuel, spare parts and food is extremely tight so that, with good planning, long trips along the coast or from island to island can easily be undertaken even by smaller yachts.

Chartering boats along the Croatian coast is ideal: in just about every marina boats of every type can be rented, and they can be hired with or without a skipper. In this way it is possible even for the average consumer to become master of a twelve-meter cabin cruiser. Clubs and organizations making use of these services can enjoy individualized vacations when traveling together.

In addition to the other kinds of boats on offer, sailing trips are also readily available. There are travel agencies specializing in romantic two- and three-masted schooners. No one has to miss the comfort of hotels on these trips, either, since everything has been thought of; the crews take care not only of transportation and lodging, but also of providing tasty meals. You can pretty much drop anchor anywhere you please, and take heavenly swims in deserted, picturesque bays, far from the masses of tourists.

For sightseeing or shopping, your itinerary might include larger ports, such as Zadar, Split or Dubrovnik, depending on how long or how far to the south the trip being made is. Most of these tours are taken in one direction only – either to the south or to the north – and at the final port passengers are exchanged for the return trip.

Early summer is the best time of year for sailing here; in May and June the winds are most favorable. Mid-summer brings dead calm; although a dreaded sirocco may blow in, with the corresponding effect on the sea.

For those who only want to have a quick whiff of the sailor's life, a "pirate's voyage" can be taken from just about any larger town which has its own marina. Normally this is simply a mundane dinner of fish and seafood aboard an older sailing vessel, which doesn't have much to do with pirates, really, except perhaps for the table manners which might be seen on board.

The Dalmatian coast also offers paradisical conditions to scuba divers. The underwater world here shows itself to be in a marvellous state, especially around the islands: the general maritime routes don't touch them, leaving the flora and fauna of the sea undisturbed. There are plenty of places where air tanks can be refilled, although it is better to bring your own equipment with you if you can, as this service is not available everywhere. Keep in mind that harpooning is strictly forbidden!

Water Sports

Those who prefer snorkeling to scuba diving will also get their money's worth here, as most sections of the interesting coastline are rocky and karstic. There is plenty of coral, and many different species of fish have made their homes in the nooks and crannies of the mussel-covered reefs. For snorkeling it is best to avoid areas with lots of beachfront and the usual crowds, and to look for desirable out-of-the-way spots.

The Dalmatian coast is ideal above all for swimming: the high waves can hardly get into many of the bays and the surface of the water can be absolutely mirror-like. The best-known swimming areas are Mali Lošinj, the Kornats and Korčula.

The wind on the Croatian coast provides ideal conditions for windsurfing. There are wind-protected bays for beginners, and for experienced windsurfers the islands of Pag, Murter and Brač are especially popular. Most hotels which have their own beaches rent out surfboards, as do many campgrounds. Those who want to customize and maintain their own equipment might have a hard time of it in Croatia, as there are hardly any specialty stores here.

Water skiing is only available in the larger tourist areas and is, therefore, accordingly expensive.

Regarding the Wind

The typical winds of the Adriatic are the *bora*, the *sirocco* (also called the *yugo*), the *mistral* and the *nevera*. The most-feared wind of all, the northeast bora, comes about most commonly when there is high pressure over the Balkan mainland. The bora creeps over the high coastal mountains and drops with immense force onto the sea. Bora-endangered areas are those where the wind hits hardest, such as valleys, and those where the wind creates huge differences in temperature while ploughing its

Above: The Adriatic waters are ideal for snorkelers. Right: Wind conditions along the coast make this a paradise for windsurfers.

way over mountain ranges: the Gulf of Trieste, the Kvarner Gulf, the Velebit Channel, Šibenik and surroundings, Split, the Pelješac Peninsula and Dubrovnik belong to these regions.

The bora is treacherous: it appears very suddenly and can therefore be dangerous. The bora's appearance cannot be precisely predicted, though residents can often read the first signs of its arrival; for example, the dark rolling clouds covering the mountain peaks when everywhere else the sun is shining, or the first foam on the waves rolling in from the northeast. When the bora comes blowing in, smaller boats are very likely to soon find themselves in distress. The further away from the coast you are, the more the effects of the bora can be felt. In the summer, the bora often lasts only a few hours; in the winter, on the other hand, it can last an entire week, and can bring extremely cold temperatures in its wake.

The other ill wind that blows no good is the sirocco, which blasts in from the south. A heavily-clouded sky, warm air mass and sometimes even desert sand accompany a considerable movement of the sea, which has made the safe entry into a marina difficult for many a boat. A sirocco often lasts for several days, and it has also been known to happen that a sirocco alternates with a bora.

But not all winds are bad winds: there are also friendly ones, like the mistral, which by and large brings pleasant weather along with it. The mistral generally blows in from the northwest, begins gusting around noon, and quiets down again in the evening, so that a planned warm evening stroll need not be put off by any means.

The nevera is a severe western wind that often brings heavy thunderstorms with it and is most common in the summer months. The thunderstorms are normally of short duration and tend to cool things off pleasantly.

If there is such a thing as a rule when it comes to the wind, it is this: During the day the wind normally comes from the sea; during the evening, from inland.

WHAT'S COOKING

The gastronomic pedigree of the Adriatic coast is just as interesting and varied as its history. First there were the fishermen and shepherds who prepared their simple meals over macchia fires, then oriental elements brought by the Turks, and finally influences from Venice and later from the Habsburg monarchy. This gave rise to a wide range of culinary delights that are full of surprises for the foreign palate. The particular living conditions on the islands, and the very limited agricultural possibilities, especially when it came to cultivating certain types of vegetables, gave rise to a specific type of nutrition for the people along the coast. As the ground became increasingly karstic (see the feature on page 224), the fields produced less and less. Putting nourishing and tasty dishes on the table required

Above: Herbal spirits, a treat for the eye and the palate. Right: Fresh fish is always the best bet along the coast.

a considerable degree of imagination on the part of generations of cooks. Especially on the islands of the Kvarner Gulf, which have very poor soil in many spots, very little meat was eaten. There were simply not enough fields to keep large animals, and the uneven and jagged karst floor, with its ruts and sharp edges, was too dangerous for cattle.

Vegetables, fresh salads and, naturally, fish wound up on the table, as well as a little mutton and wine. A solid helping of meat was something for holidays, weddings and days of heavy physical labor. The dishes were prepared with olive oil, wine vinegar, and local herbs.

A typical Istrian "mainland" dish is a strong minestrone (*minestra*), often made with corn and beans. One of the classic recipes of the islands is barley stew with lamb chops – showing exactly what ingredients the islands have to offer; barley, which is easier to grow than wheat, mutton, onions, garlic, bay leaves, parsley and salt. *Peka*-style roast lamb, prepared in a casserole with potatoes and vegetables and cooked on wood coals, or lamb roasted on a spit, are still the traditional feasts on the islands and along the coast. The roast is kept juicy by being covered with bacon and basted with beer. The most famous lamb roasts are on the islands of Plavnik (south of Krk) and Cres.

The Courses of a Meal

Čorba is one of the more typical soups (*juhe*) you will find. It tastes slightly sour, and is usually prepared in a myriad of variations. A perennial favorite is a soup made with lamb known as *juha od junjetine*. *Riblja juhe*, which is prepared with fish, is particularly popular along the coast. However, do not confuse this dish with *brodet*, a fish stew that makes use of mostly small fish, such as anchovies. The stew is slow-cooked with olive oil, onions and tomatoes, and is flavored with wine, parsley and garlic. *Brodet* is eaten with bread or polenta.

Hors d'oeuvres are not nearly as varied and phenomenally numerous as in neighboring Italy. Popular openers are sausage or ham. *Pršut* – savory Dalmatian air-cured or Istrian smoked ham, served in paper-thin slices – is one of the great favorites when it comes to appetizers. Often hot peppers, mushrooms and a variety of cheeses are eaten with the ham.

Among the various cheeses, *paški sir*, an aromatic sheep's cheese from the island of Pag, has a special rating. A truly fine delicacy, too, is *kajmak*, the cream of cooked milk, salted and stored in wooden barrels, and then either eaten spread on bread, or used in baking. On the southern Dalmatian islands of Brač, Hvar and Korčula, marinated fish (anchovies and mackerel) are served as appetizers. Another delicacy that is often in the hors d'oeuvres category is fried peppers, pickled with garlic.

Fish has always been the main ingredient in traditional cooking along the coast. One way of preparing any type of fish is

charcoal-grilling. Among the finest, and hence most expensive varieties of fish are the breams, *zubatac* (toothed bream) and *orada* (gold bream), and *brancin* (sea perch). Somewhat cheaper and always good is the *tabinja* (sole). Red dragon fish (*škarpin*) cooked in broth is also highly recommendable. Special delicacies include oysters on ice with lemon (around Limski Fyord and in Ston), *prstaci na buzaru* (Buzara-style mussels) and *šcampi na buzaru* (scampi in its own stock with olive oil, onion, diced tomato, bread crumbs, pepper and wine). In inner and north Istria, the pasta or lamb chops with truffels should be sampled.

Among the crustaceans, which are also found in on the rocky seabed of the Adriatic, lobster is not as frequently found on menus as spiny lobster is. Lobster (*jastog*) is boiled and basted with a paste of herbs and white wine (*kuhani jastog*). For those on a budget, pasta and risotto (*rižoto*) with mussels or scampi (or both), and *crni rižoto* (black risotto) with squid are recommended.

Unfortunately, squid is often unimaginatively dunked in batter and deep-fried, though it is now and then served as *punjene lignje* (stuffed squid), or else as *lignje na žaru* (grilled), served with a dip of olive oil, garlic and parsley.

In the restaurants specializing in fish, you usually choose your fish first and then the recipe. You should not feel it impolite to take a very careful look at the fish. Your nose might tell you enough right off the bat. If the eyes are filmy, you can assume the animal is not fresh. To be absolutely sure, check behind the gills, which should show a healthy red color. The gill lamellae should not be stuck to each other, either. If the fish fails to pass muster on all three counts, discreetly choose another.

Where meat is concerned, the coastal regions have mainly produced dishes using lamb (*janjetina*) and goat. Beef and

Above: The more the merrier at mealtime.
Right: Western Istria and Peljesac have a reputation for good wines.

pork dishes come from inland Croatia. Balkan dishes include *čevapčiči, pleskavica* (both made of ground meat) and *ražnjiči* (a meat kebab). Often you will find stuffed peppers, stuffed cabbage (*sarma*) and *hajdučki čevap*, which consists of marinated lamb and other kinds of meat with onions. Mousaka (*musaka*) is a favorite dish in Dalmatia born in Greece; and *pilav* (rice with chicken or meat) from the Orient has also established itself in the local gastronomy. A number of other rice dishes also appear on the menus, generally derived from various Italian risottos. *Đuveč* – vegetable risotto seasoned with paprika – is often served as a side dish. Another spicy side dish based on paprika is the hot red mousse *ajvar*.

What influenced desserts was the art of *patisserie* introduced by the Austrians. This is particularly true of the Kvarner Gulf. Puff pastry items, such as strudel, and *palačinka* (sweet omelets) dominate the range. Highly recommendable is the *kremšnite*: puff pastry filled with vanilla or cream pudding.

Wines

The tastiest foods would be of little interest were it not for the appropriate liquid accompaniment. Istria and Dalmatia both offer a broad and yet easily available supply of native wines. As usual, if you can't decide, the best thing to do is ask for the local house wine.

There are some very fine quality wines (*čuveno vino* and *vrhunsko vino*), and a classification by region similar to the system of Italian DOC wines. The Istrian wines are on the fruity side and don't have such a high sugar content as the Dalmatian wines, which is why they are such a relish to the drinker.

"Heavy caliber" Dalmatian red wines, such as the *dingač* or *postup*, are by no means a rarity. Their alcohol content is about 14 percent, which is well above the French, Italian or German norm. On the other hand, Croats normally only drink their wine straight with meals. Wine mixed with tap water (*bevanda*) or mineral water (*gemišt*) makes a very refreshing drink for locals and tourists alike on a hot summer day.

Native wines are normally not diluted, and hence retain their pure, unadulterated character. Red wines have a very dark color and a full-bodied – and at times dry – bouquet. White wines are similar in character and are also somewhat heavy.

The best wines come from western Istria and from the Pelješac Peninsula in southern Dalmatia. Istrian red wines include: *porečki merlot*, *porečki teran*, *teran* (Pazin) and *cabernet sauvignon porečki*. Among the most popular Istrian white wines on the market are *malvazija rovinjska* and *pinot*.

Dalmatia's red wines are called *dingač*, *postup*, plavac and vranac. The best-known white wines from Istria include *grk*, *pošip*, *maraština* and *malvazija*.

To top off an opulent meal, the coastal folk are in the habit of drinking a dessert

wine. The *prošek* is famous. Its special features are a coppery, dark yellow color and high sugar content (100 grams per liter). The ancient Romans were familiar with this wine, calling it *vinum sanctum*, or sacred wine. The grapes are dried in the sun before being pressed for a sweet must (28 percent sugar), which is then fermented. The wine is stored in bottles that are stuck in the sand. The older the wine, the better the quality. The *prošek dioklecijan* from Split enjoys widespread distribution.

What remains after grape pressing, the pomace, is distilled into a drink known as *lozovača* (sometimes simply called *loza*), which is similar to grappa. *Travarica* is a very popular spirit flavored with herbs. And known well beyond Croatia's borders is *šljivovica*, the tasty plum brandy that has caught many a traveler to Croatia unawares and left them with a mighty hangover.

Maraskino is a transparent liqueur distilled from wild cherries. It is usually sipped as a digestive.

METRIC CONVERSION

Metric Unit	US Equivalent
Meter (m)	39.37 in.
Kilometer (km)	0.6241 mi.
Square Meter (sq m)	10.76 sq. ft.
Hectare (ha)	2.471 acres
Square Kilometer (sq km)	0.386 sq. mi.
Kilogram (kg)	2.2 lbs.
Liter (l)	1.05 qt.

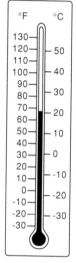

SLOVENIA

TRAVEL PREPARATIONS

Information

Slovenian Tourist Offices abroad:
UK: 2, Canfield Place, London NW6 3BT, tel. 0171/ 372-3767, fax. 0171/ 372-3763. *US:* 345 East 12th Street, New York, NY 10003, tel. (212) 358 96 86, fax. (212) 358 90 25; e-mail: slotouristboard@ sloveniatravel.com

IN SLOVENIA: Dunajska 156, SLO-1000 Ljubljana, tel. 61/ 189 18 40, fax. 61/ 189 18 41. *INTERNET:* Interactive information at www. tourist-board.si

The embassy, consulate or other diplomatic representation of Slovenia nearest you will also be able to guide you further. Slovenian diplomatic representatives: *AUSTRALIA:* Level 6, Advance Bank Center, 60 Marcus Clarke St., Canberra, ACT 2601, tel. (6) 243-4830, fax. (6) 243-4827. *CANADA:* 150 Metcalfe St., Suite 2101, Ottawa, Ontario K2P 1P1, tel. (613) 565-5781, fax. (613) 565-5783. *NEW ZEALAND:* Consulate of the Republic of Slovenia, PO Box 30247, Eastern Hutt Rd., Pomare, Lower Hutt, Wellington, tel. (4) 567-0027, Fax. (4) 567-0024. *U.K.:* Suite One, Cavendish Court, 11-15 Wigmore St., London W1H 9LA, tel. (171) 495-7775, fax. (171) 495-7776. *U.S.:* 1525 New Hampshire Ave. NW, Washington, D.C. 20036, tel. (202) 667-5363, fax. (202) 667-4563.

Customs

Personal items are not subject to any duties on entering the country. You can bring in the following duty free: 200 cigarettes or 50 cigars, 1 l of wine, 0.75 l of spirits, 50 ml of perfume, 250 ml of eau de toilette. Gifts valued at over US $60 must be declared at the border. There are duty free shops all border crossings, where you can buy a host of foreign products. By and large, however, prices are not a great deal lower than at home.

All foreigners purchasing over 9,000 SIT worth of goods will be reimbursed the 13 percent VAT (value added tax) at the border; this does not apply to cigarettes or alcohol, however. In order to get your money back, you will need a receipt printed on so-called ETS forms (Tax-cheque). On leaving the country you will receive the VAT – minus a fee.

Entry Requirements

For a stay of up to three months you must have a valid passport. Residents of EU countries traveling with only an identity card can stay up to 30 days. If staying more than three months, you will need a visa, which can be obtained at any Slovene diplomatic representation.

Children require their own passports or must be entered in the passport of one of their parents. Since you will be asked to leave your passport at your hotel, pension or camping site, bring a photocopy of it and/or your identity card along.

If coming by car or motorcycle, you will need a green international insurance card. If you forget it, you will be asked to purchase additional coverage at the border for up to US $50. If driving someone else's car, have a notarized statement of permission from the car's owner.

If you bring your dog or cat along, you will be asked to show a certificate of rabies vaccination for the animal.

PRACTICAL TIPS
FROM A TO Z

Accommodation

Hotels in Slovenia are divided into categories. Category A (⑤⑤⑤) is the highest, which is reflected in the prices. A single room costs between about US $50 and $90, depending on the city or town it's in. These hotels offer TV, elevators, restaurant, garage, swimming pool and sauna; some even have spa facilities.

Category B (⑤⑤) hotels are only slightly below the A class, with prices starting at around US $40 per night.

Category C (⑤) hotels are cheaper, their standard lower, and the difference between them and pensions hardly noticeable.

Pensions cost around US $18 per night. If you want to lodge particularly cheaply, then try a private room (*sobe*) for about US $7 to $12 per night. Since the state has nothing to do with them, the price is open to negotiation, especially if you wish to stay longer.

Youth Hostels can only be found in towns and cities, but they are generally booked out, since local young people often travel during the peak season. Finding a cheap pension or a private room is often a lot easier.

Camping: During the peak season, the camping sites are often filled to the rafters, and during other times of the year season they are frequently closed. Istria even has a few nudist camping sites; on some other sites a nudist section has been marked off. Slovenia has plenty of campgrounds, especially along the coast, though there are many at inland tourist centers as well.

Camping is strictly prohibited outside of registered campgrounds because of the danger of forest fires. The police are particularly vigilant in both Slovenia and Croatia, and fines for camping rough are extremely high!

Car Rentals

National and international rental companies have offices in most tourist centers. Drivers must be at least 25 years old.

Driving

Speed limits are: 50 kph in towns and villages, 80 kph outside towns, 120 kph on highways. Superhighways are toll roads. Gas stations and service stations are European standard.

If you are involved in an accident in Slovenia, you may have to extend your stay involuntarily. Whether guilty or not, foreigners are often asked to turn in their passport, as the police tend to favor summary proceedings. This generally entails spending an extra night or two in the country.

In case of minor accidents, avoid calling the police if possible, and fill out a European accident report with the other party (available from automobile clubs). Otherwise, every accident should be reported to the police.

Foreign breakdown insurance is recommended, with which you can turn to the Slovenian automobile club (AMZS, emergency tel. 987). The AMZS works well with its foreign affiliates, though you may have language problems with the person on the phone.

Contact: AMZS, Dunajska 128, SLO-1000 Ljubljana, Slovenia, tel. +368-61/ 341341, fax. +386-61/ 342378, Internet: www.amzs.si

Embassies and Consulates

AUSTRALIA: Trg Republike 3/XIII, Ljubljana, tel. 61/ 125-4252, fax. 61/ 126-4721.

CANADA: Miklosiceva 19, Ljubljana, tel. 61/ 130 3570, fax. 61/ 130-3575.

U.K.: British Embassy, Trg Republike 3, 4th floor, Ljubljana, tel. 61/ 125-7191, fax. 61/ 125-0174, e-mail, info@british-embassy.si

U.S.: Pražakova 4, Ljubljana, tel 61/ 301-485, fax. 61/ 301-401.

Food and Drink

Eating and drinking are pleasant activities in Slovenia, and the quality corresponds to the price. If you want to have a good fish dinner along the coast, count on US $18 to $30 without wine. Prices are, in fact, comparable to other European countries. The range of dishes offered (see "What's Cooking" on page 232) leaves hardly any wish unfulfilled. Slovene cooking has Italian, Alpine and Balkan influences.

To help make yourself understood in restuarants, the glossary of Croatian on page 247 should help you out. Thanks to their common past, Croatian is also understood in Slovenia. Besides restaurants (*restavracija*), you will also find plenty of inns (*gostišče, gostilna*); these are usually family operations and are quite cozy, as they are generally smaller and more intimate. A *kavarna* is a traditional Viennese-type coffeehouse. The *bife* (buffet) is a kind of snack bar. There are a number of self-service restaurants (*samopostrežna restavracija*) in larger towns where you can get inexpensive meals.

Health

Slovenia's health care is on par with other European countries, and conventions with some European countries make it possible to receive treatment there with an international insurance form. Citizens of other countries (including the U.S., Canada, Australia, and New Zealand) should consider purchasing travel insurance.

Larger towns all have hospitals or medical centers, the coastal region is also well equipped with doctors. Pharmacies are equipped as in most European countries, nevertheless, if you take regular medication, you are advised to take along an adequate supply just in case..

Money Matters

The Slovene currency is the *tolar* (SIT) The rate of exchange to the U.S. dollar was around 160 SIT in late 1998, and 267 SIT to the pound sterling. There is no limit on the import of foreign currency. The export of SIT, however, is limited to the equivalent of about US $600. Banknotes are 10, 20, 50, 100, 200 and 1,000 tolar.

Banks in Slovenia are open from 8 a.m. to noon and from 2 to 5 p.m., Saturdays from 8 a.m. to noon. Eurochecks are accepted up to a limit of about 130 pounds sterling. A two percent commission is charged for cashing Eurochecks and traveler's checks.

Credit cards are generally accepted only at hotels, car rental agencies, exclusive restaurants and luxury shops. The best way to pay is with cash. If you run out of the local currency, foreign money is sometimes accepted; take a sufficient amount of this along, preferably in small bank notes.

Post Offices / Telephones

Post offices are open from 8 a.m. to 6 p.m., Monday through Friday, and Saturdays from 8 a.m. to noon.

The international prefix for Slovenia is 00386. International calls can be made from post offices, hotels, pay phones and private phones.

CROATIA

TRAVEL PREPARATIONS

Climate / Travel Season

Basically you can travel along the Croatian and Slovene coast at any time of year. Traveling in winter, however, you should pack some warm clothing in spite of the Mediterranean climate. The temperature seldom drops below the freezing point, but solid winds carrying lots of dampness can make for unpleasant weather. When the famous bora blows, it can bring frosts.

The prime travel season is from April to October. Peak temperatures in summer can reach 38° C. The water surface at that point reaches a comfortable 26° C. In spring, count on frequent rain showers, but the autumn months of September and October are ideal for travel. In the off season the beaches are empty and the prices lower, weather, however, remains stable and the water is still agreeably warm.

Customs

Personal items are not subject to any tolls on entering or exiting the country. You are allowed to bring in the following duty free: 200 cigarettes or 50 cigars, 1 l of wine, 0.75 l of spirits, 50 ml of perfume, 250 ml of eau de toilette. Sports articles, cameras, video cameras and other electronic gear must be declared. Car phones must be fully installed in the vehicle.

There are special regulations concerning cellular phones, which must be declared at customs even if they are not functioning. For CB radios, you will need a special permit from the Croatian embassy.

Information / Tourist Offices

The Croatian National Tourist Office has a fair amount of literature and information on the various destinations in the country. The organization is also very helpful in assisting you in your travel plans. They have offices in the larger tourist centers that can help in all sorts of situations. These offices are open from 8 a.m. to 10 p.m. in the summer months (see *Info* at the end of each chapter for addresses and phone numbers).

Croatian National Tourist Offices – *U.K.:* 2, Lanchesters 162-164 Fulham Palace Road London, W6 9ER tel. (181) 563-7979 fax. (181) 563-2616; *U.S.:* 300 Lanidex Plaza, Parsippany, NJ 07054, tel. (201) 428-0707 fax. (201) 428-3386. *IN CROATIA:* Ilica 1a, 410000 Zagreb, tel. +385-1/ 456-455, fax. +385-1/ 428-674.

Entry Requirments

A valid passport is necessary for a stay of up to three months. EU residents can stay for up to one month with an identity card. For a stay of more than three months, you will need to apply to a consular representative for a visa (addresses on page 244).

Children must have their own passport or be entered in the passport of one of their parents. Since you will be asked to leave your passport or identity card at the hotel, pension or camping site, bring a photocopy of one or both along with you.

Animals must be vaccinated against rabies, the vaccination should be no older than six months and no more recent than 14 days. A certificate of vaccination and of veterinary checkup must be provided.

Note: Consult your Foreign Office, the Croatian Tourist Office or Croatian embassy for travel advisories. The U.S. State Department, for example, has issued a travel advisory to Croatia's inland areas, telling people to stay on paved roads as there is a danger of unexploded land mines in the country.

TRAVEL TO AND IN CROATIA

By Air

Scheduled flights from abroad only land in the capital, Zagreb, where you can transfer to domestic flights. Croatia Airlines and a host of international airlines fly to Zagreb daily.

During the peak season, the number of flights is increased. All kinds of charter flights are then offered to the most important destinations along the coast directly: Pula, Rijeka, Split, Brač and Dubrovnik. There are plans to build an airport in the next few years on the island of Korčula.

Croatia Airlines Offices/Agents:

AUSTRALIA: Sky Air Service, 7/24 Albert Road South, Melbourne, Vic. 3205, tel. (3) 9699-9355, fax (3) 9699-9388.

CANADA: Adria Travel Service, Ltd., 2175 Bloor Street West, Toronto, Ont. M6S 1N2, tel. (416) 767-2196, fax. (416) 762-2514.

U.K.: 2, Lanchesters, 162-164 Fulham Palace Road, Hammersmith, London W6 9ER, tel. (181) 563-0022, fax. (181) 563-2615.

U.S.: Croatia Travel Agency, Inc., 3207 Broadway, Suite 1, Long Island City, NY 11106, tel. (718) 726-6700, fax. (718) 956-3988; Adria Travel-Croatia Tours, 5147 N. Lincoln Ave., Chicago, IL 60625, tel. (773) 271-1800, fax. (773) 271-2127.

IN CROATIA: Town Office, Savska 41, 10000 Zagreb, tel. 01/ 427751, fax. 01/427935. Universal access number for central reservations: 062/ 777777.

By Train

Trains to the Istrian peninsula go via Ljubljana and then on to Pula, Koper or Rijeka. Times from Munich, for example, to Rijeka, about nine hours, and to Pula 13 hours. Count on about five hours for trains from Vienna.

If you are going any further south, get ready for a rough ride: the Dinaric range cuts off the coast from the hinterlands, and the tracks are built more for freight than for humans. Most stretches of track date from pre-1945 days. Still, though they are very winding, they boast wonderful scenery.

Just past Split, the train crosses a bit of Bosnian territory, which it also does after Ploče at the Neretva Delta, the southernmost station. There is no railroad line running along the coast. For traveling within Croatia, trains are not recommended as your primary means of transportation.

By Boat / Ferry

For central and norther Europeans, traveling to Croatia by ship is recommended only for its nostalgic value; while from central or southern Italy or Greece it still makes a lot of sense. Docks are located in the numerous port cities along the coast and on the islands. Passenger ships, barring cruise ships, usually sail in from Venice, Trieste, Ancona, Pescara and Bari.

The most important Croatian harbors are Rijeka, Zadar, Šibenik, Split and Dubrovnik, followed by Vis, Stari Grad (Hvar), Vela Luka (Korčula) and Brbir (Dugi Otok), depending on your subsequent itinerary. The other harbors, in particular those on the islands, are accessed by the state-run shipping company *Jadrolinija*.

The **ferries** leaving from Rijeka and heading south are an interesting proposition for drivers, who thereby avoid the difficult and dangerous drive along the coast, and arrive at their destination rested. Information (also for routes from Ancona to Dugi Otok, Zadar, Šibenik, Split, Vis and Hvar, and from Bari to Dubrovnik) is available from: Jadrolinija, 51000 Rijeka, Riva 16, Croatia, tel. +385-51/ 330899, fax. +385-51/ 213116. Otherwise, contact the Croatian Tourist Office or your travel agent.

By Bus

The cheapest way to travel to Croatia from within Europe is by bus, and it's not as uncomfortable as some people might think. Since a lot of foreign workers travel home on the weekends, numerous bus companies, mostly Slovenian and Croatian, have specialized in this route, especially from southern Germany and Austria.

If coming from Germany, inquire at one of the offices of the Deutsche Touring company in any large German train station. Tickets are available from train station ticket offices and travel agencies.

Croatia itself has a vast national bus network that will take you to the remotest of villages, though service may not be very regular.

By Car / Motorcycle

Coming from Austria, Italy, Switzerland, or southern Germany, you can reach some of the closer destinations in Istria and along the Kvarner Gulf faster by car than by train. During the summer months, however, traffic at the borders is very heavy, and that can delay you somewhat. The main routes into Croatia and Slovenia are via the Tauern autobahn, the Tauernschleuse (car transport by train between Böckstein and Mallnitz; book early) and the normal road, the so-called Felbertauern Bundesstrasse.

Austria's autobahn is not free of charge anymore (as of January 1, 1997). You can pick up an autobahn sticker (officially *Autobahnvignette*) at the Austrian border or at gas stations, automobile club offices and sometimes tobacco shops in all countries bordering Austria. These stickers can be purchased for periods of time from a week to a year. Fines for not having the sticker are high. The Tauern Tunnel, Katschberg Tunnel, Tauernschleuse, Felbertauern Tunnel and the Karawanken Tunnel charge tolls. Some pass roads in Austria are also toll roads.

From Villach, there are several roads to Slovenia and Croatia. The Wurzen pass (1,073 meters) has an 18 percent gradient and is closed to vehicles with trailers. The landscape is beautiful, but you will save time by using the Karawanken Tunnel.

An alternative is the Loibl pass to the east (1,396 meters), with a 17 percent gradient, and the Seebergsattel (1,218 meters; twelve percent gradient). All roads then pour into the toll road to Ljubljana, from where a highway goes off in the direction of Postojna – Trieste; if you are planning to go straight to the Kvarner Gulf or Dalmatia without passing by western Istria, then pick up the regular road to Rijeka at Postojna. In Italy, you can pick up the *autostrada* (toll) to Trieste, and then pick any one of a number of border crossings (Lipica and Koper, among others); traveling toward the Istrian west coast, the crossing near Škofije is recommended. After another 40 kilometers you reach the Croatian border near Kaštel.

For motorcyclists who love the winding Alpine roads, the drive can be particularly exhilarating across the following passes: Grossglockner (2,577 meters), Iselsberg (1,204 meters), Kreuzberg (1,077 meters) Nassfeld (1,530 meters), Predil (1,156 meters); or across the Vršič Pass (1,611 meters) and on to Novi Gorica in Slovenia.

To enter Croatia, you will require a green international insurance card. Get it from your insurance company at home or the car rental agency. If you forget it, you will be asked to purchase additional – expensive – coverage at the border. You must also have your vehicle registration card with you.

Fuel is noticeably less expensive here than in the rest of Europe. Lead-free is called *bezolovni*. Carting out canisters of fuel from Croatia is not allowed.

Driving in Croatia can be tiring owing to the state of the roads. The coastal road (Magistrala) is particularly dangerous, especially when it rains and the asphalt becomes slick; motorcyclists especially are at risk. When the terrible bora wind blows, it might be a good idea to take a break: it can even push heavy cars out of their lane suddenly. Many roads have a lot of curves, and therefore poor visibility; which doesn't always deter the locals from taking some dangerous chances when passing.

The speed limit in towns is 50 kph, out of town 80 kph, on expressways 100 kph, and on highways 130 kph. Be aware that the police (*Policija*) keep a sharp lookout with radar. The amount of the fine depends on the extent of the infraction committed. The blood-alcohol limit is 0.5 ppm.

Accidents must be reported to the police at all times. In case of more serious accidents or damages, you should have the police fill out a protocol (*potvrda*): cars with major body damage will not be allowed out of the country without such a form.

Special traffic regulations: When passing another vehicle, keep your blinker on until the maneuver is completed. "Queue jumping" is not allowed. School buses or other vehicles with children may not be passed if they are stopped. If you are being towed, the towing vehicle must carry a warning triangle in front; the towed vehicle one in back.

Breakdown Assistance in Croatia: The Croatian automobile club HAK (*Hrvatski Autoklub*) works together with other international automobile clubs. HAK, Draškovičeva 25, 10000 Zagreb, tel. 01/ 455-4433, fax. 01/ 448-630).

Find out from your own automobile club what arrangements they have. If renting a car, make sure you are covered for breakdowns and towing. Road service of the HAK is available around the clock by dialing 987.

PRACTICAL TIPS FROM A TO Z

Accommodation

Croatia's coast was one of Europe's most popular tourist destinations before the war. The supply of lodgings is correspondingly ample, but you have to be a little careful. Never forget that much of the local hotel business was built up during the Socialist era for a clientele that sought cheap lodgings.

Hotels are the most expensive way to go. There are four categories:

Category A (💲💲💲): Top comfort, close to the sea, separate swimming pools (often an indoor one as well), sauna, gym, tennis courts, mini-golf, sports equipment rentals, restaurant, bar and discotheque. In the larger complexes you will also find shops. Prices range, depending on city and surroundings, from about US $50 to $90 for a double room. In Opatija, for example, you will pay more than in Biograd.

Category B (💲💲): Similar to the Category A hotels, but usually minus the pools inside and out, and with less in the way of sports. Most of the hotels along the coast belong to this category. Prices are between about US $40 and $70 for a double room in the peak season.

Category C (💲💲): Generally the annexes of the hotels are in this category. For a somewhat longer walk to the restaurant or to the beach you can enjoy lower prices, and evenings are a lot quieter. Prices range from about US $35 to $45

Category D (💲): This has become a very rare category indeed, as it is in fact a strong rival of the private room, without, however, the personal contact to the host. A simple room, with the shower in the hall and no breakfast, usually goes for between US $18 and $35.

Prominent in the categorization of the hotels, which does not follow international standards, is the furnishing of the rooms, the location and the level of comfort of the hotel. Often the ranking given to new hotels was not changed even ten or fifteen years later, although they were never renovated. This means that a "Category A" hotel may not necessarily be what you expected; you might find worn-out mattresses, defective bathroom fixtures and threadbare carpets. Inspect a room carefully before taking it. Newer hotels are generally in better condition that the older ones; even if an older one might have a higher catergory rating. Breakfast is usually included in the price of the room.

You should also consider that the price in the off season is a lot lower than in the peak season. Since the hotels are still state run, it is no use trying to bargain the price down. Prices are also a lot higher for individual travelers than for those booking through a travel agent. Therefore, if you are planning to spend your vacation at only one or two different places, see if you can find a travel agent who has the kind of hotel you envision in his or her catalogues.

Families with children are best off booking an **apartment**. This offers the possibility of doing your own cooking. Large hotel complexes also have apartments for rent. These are usually sufficient for four people, and include a kitchen and bathroom, and sometimes a small terrace. There are categories here, too. For first category lodgings, the price for two people is about US $40, in the second category around US $30 to $35.

Private rooms can be found everywhere. Just keep an eye out for houses bearing a sign saying "Sobe, Zimmer, Rooms." Owners of some beautifully situated villas or centrally-located apartments like to make a little extra money in this manner. If you come by bus or by train, you will often be approached in the station by women trying to rent out rooms, and be invited to have a look at one or two. Besides the fact that private rooms are often of the same quality as hotel rooms (sometimes even better) but are a lot cheaper, the personal contact with Croatian hosts may also be a factor in your decision to take a room.

Indeed, private rooms have become a significant aspect of tourism on the Adriatic coast. Many guests return every year to the same family. They become integrated into the families, get invited to coffee, and even become involved in their host's everyday life.

All private landlords are registered and required to pay income ax on their rooms. They must also keep the passports of their guests, unless the room was booked through a tourist office, in which case the tourist office takes charge of this.

Youth hostels are quite rare and are usually only found in bigger cities. Since Croatians like to organize school field trips during the holidays, the hostels are filled to the brim at those times. Travelers up to 27 years of age are eligible for lodgings in youth hostels. For further information, inquire at the youth hostel organization in your country.

Camping: Croatia boasts 277 camping sites, about 90 percent of which are located on lakes, on the islands, and along the Adriatic coast. The most developed areas are the Istrian peninsula and the Kvarner Gulf. Some campgrounds, especially in Istria, are strictly for nudists. The furnishings and amenities are of European standard. These large sites are usually set in beautiful bays in the midst of typical Mediterranean vegetation. Sports facilities and a private marina are no rarity; there are also restaurants and even shopping facilities.

Most camping sites are open from May to the end of September. At some places you can rent bungalows, caravans or tents. Prior booking during the peak season is advised (from mid-June until the end of August) in order to avoid disappointment.

The tourist office has a free brochure, with pictures that don't tell you very much about the places, but with excellent information. The price per person per night ranges from US $4 to $6, a car costs about US $4, and a caravan costs somewhat more. Private campgrounds are usually a little cheaper.

Camping rough is strictly forbidden! This is intended to help avoid forest fires and to keep the environment unspoiled.

Car Rentals

The person renting the vehicle must be at least 23 years old; a national driver's licence is sufficient. Most international rental agencies have offices in Croatia's larger towns.

Diplomatic Representation Abroad

Besides its diplomatic representation, Croatia has numerous national organizations abroad, especially in the U.S.

AUSTRALIA: Embassy of the Republic of Croatia, 6 Bulwarra Close, O'Malley Act 2606, Canberra, tel. (06) 286-6988, 286-2427, fax. (06) 286-3544, 286-6621; Consulate General, 9/24 Albert Road, South Melbourne 3205, Victoria, tel. (03) 699-2633, fax. (03) 696-8271; Consulate General M.A 78 Mill Point Road, South Perth 6151, West Australia, tel. (09) 474-1620, fax. (09) 474-1621; Consulate General, 379 Kent Street, Level 4, Sydney NSW 2000, tel. (02) 299-8899, fax. (02) 299-8855, 299-8889.

CANADA: Embassy of The Republic of Croatia, 130 Albert Street, Suite 1700, Ottawa, Ontario K1P 5G4, tel. (613) 230-7351, fax. (613) 230-7388; Consulate General, 918 Dundas Street East, #302, Mississauga, Ontario, L4Y 2B8, tel. (905) 277-9051, fax. (905) 277-5432.

NEW ZEALAND: Consulate General of the Republic of Croatia, 131 Lincoln Road, P.O. Box 83200, Edmonton, Auckland, tel. (09) 836-5481.

U.K.: Embassy of the Republic of Croatia, 18-21 Jermyn Street, London SWY 6HP, tel. (171) 434-2946, fax. (171) 434-2953.

U.S.: Consulate General of Croatia, 369 Lexington Avenue, New York, NY, 10017, tel. (212) 599-3066, fax. (212) 599-3106; Embassy of the Republic of Croatia, 2343 Massachusetts Ave. NW, Washington DC, 20008, tel. (202) 588-5899, fax. (202) 588-8936; Honorary Consulate to the Republic of Croatia, 4119 White Bear Pkwy., Saint Paul, MN 55110, tel. (612) 429-6183.

Diplomatic Representation in Croatia

CANADA: Canadian Embassy, Hotel Esplanade, Mihanoviceva 1, 10000 Zagreb, tel. 1/ 4577-885, 4577-754, 4577-884, fax. 1/ 4577-913. *U.K.:* British Embassy, Vlaska 121, 3rd floor, PO Box 454, 1000 Zagreb, tel. 1/ 455-5310, fax. 1/ 455-1685, e-mail, britishembassy@zg.tel.hr *U.S.:* Embassy of the United States of America, Hebrangova 2, 10000 Zagreb, tel. 1/ 4555 500, fax. 1/ 455-8585.

Electricity

Electricity is 220 volts. If you are coming from the U.S., you may want to equip yourself with a transformer or bring electrical equipment than can be switched from 110 to 220 volts.

Emergency Phone Numbers

Police: 92
Fire: 93
Ambulance: 94

Food and Drink

Croatian cuisine is described in the feature "What's Cooking" on page 232.

Health

Just about all larger towns have a hospital (*bolnica*), some hotels have their own infirmary to take care of small emergencies. The distribution of doctors is good throughout the country. All cities have well-stocked pharmacies. They are open from 9 a.m. to 7 p.m.

Conventions with some European countries make it possible to receive treatment there with an international insurance form. Citizens of other countries (including the U.S., Canada, Australia, and New Zealand) should consider purchasing travel insurance.

Media

The tourist offices have material in English relating directly to the country – and to travel, of course. International

English-language papers (the *Herald Tribune*, the *Guardian*, the *Independent*, and so on) are available in the larger towns and resorts. The better hotels also have satellite access to CNN.

The state news agency, HINA (Croatian Information and News Agency, Zagreb), produces material in English for international distribution on a daily basis. The state TV-Radio station, HRT, also produces a daily program from 5 to 11 p.m., including news in English.

BBC World Service and Voice of America frequencies (subject to change): BBC: 1209, 1557, 6195, 9410 MHz; VOA: 6040, 9760, 1197, MHz.

Money Matters

Just about any standard currency is accepted as payment in Croatia. The Croatian kuna (HRK) is divided up into 100 lipa. HRK 100 is equivalent to about US $15, i.e., one dollar equals 6.2 kuna. The currency is stable. You can only move up to HRK 2,000 in bills of up to HRK 500 across the border in either direction. There is no limit to the export or import of foreign currencies. Changing cash is a quick affair, and a commission is always charged. The German mark is often used as a means of payment.

Eurochecks can only be cashed up to HRK 1,500. Checks should be made out in kuna. In general, only banks and currency exchanges accept Eurochecks, but they can sometimes be used in some of the larger tourist centers, e.g., in hotels and expensive shops. A two percent commission is charged on them. There are few ATMs offering the possibility of withdrawing cash with an EC card.

Traveler's checks are a safe method of payment, and they are accepted by banks and currency exchanges as well as many hotels, restaurants and shops. A two percent commission is normally charged for cashing a traveler's check. All standard credit cards – Visa, Eurocard/Mastercard, American Express, Diners Club – are accepted at banks, hotels, yacht clubs, car rental agencies and upscale restaurants and shops.

Banks are open weekdays from 8 a.m. to 7 p.m., Saturdays from 8 a.m. to noon. In summer they are open weekdays from 7 a.m. to 7 p.m., Saturdays from 7 a.m. to 1 p.m.

National Holidays

On a number of holidays, banks and shops close. Official holidays are: January 1 (New Years Day); January 6 (Epiphany); Easter Monday; May 1 (Int'l Workers Day); May 30 (National Holiday); June 22 (Day of Anti-fascist Struggle); August 5 (Homeland Day); August 15 (Assumption Day); December 25 and 26 (Christmas).

Photography

The usual brand-name films are available all over, but they can be somewhat expensive in Croatia. In the tourist resorts there are often photo shops that offer good 24-hour developing service. Photographing military installations is strictly forbidden, otherwise there are no restrictions on photo subjects. It's a good idea to ask for their permission before photographing people.

Post Offices

Post offices in Croatia have blue and yellow signs with the lettering HPT. In tourist centers, post offices are open Monday to Saturday from 7 a.m. to 10 p.m., and Sundays from 7 a.m. to 2 p.m.

Phone calls can be made from post offices (with a phone card as well), they also offer telegram and fax services, as well as currency exchange. Stamps are also available in hotels and in souvenir shops.

Sports

The Croatian coast, with its countless and beautiful coves, wonderful beaches, and numerous swimming pools, is a paradise not only for swimmers; a wide range of other aquatic sports are also on offer (see feature on page 228).

Yachters will also enter a seventh heaven exploring the thousands of coves around the islands, which make for some fabulous sailing trips. The privately operated marinas (yacht harbors) structure their prices according to free-market criteria. The marinas of the **Adriatic Croatia International Club** (ACI) are well equipped, with a ten-ton crane, fueling station, repair shops, and a restaurant.

Croatia has 42 marinas in all, not counting the docking facilities of the seaside campgrounds. The berths of the larger marinas also have electricity and running water.

Prices rose in 1996. For long-term berthing, they went up about 20 percent. The especially popular marinas are, of course, more expensive. The good news is that other marinas have lowered their prices in order to attract clientele. The ACI has justified its price increase by explaining that it intends to improve the quality of its marinas in the near future, and will invest around US $4 million in the project.

The ACI has central offices at: Maršala Tita 221, 51410 Opatija (Istria/Kvarner Gulf), tel. +385-51/ 257214, fax. +385-51/ 27201-824. The Croatian Tourist Office also has a good brochure on aquatic sports in Croatia. Check the Internet link at www.htz.hr

Anglers will need a fishing permit to indulge in their sport. Fishing methods are restricted (harpooning, for example, is not allowed), as is the catch size. You may only fish in rivers with a fishing permit, as well, which can be quite expensive. Around Plitvice, for example, it can cost as much as US $50. These high prices are justified by the high catch quota allowed.

The sea along the coast contains about 300 species of fish – quite a challenge for the passionate sport fisherman. This sub-ject is also well covered in a free brochure available at most tourist offices.

Tennis is a national sport in Croatia, so expect to find many good courts. Hotels in the two top categories almost always have one or two courts on the premises. Tennis lessons are frequently available, and the teachers usually know their stuff. Keep in mind that such top players as Goran Ivanisevič and Iva Majoli both come from Croatia, as does the former trainer of the German Davis Cup team Niki Pilič.

The Dinaric mountains offer a lot of possibilities for another sport, **hiking**, which can be done at all levels from easy to very tough. Trails are marked, though not quite as well as in they are in the Alps. This kind of recreational activity is relatively new to Croatia. For some hikes it is advisable to bring along a compass and very good boots; the karstic mountains are known for their jagged ground, and twisting an ankle in a fissure is not a rarity. If hiking boots are not at least ankle high, you could suffer severe injury. In some more remote areas you may come across snakes, not all of which are poisonous.

Winter sports, especially skiing, are still very much in their infancy. Skiers find the best slopes on the Učka, the Risnjak and the Velebit.

Telecommunications

Long-distance calls (international as well) are possible from post offices, hotels and phone booths. The cheap period is between 10 p.m. and 6 a.m. Telephone booths take cards, which are available from post offices, tobacconists and kiosks, or tokens (*žetons*).

To phone **to Croatia** from abroad, dial **00385** and then the number without the "0" before the local prefix. To phone **from Croatia** abroad, dial 99 followed by the country code: 1 for the U.S. and Canada, 44 for Great Britain, 61 for Australia, etc.

Tipping

A tip is *not* included in the price of meals and hotels. Hence you should give waiters a tip of somewhere around ten percent of the bill: provided they deserve it, of course.

Often a small cover charge may be levied in restaurants for bread, condiments, and such. Service in private restaurants, bars, and cafés is often top quality, while the personnel in some of the state-run hotels tend to demonstrate a certain slowness. Businesses that are open year-round tend to be particularly afflicted with this problem of "fatigue." Sometimes a small tip in advance helps raise the level of hospitality.

GLOSSARY

English is the second language spoken in the tourist resorts, but Italian and German are also fairly widespread. Just in case, however, we have listed some of the most important terms and expressions here.

Pronunciation of some of the words is a little difficult, since vocalized consonants tend to be strung together in Croatian (for example, *Brdo;* mountain).

Pronunciation

aj.	ay (as in I)
c	ts
č	ch
ą.	j (as in jug)
e	eh
ej	ey (as in day)
h	(heavily aspirated h)
š.	sh
z	z (as in zoom)
ž	j (as in Jacques in French)

General Vocabulary

Please.	*molim*
Excuse me	*molim*
How much is...?	*koliko stoji?*
Thank you.	*hvala*
I'd like/I need	*želio bih, trebam*

When?	*kada?*
Where is...?	*gdje je...?*
Before	*prije*
After	*poslije*
A little	*malo*
A lot.	*puno, mnogo*
Fast.	*brzo*
Yes	*da*
No	*ne*
What	*što*
I don't understand	*ne razumijem*
What time is it?	*koliko je sati?*
In the morning	*ujutro*
In the evening	*na večer*
Good morning	*dobro jutro*
Good evening	*dobro večer*
Goodbye	*doviđenja*
Good night.	*laku noč*
Yesterday	*jučer*
Today	*danas*
Tomorrow	*sutra*
Right away.	*odmah*
Left	*lijevo*
Right	*desno*
Forward	*naprijed*
Backward	*natrag*
Bus stop.	*postaja*
Exhibition	*izložba*
Male	*muški*
Female	*ženski*
Church	*ckrva*
Drive.	*vožnja*
Street/road.	*ulica*
Number.	*broj*

In the Restaurant

Eat	*jesti*
Drink	*piti*
Breakfast	*doručak*
Lunch	*ručak*
Dinner	*večera*
Table	*stol*
Chair	*stolica*
Spoon	*žlica*
Fork	*viljuška*
Knife	*nož*
Glass	*čaša*
Bottle	*boca*
Waiter	*konobar*

Bread . . . . *kruh*
Butter . . . . *maslac*
Honey . . . . *med*
Milk . . . . *mlijeko*
Coffee . . . . *kava*
Tea . . . . *čaj*
Water . . . . *voda*
Mineral water . . . . . *mineralna voda*
Fruit juice . . . . *voćni sok*
Cold . . . . *hladno*
Hot . . . . *vruće*
Soup . . . . *juha*
Boiled ham/cured ham . . . *šunka/pršut*
Eggs . . . . *jaja*
Meat . . . . *meso*
Beef . . . . *govedina*
Veal . . . . *teletina*
Pork . . . . *svinjetina*
Lamb . . . . *janjetina*
Game . . . . *divljač*
Chicken . . . . *pile*
Duck . . . . *patka*
Turkey . . . . *purica*
Fish . . . . *riba*
Potatoes . . . . *krumpir*
Noodles . . . . *rezanci*
Rice . . . . *riža*
Salad . . . . *salata*
Lettuce . . . . *zelena salata*
Cake . . . . *kolač*
Cheese . . . . *sir*
Fruit . . . . *voće*
Ice cream . . . . *sladoled*
Sweet . . . . *slatko*
Sour . . . . *slano*
Hot (spicy) . . . . *pikantno*
Sour . . . . *kiselo*
Wine . . . . *vino*
Beer . . . . *pivo*
Brandy . . . . *lozovača*
Plum brandy . . . . . . *sljivovica*
Cheers! . . . . *živjeli*

Fish and Sea Food

Mussels . . . . *dagnje*
Oysters . . . . *oštrige*
Squid . . . . *lignje*
Octopus salad . . . *hobotnica na salatu*
Crabs . . . . *rakovi*

Scampi . . . . *račići*
Toothed bream . . . . *zubatac*
Dried cod . . . . *bakalar*
Mackerel . . . . *skuša*
Mullet . . . . *cipal*
Red bream . . . . *arbun*
Tuna . . . . *tuna*
Gold bream . . . . *orada*

Shopping

Shop . . . . *prodavaonica*
Market place . . . . *tržnica*
Pastry shop . . . . *slastičarna*
Buy . . . . *kupiti*
Trousers . . . . *hlače*
Shirt . . . . *košulja*
Dress . . . . *haljina*
Coat . . . . *kaput*
T-shirt . . . . *majica*
Cotton . . . . *pamuk*
Wool . . . . *vuna*
Shoes . . . . *cipele*
Leather . . . . *koža*
Bigger . . . . *veće*
Smaller . . . . *manje*
Cheap . . . . *jeftino*
Expensive . . . . *skupo*
Silver . . . . *srebro*
Gold . . . . *zlato*
Hand-made . . . . *ručni rad*
Open . . . . *otvoreno*
Closed . . . . *zatvoreno*
Let's go . . . . *idemo*

Numbers

One . . . . *jedan*
Two . . . . *dva*
Three . . . . *tri*
Four . . . . *četiri*
Five . . . . *pet*
Six . . . . *šest*
Seven . . . . *sedam*
Eight . . . . *osam*
Nine . . . . *devet*
Ten . . . . *deset*
Twenty . . . . *dvadeset*
Fifty . . . . *pedeset*
Hundred . . . . *sto*
Thousand . . . . *tisuč*

Times / Days

Hour	*sat*
Noon	*podne*
Morning	*prijpodne*
Afternoon	*popodne*
Sunday	*nedijelja*
Monday	*ponedjeljak*
Tuesday	*utorak*
Wednesday	*srijeda*
Thursday	*četvrtak*
Friday	*petak*
Saturday	*subota*

Driving

Could you please give me ... liters
of leadfree gasoline. . . . . . . *dajte mi,*
molim vas, ... litara bezolovnog benzina
I have a problem . . . . . *ja imam jedan*
problem
Garage . . . . *automehaničar*
Something's wrong with the engine/
breaks/starter.... . . . . *nešto nije uredu*
sa motorom/sa kočnicama/sa starterom
Headlight . . . . *reflektor*
Windshield wiper . . . . . *brisač stakla*
Oil. . . . . *ulje*
Battery . . . . *baterij*
Radiator . . . . *hladnjak*
Tire. . . . . *Autoguma*
Accident . . . . *nezgoda*

AUTHORS

Alexander Sabo studied history and
has traveled the Balkans extensively, not
only professionally as a guide for educational charters tours, but also because of a
profound love and appreciation for the
region.

Istria's and Dalmatia's fascinating historical ties with Venice, in particular,
caught his fancy, and he has focused a
great deal of energy on studying these
two regions.

Darja Peitz-Hlebec is a Balkan specialist and travel book writer. She provided information for the update of this
guide.

PHOTOGRAPHERS

Amberg, Gunda 146, 196-197
Amberg, Dr. Hellmuth 204
Archiv für Kunst und Geschichte,
Berlin 14-15, 17, 23, 26, 27, 28, 30,
32, 35, 37, 40, 41
Bersick, Dr. Gerhard 8-9, 16, 29, 33, 36,
80, 83, 91L, 91R, 154, 160,
161, 175, 176, 178,
188, 189, 190, 200, 208,
211, 212, 234, 235
Brey, Dr. Hansjörg 213
Hackenberg, Rainer 48-49, 52, 56
Heinzelmann, Ingrid (Freelance Press)
228
Hinze, Peter 10-11, 46/47, 64, 73, 78,
98-99, 100, 103, 109, 111,
112, 113, 115, 116, 132
Hrvatska zuristićka zajednica
18, 210, 226
Janicek, Ladislav (Mainbild) 193
Janicke, Volkmar E. 221
Kalmár, János 20, 85, 86, 87, 92,
138, 191, 201
Lesire, P. (Club Mediterranée,
Deutschland GmbH) 150
Möhn, Dieter (Photo-Press) 122
Müller, Kai-Ulrich 21, 50, 54, 55,
58, 74, 126, 128, 129, 224, 225
Münker, Burkhard (Silvestris) 149
Peitz-Hlebec, Darja cover
Redeker, Hans-Joachim (Silvestris) 230
Russ, Andrea 59
Scholten, Jo 62-63, 66, 75, 77, 79,
89, 93, 94, 106, 124,
136-137, 232, 233
Schröder, Dirk 39, 60, 134, 145,
180-181, 184, 194, 227
Schwarz, Berthold 12, 43, 67, 117
Skupy-Pesek, Jitka 216
Stankiewitz, Thomas 24, 42, 44, 45,
71, 76, 110, 140, 147, 152-153,
157, 158, 164, 166-167,
168, 170, 172, 177, 182, 198,
205, 207, 209, 231
Stuhler, Werner 127, 131, 133
Vahl, Wolfgang (Photo-Press) 120-121
Ziegler, Dieter (Mainbild) 215, 218.

INDEX

INDEX

Explore the World

AVAILABLE TITLES

Afghanistan 1 : 1 500 000
Australia 1 : 4 000 000
Bangkok - *and Greater Bangkok*
1 : 75 000 / 1 : 15 000
Burma → *Myanmar*
Caribbean - *Bermuda, Bahamas,
Greater Antilles* 1 : 2 500 000
Caribbean - *Lesser Antilles*
1 : 2 500 000
Central America 1 : 1 750 000
Central Asia 1 : 1 750 000
China - *Northeastern*
1 : 1 500 000
China - *Northern* 1 : 1 500 000
China - *Central* 1 : 1 500 000
China - *Southern* 1 : 1 500 000
Colombia - **Ecuador** 1 : 2 500 000
Crete - *Kreta* 1 : 200 000
Dominican Republic - **Haiti**
1 : 600 000
Egypt 1 : 2 500 000 / 1 : 750 000
Hawaiian Islands
1 : 330 000 / 1 : 125 000
Hawaiian Islands – **Kaua'i**
1 : 150 000 / 1 : 35 000
Hawaiian Islands – **Honolulu**
- **O'ahu** 1 : 35 000 / 1 : 150 000

Hawaiian Islands – **Maui - Moloka'i**
- Lāna'i 1 : 150 000 / 1 : 35 000
Hawaiian Islands – **Hawai'i, The Big**
Island 1 : 330 000 / 1 : 125 000
Himalaya 1 : 1 500 000
Hong Kong 1 : 22 500
Indian Subcontinent 1 : 4 000 000
India - *Northern* 1 : 1 500 000
India - *Western* 1 : 1 500 000
India - *Eastern* 1 : 1 500 000
India - *Southern* 1 : 1 500 000
India - *Northeastern* - **Bangladesh**
1 : 1 500 000
Indonesia 1 : 4 000 000
Indonesia *Sumatra* 1 : 1 500 000
Indonesia *Java - Nusa Tenggara*
1 : 1 500 000
Indonesia *Bali - Lombok*
1 : 180 000
Indonesia *Kalimantan*
1 : 1 500 000
Indonesia *Java - Bali* 1 : 650 000
Indonesia *Sulawesi* 1 : 1 500 000
Indonesia *Irian Jaya - Maluku*
1 : 1 500 000
Jakarta 1 : 22 500
Japan 1 : 1 500 000

Kenya 1 : 1 100 000
Korea 1 : 1 500 000
Malaysia 1 : 1 500 000
West Malaysia 1 : 650 000
Manila 1 : 17 500
Mexico 1 : 2 500 000
Myanmar (Burma) 1 : 1 500 000
Nepal 1 : 500 000 / 1 : 1 500 000
Trekking Map *Khumbu Himal -
Solu Khumbu* 1 : 75 000
New Zealand 1 : 1 250 000
Pakistan 1 : 1 500 000
Peru - **Ecuador** 1 : 2 500 000
Philippines 1 : 1 500 000
Singapore 1 : 22 500
Southeast Asia 1 : 4 000 000
South Pacific Islands 1 : 13 000 000
Sri Lanka 1 : 450 000
Taiwan 1 : 400 000
Tanzania - *Rwanda, Burundi*
1 : 1 500 000
Thailand 1 : 1 500 000
Uganda 1 : 700 000
Venezuela - *Guyana, Suriname,
French Guiana* 1 : 2 500 000
Vietnam, Laos, Cambodia
1 : 1 500 000

Nelles Maps are top quality!
Relief mapping, kilometer charts and tourist attractions.
Always up-to-date!

Explore the World

NELLES GUIDES

AVAILABLE TITLES

Australia
Bali / Lombok
Berlin and Potsdam
Brazil
Brittany
Burma → Myanmar
California
 Las Vegas, Reno,
 Baja California
Cambodia / Laos
Canada
 Ontario, Québec,
 Atlantic Provinces
Canada
 Pacific Coast, the Rockies,
 Prairie Provinces, and
 the Territories
Caribbean
 The Greater Antilles,
 Bermuda, Bahamas
Caribbean
 The Lesser Antilles
China – Hong Kong
Corsica
Crete
Croatia – Adriatic Coast
Cyprus
Egypt
Florida
Greece – The Mainland
Hawai'i

Hungary
India
 Northern, Northeastern
 and Central India
India – Southern India
Indonesia
 Sumatra, Java, Bali,
 Lombok, Sulawesi
Ireland
Israel - with Excursions
 to Jordan
Kenya
London, England and
 Wales
Malaysia - Singapore
 - Brunei
Mexico
Morocco
Moscow / St. Petersburg
Munich
 Excursions to Castles,
 Lakes & Mountains
Myanmar (Burma)
Nepal
New York – City and State
New Zealand
Paris
Philippines
Portugal
Prague / Czech Republic
Provence

Rome
Scotland
South Africa
South Pacific Islands
Spain – Pyrenees, Atlantic
 Coast, Central Spain
Spain
 Mediterranean Coast,
 Southern Spain,
 Balearic Islands
Sri Lanka
Syria – Lebanon
Tanzania
Thailand
Turkey
Tuscany
U.S.A.
 The East, Midwest and South
U.S.A.
 The West, Rockies and Texas
Vietnam

FORTHCOMING

Canary Islands
Costa Rica
Greek Islands
Maldives
Norway
Poland
Sweden

Nelles Guides – authoritative, informed and informative.
Always up-to-date, extensively illustrated, and with first-rate relief maps.
256 pages, approx. 150 color photos, approx. 25 maps.